The Contested Country
*Yugoslav Unity and Communist
Revolution, 1919–1953*

Russian Research Center Studies, 85

Harvard Historical Studies, 108

The Contested Country

Yugoslav Unity and Communist Revolution, 1919–1953

Aleksa Djilas

Harvard University Press
Cambridge, Massachusetts
London, England
1991

Library of Congress Cataloging-in-Publication Data

Djilas, Aleksa, 1953–
   The contested country : Yugoslav unity and communist revolution,
1919–1953 / Aleksa Djilas.
      p.   cm. — (Russian Research Center studies, 85) (Harvard
historical studies, 108)
   Includes bibliographical references and index.
   ISBN 0-674-16698-1 (alk. paper)
      1. Yugoslavia—Politics and government—1918–1945. 2. Yugoslavia—Politics
and government—1945– 3. Komunistička partija Jugoslavije. 4. Nationalism—Yugoslavia. I. Title. II. Series. III. Series: Harvard historical studies, 108.
DR1291.D57   1991   90-46006
949.702—dc20   CIP

*To the memory of
my mother's parents,
Leonard and Marija Barić*

Acknowledgments

While working on this book, as well as on earlier essays, articles, and lectures on the national question in Yugoslavia, I was much helped with advice, comments, and encouragement from Yugoslav, British, American, and German friends. There are too many of them to thank individually; I therefore express my gratitude to all of them together. I would like, however, to mention some who have been of particular assistance. Vane Ivanović and Desimir Tošić have made many very useful comments. Stevan K. Pavlowitch, of the Department of History, University of Southampton in Great Britain, with his characteristic feeling for historical nuance and detail, gave valuable suggestions in the final stages of preparation of the manuscript. Anthony D. Smith, of the Department of Sociology, London School of Economics and Political Science, offered much useful advice and criticism while I was writing an early version. George Schöpflin, Lecturer in East European Political Institutions, London School of Economics and Political Science, made helpful comments on the early drafts of three chapters. I also thank Margaret Smith and Jane Prokop for their editorial assistance.

It is a pleasure to acknowledge my debt to the Russian Research Center, Harvard University, for providing me with an excellent working environment and to the John M. Olin Foundation for two years of financial support. I thank my Harvard colleagues for their genial and stimulating company.

My special gratitude goes to my parents and to my godmother, Milica Dragić, for their love and their support of my work.

Contents

Maps

The Contested Country

Introduction

Yugoslavia is a difficult country to understand. Its many nations, languages, and religions generate centrifugal tendencies.[1] At the same time there exist powerful centripetal forces: the common South Slav origin of the majority of the population is the basis for many ethnic, linguistic, and cultural similarities; and there are also many shared historical experiences.

According to the 1981 census, in today's Yugoslavia (255,804 sq km) there are only two non–South Slav national minorities of any significant number: 427,000 Hungarians, living in Vojvodina (21,506 sq km), the northern autonomous province of Serbia; and 1,731,000 Albanians, mainly in Kosovo (10,887 sq km), the southern autonomous province of Serbia, but also in western Macedonia and in southeastern Montenegro. The total population of Yugoslavia was 22,352,000 at the time of this census.[2] The South Slavs thus make up the vast majority of the population. Yugoslavia is, indeed, what its name means in all three of its South Slav languages (Macedonian, Croato-Serbian or Serbo-Croatian, and Slovenian): the land of the South Slavs.[3] The League of Communists of Yugoslavia (Savez komunista Jugoslavije), as the Communist party was officially known from 1952 until its disintegration into Communist parties of the six republics in 1989, recognized six South Slav nations as constituting Yugoslavia: Croats (4,428,000), Macedonians (1,341,000), Montenegrins (577,000), Muslims (2,000,000), Serbs (8,136,000), and Slovenes (1,754,000). The 1981 census also showed that 1,216,000 people declared themselves "Yugoslavs."[4] This group might well be considered the seventh South Slav nation of Yugoslavia. Officially, self-declared Yugoslavs enjoy only partial recognition: they are recorded separately in statistics but are not recognized as a nation.

Nationalisms of the different nations of Yugoslavia are most often and rightly considered, both by outside observers and in the country itself, to be the main cause of political instability in Yugoslavia. Not all the nationalisms, however, pose an equal threat. Apart from differences in their goals and mobilizing power, some are geographically peripheral and numerically weak. For example, in the unlikely event that militant Albanian nationalists realized their most ambitious separatist demands, Yugoslavia would lose to Albania a considerable part of its territory: the province of Kosovo, a large part of western Macedonia, and perhaps some other, smaller territories too. There would also be ripple effects: separatism would be encouraged in other parts of the country, and Serbs and Macedonians, whose national interests and pride would be injured, could turn toward extremism. Still, it would not mean the end of Yugoslavia. Another example could be provided in connection with the Hungarian minority, living mostly in Vojvodina, which has a Serbian majority. There is no significant conflict between Hungarians and Serbs, and there are no Hungarian separatist organizations seeking the secession of Vojvodina to Hungary. But even if one were to imagine such a secession, it is again clear that Yugoslavia would not cease to exist.

Two South Slav nations and their republics might also be lost without bringing an end to Yugoslavia: the Macedonians, who live in the southeastern republic of Macedonia (25,347 sq km), and most of whom want their republic to remain part of Yugoslavia; and the Slovenes, who inhabit the northwestern republic of Slovenia (20,251 sq km), and among whom separatism has been on the increase in recent years. The Macedonian and Slovenian republics have some common characteristics that differentiate them from the other five South Slav nations and the four central republics (Bosnia and Herzegovina, Croatia, Montenegro, and Serbia). Both are ethnically and linguistically homogeneous (except for the Albanian minority inside Macedonia), and in this sense resemble the nineteenth-century European model of the nation state.

Strictly speaking, after the departure of Macedonia and Slovenia, Yugoslavia would cease to be "the land of the South Slavs," since two of the Yugoslav nations would be excluded. But most of its territory and most of its population would remain. Thus, without Kosovo, Macedonia, Slovenia, and Vojvodina, a large part of the territory and population of present-day Yugoslavia would remain intact, as four republics: Bosnia and Herzegovina, Croatia, Montenegro, and Serbia (without its two autonomous provinces, Vojvodina and Kosovo).

Albanians, Hungarians, Macedonians, and Slovenes have their own languages. But Croats, Montenegrins, Muslims, Serbs, and declared Yugoslavs all speak one language, officially called Croato-Serbian or Serbo-Croatian. (The Croats call this language Croatian; Serbs and Montenegrins call it Serbian; most Muslims use one of the official names.) Croato-Serbian or Serbo-Croatian is written in both Cyrillic and Latin. Most Serbs and Montenegrins use Cyrillic, which is part of their Eastern Orthodox Christian heritage. But use of the Latin script has become quite widespread in the last few decades, mostly as a result of western cultural influences. The Croats, who are almost all Roman Catholic, use the Latin script, as do most Muslims. (There is no precise information about the script preferred by declared Yugoslavs, but it seems likely that they would choose Latin as the more international and "modern.")

There are, then, no linguistic barriers between Croats, Montenegrins, Muslims, Serbs, and declared Yugoslavs. Even the most zealous Croatian and Serbian nationalists do not dispute this fact. The Croats and Serbs, however, do have independent national literatures, although they share some literary movements and traditions. There are also great differences among dialects and regional subdialects within the Croatian and Serbian nations. The *štokavski* dialect became in the nineteenth century the basis for literary Croato-Serbian (or Serbo-Croatian), and the differences between its Croatian and Serbian versions are both minimal and insignificant in comparison with, say, the differences between it and the Croatian *kajkavski* dialect (spoken mostly in the region around Zagreb and Varaždin) and the Croatian *čakavski* dialect (spoken mostly in Istria and in some coastal regions south of it). (The names of the dialects stem from the three different ways of saying "what": *što* or *šta, kaj,* and *ča.*) The differences between *kajkavski* and *čakavski* are so great that conversation between speakers of the two dialects is difficult.

The Serbs, the largest nation of Yugoslavia, outnumber the second-largest population, the Croats, almost two to one. Altogether the two groups number 12,564,000, representing 56 percent of the population of Yugoslavia. Croats and Serbs live in the three central republics of Croatia (56,538 sq km), Bosnia and Herzegovina (51,564 sq km), and Serbia with its autonomous provinces (88,361 sq km). These republics, along with Montenegro (13,967 sq km), represent 82 percent of the territory of Yugoslavia.

Although the Montenegrins are relatively small in number and are officially designated as a separate nation, Montenegro must be considered one of the central republics of Yugoslavia. Not only is it bordered by Bosnia and Herzegovina, Croatia, and Serbia; significant numbers of Montenegrins insist that nationally they are Serbs, and since the creation of Yugoslavia they have taken an active part in the conflict between Croats and Serbs.

Many Croats (974,000, or 22 percent of the entire Croatian population) and many Serbs (1,958,000, or 24 percent of the total Serbian population) live outside Croatia and Serbia (and the latter's two provinces). (Montenegrins are not counted as Serbs in this figure.) In many regions Croats and Serbs live mixed together. There is a Serbian minority in Croatia of 532,000, and a Croatian minority in Serbia (mostly in Vojvodina) of 148,000. Bosnia and Herzegovina, the most central Yugoslav republic, contains the greatest mixture of populations. There the Muslims (recognized as a nation for the first time in the 1971 census) are the most numerous group (1,629,000), followed by Serbs (1,320,000) and Croats (758,000). There is a sizable minority of Muslims in Serbia— 215,000—mostly in Serbia's part of what was, under the Ottoman Empire, the Sandžak of Novi Pazar (commonly known today as Sandžak). (A smaller part of Sandžak belongs to Montenegro.)

The comparative numerical strength of the Croats and Serbs and the size and central location of the territories they inhabit make any conflict between them the most important threat to Yugoslavia's continued existence. All problems between the two groups are aggravated by the fact that so many Serbs and Croats live mixed together, often with Muslims also; it would be impossible to draw any border that would create ethnically homogeneous states.

Since the creation of Yugoslavia in 1918, the conflict between Croats and Serbs has posed the greatest threat to the Yugoslav union. Its causes can be traced to their development of separate cultural and political identities as they took crucial steps toward becoming modern nations in the nineteenth century.

Non-Slav observers did not distinguish between Croats and Serbs until the ninth century. These two names became established when the first forms of political organization appeared. The Croatian and Serbian tribes, though identical in ethnic and linguistic origin, developed distinct political organisms.[5] The formation of two separate polities was, from the beginning, an important differentiating force between Croats and Serbs. But in later centuries and even today foreign visitors and observers have frequently been confused by the absence of observable differences between Croats and Serbs and have used the name *Croatian* for the Serbian population, and vice versa.

From the time of their settlement in southeastern Europe during the sixth and early seventh centuries, Croatian tribes were influenced by Latin and Germanic political orders and cultures. The Croats were at the periphery of this western civilization. To the east lived the Serbian tribes, adjacent to the Byzantine world. In the following centuries these eastern and western influences, especially Eastern Orthodox and Roman Catholic, frequently transgressed the borders—which were never firmly established anyway—between Croatian and Serbian tribes and Croatian and Serbian states, creating a pluralistic mosaic rather than a simple division between "western Croats" and "eastern Serbs."[6]

Between the eighth century and the first half of the tenth, Bulgarian, Croatian, Hungarian, and Serbian feudal states were established. These four polities and the political entities that succeeded them, remained into modern times crucial political and military forces in southeastern Europe. In the nineteenth and twentieth centuries the memories of their existence and the traditions they left behind played an important role in the formation of modern Bulgarian, Croatian, Hungarian, and Serbian national consciousnesses. The zones of conflict remained unchanged for almost a millennium: Croatia versus Hungary over territories north of the river Sava, Croatia versus Serbia over Bosnia, and Serbia versus Bulgaria over Macedonia (except in the fourteenth century, when Serbia fought Byzantium over Macedonia). These medieval polities expanded and contracted, acquiring additional territories when internal unity coincided with weakness in neighboring states, then losing territories with the onset of domestic strife. The name "Croat" or "Serb" would sometimes spread in this way, especially if the conquered territories were ethnically and linguistically South Slav.[7]

Medieval Croatian kings retained their independence even under the suzerainty of the Byzantine emperor, or under the strong influence of Frankish kings. Although Croatian kings often called their territories their *regnum,* there was no proper state organization. Rather than a political ruler, the king was more of a supreme military commander of an alliance of feudal armies. Almost all the resources at his disposal, which were collected through taxation, were spent on the army and the fleet.

The homogeneous and expansionist Hungarian kingdom was a powerfully attractive force for less well-organized neighboring states. In 1102 the Croatian nobility established agreements called the Pacta Conventa with Koloman, the Hungarian king, making him also king of Croatia. The nobles were exempted from paying taxes and in general strengthened their power. Their only duty was service in the king's armies, and they enjoyed equal status with the Hungarian nobility. Not until the eighteenth and nineteenth centuries would Hungary, always the more cohesive state, attempt to impose its hegemony over Croatia and assimilate Croats. The Pacta Conventa remained formally valid until the dissolution of Austria-Hungary in 1918.

From 1102 on, Croatia's sovereignty was limited, but Croatia had its own diet (Sabor); a military organization of feudal armies that, though under the supreme command of the Hungarian king, were still partly independent; and a separate system of currency and taxation. It was in the twelfth century that the foundations were laid for the idea that the kingdom of Croatia was a triune kingdom (*trojedno kraljevstvo*), consisting of three separate yet united kingdoms: Dalmatia, Slavonia, and (inner) Croatia.

As early as the twelfth century Bosnia and southern Croatia were centers and sanctuaries for a neo-Manichean sect of Christians known as Bogumils. Like their western counterparts the Patarins and Catharists, they rejected institutionalized religion and church hierarchy, and often lived in small communities.[8] During the thirteenth century the papacy organized crusades against the Bogumils. The persecution of the old Slavonic church and the deep alienation of the people of Croatia and Bosnia from the official church with its Latin hierarchy had created favorable conditions for the dissemination of Bogumil teachings. By giving Bosnia religious individuality this heresy played a role in the development of a separate Bosnian state, which toward the end of the fourteenth century became a powerful kingdom. Tvrtko I (ruled 1353–1391) threw off Hungarian domination, expanded his realm in all directions, and assumed the title of king of Serbia, Bosnia, Croatia, and Dalmatia (Slavonia remained part of Hungary). By uniting the majority of Croats and Serbs in one kingdom he became a proto-Yugoslav ruler. Tvrtko's state disintegrated after his death. It had not lasted long enough to become a basis for the integration and unification of Croats and Serbs. In the middle of the fifteenth century Bosnia fell under Ottoman rule.[9]

Southeast of Croatia and Bosnia lay the Serbian medieval kingdom, with its center in what are today southern and western Serbia, Montenegro, Kosovo, and northern Macedonia. In the thirteenth century it was a strong kingdom with ecclesiastical independence. The Serbian kingdom reached its peak under Stefan Dušan, who ruled over a territory encompassing most of today's Serbia, Macedonia, Albania, and Greece. He was crowned emperor in 1346, but soon after his death in 1355 his empire broke apart into smaller kingdoms and principalities.[10]

From the fourteenth through the sixteenth centuries the Ottoman Turks expanded into southeastern and central Europe. Although they reached the gates of Vienna in 1683, in the seventeenth century they were already on the defensive. At that time the Ottoman Empire underwent progressive internal decadence and decline, accompanied by territorial losses, although it was not until 1912 that an alliance of Balkan states all but expelled Turkey from southeastern Europe.

The medieval feudal armies of the southeastern European states were no match for the more numerous Turks. The Serbs met defeat in the battle of Kosovo in 1389, the Croats in the battle of Krbava in 1493, and the Magyars in the battle of Mohács in 1526. In 1527 the Croatian nobles elected Ferdinand of Habsburg, archduke of Austria, as the king of Croatia, thus acknowledging the futility of an independent struggle against the Turks. Even so, the territory of Croatia was reduced from around 50,000 square kilometers in 1526 to 16,000 square kilometers by the end of the sixteenth century. The Serbian polity retained some independence until the second half of the fifteenth century, and its province

Zeta, later called Crna Gora (Montenegro), remained independent until the end of the century. The Serbian feudal political system and ruling class were all but eradicated by the Ottoman Turks. Some of the surviving nobility reverted to the peasant way of life, and there was a revival of the traditional tribal system. For the Serbs, the break with the medieval state might have been complete had the Orthodox church not preserved memories of it.[11]

The Serbian Orthodox hierarchy was subject to the Ottoman sultan, who was at the same time the supreme secular and religious leader; however, the Ottomans rarely interfered in the dogmas and organization of the Christian churches. Most of the priests of the Serbian Orthodox church, including its senior hierarchy, were Serbs. The identification of Serbs with the Orthodox church was twofold: the Serbs regarded it as their national institution, and foreigners regarded almost all Orthodox South Slavs who were not Bulgarians as Serbs. This identification with the church increased after restoration of the patriarchate of Peć in 1557. Until it was abolished in 1766, primarily because it was a center of resistance to Turkish rule, the patriarchate had ecclesiastical authority and considerable juridical power over Serbs in Serbia, Montenegro, Bosnia, Herzegovina, and even in Serbian colonies in Habsburg, Hungarian, and Venetian lands.[12]

The higher clergy of the Catholic church in Croatia were often foreigners unable to speak or even understand the language of the people. The Croatian church was also more dependent on outside powers: on the papacy, on the Hungarian diet, and on Vienna. Thus it could give little support to the nobles' struggle to preserve the limited sovereignty of their kingdom or, in the nineteenth century, to the Croatian struggle for modern national identity and independence.[13]

Still, the Catholic church played a significant role—though unintentionally—in the formation of the Croatian national identity. First, it was often the only source of differentiation between Croats and Serbs. Second, the Catholic church was a factor that "made" many people into Croats, just as the Orthodox church "made" many into Serbs. South Slavs who had never developed a rudimentary national consciousness in the sense of historical memory of and identification with the medieval Croatian and Serbian kingdoms simply called themselves Slavs or used the name of their region or tribe, rather than calling themselves Croats or Serbs. Migration and mixing of populations as a result of Turkish invasions also made some populations lose or forget their identities. The Serbian Orthodox church could "transform" undetermined Orthodox South Slavs into Serbs, or "reawaken" those Serbs who had forgotten their identity, because it had characteristics that made it a protonational institution. (The Orthodox church had the same effect elsewhere in the Balkans, on

Greeks and Bulgarians.) The foreign-dominated, Latin-speaking, universalist Catholic church could in a similar way "transform" Catholic South Slavs into Croats or "reawaken" Croats who had forgotten their identity. Catholicism was the dominant religion of the Habsburg monarchy. Croatia, a Catholic kingdom, was part of that empire and was also the only Catholic South Slav kingdom. Over the centuries these combined factors influenced almost all the South Slav Catholics of inner Croatia, Slavonia, Dalmatia, Bosnia, and Herzegovina to identify themselves as Croats.

The Turkish conquest of southeastern Europe provoked massive movements of people. Sometimes the population of whole provinces migrated, rarely moving as organized groups, but invariably seeking areas that afforded freedom, safety, or both. Most of the movement was from southeast to northwest. But there were also migrations on a smaller scale toward the south and southwest. Jesuit attempts to convert Orthodox Serbs to Catholicism, for example, caused some to move within the boundaries of the Ottoman Empire. These population movements continued into the seventeenth century wherever the Habsburg monarchy and Ottoman Empire confronted each other. During this period the greatest mixing of Serbian and Croatian populations took place, making any later drawing of clean ethnic borders between them impossible.[14]

Croats and Serbs did not migrate only within South Slav lands. Already in the late fifteenth century overpopulation and the scarcity of arable land forced many people from Dalmatia to seek a better life in western Europe. In the nineteenth century, North and South America and Australia became preferred destinations. The availability of comparatively cheap maritime transportation and the geographic proximity of their lands to western countries made it easier for "western" Croats than for the "eastern" and more "continental" Serbs to migrate.

The Turkish conquests are regarded as the greatest tragedy in the history of the Croats and Serbs. It was largely as a result of these that the Croats lost both population and territory, sought protection in alliances with stronger foreign powers and in the process surrendered some of their identity. Their experiences under the Turks formed the basis of Croatian nationalists' almost paranoid belief, in the nineteenth and twentieth centuries, that it was the fate of Croatia to become ever smaller until it disappeared altogether. Since the nineteenth century many Croatian and Serbian intellectuals and political figures have viewed their nations in an exaggerated, romantic way, as border nations doomed to devastation by foreign armies, situated on the periphery of Europe, and never fully benefiting from European civilization. These beliefs contain elements of truth to this day, but their frequent and dramatic expression primarily reflects a persisting memory of Turkish rule.

During all the important European cultural and intellectual developments from the fifteenth to the nineteenth centuries, Croatian and Serbian lands remained little more than backward, predominantly peasant provinces, ruled partly by foreign nobles and divided among the Habsburg, Hungarian, Ottoman, and Venetian dominions. There was not a single cultural metropolis. Intellectually and artistically gifted people departed for Vienna, Rome, Venice, Budapest, and Constantinople.

During these centuries the Croats and Serbs developed a tradition of armed groups of volunteers waging fierce and enduring warfare against the Ottomans. The peasant population, living in scattered villages that were difficult to control, sometimes gave help and support to these rebels, but sometimes also organized local militias to fight against them. The tradition of such struggle continued through the Second World War (the Communist-led Partisans were the most powerful guerrilla army in occupied Europe) and, among small groups of anti-Communists, even into the 1950s. It took the advent of the modern state, with its means of transport and communication, and with its efficient control over the populace, finally to make such struggle impracticable. Early on, these rebels acquired heroic status in folk legend. Oral epic ballads and, later, literature celebrated their exploits.

The centuries of foreign domination, however, did not give birth only to rebels. There were Croats and Serbs who in various ways complied with this domination. They did so sometimes for money or power, but also through fear for their own survival and that of their families, or because loyalties were so complex and interwoven. In their legends, history, and art, Croats and Serbs were as merciless toward traitors as they were generous toward their heroes. They proclaimed traitors as absolutely evil, and heroes as absolutely good, and in general refused to see them as anything but permanently opposed forces of light and darkness. The phenomenon of treason became a veritable obsession for Croats and Serbs and a frequent theme of their literature.

Many South Slavs in Bosnia-Herzegovina and the Sandžak adopted the religion of Islam. The Islamization culminated in the sixteenth century, when the Ottoman Empire was at its peak. The motives for conversion have not yet been fully explained. Apparently some nobles who had previously embraced the Bogumil heresy found the Muslim religion and the Ottoman Empire a better protector of their way of life than the Christian kingdoms of southeastern Europe. Their peasants then followed. For low-born converts, acceptance of Islam often meant social advancement. By becoming Muslims they became legally equal members of both a ruling religious community and a powerful empire. In contrast, Christians in areas under Ottoman dominion remained second-class subjects. They were prohibited, for example, from riding horses, carrying weapons, and wearing certain types of clothing, and their choice of occupation and freedom of movement were severely limited.

For South Slav Muslims, membership in the religious community was more important than feelings of solidarity based on a common language or common ethnic characteristics. Religion was paramount in determining political loyalty. Even so, some ethnic and linguistic bonds persisted. Everyone was well aware who was a Muslim colonist from Anatolia and who was a native South Slav Muslim. The South Slav Muslims spoke their own language, and the large majority understood neither Turkish nor Arabic. Periodically the Bosnian nobles revolted against the central power.

Over the centuries the religion and civilization of Islam have formed the South Slav Muslims into a distinctive group. Their way of life, customs, dress, architecture, traditions, and historical memories became a basis for the development of a national identity. Islam, however, is explicitly antinational; it asserts that Muslims should not commit themselves to any nation, since belonging to any community other than that of Islam is unworthy of a true believer. During the nineteenth century and well into the twentieth, religious leaders of the Bosnian Muslims tried to prevent them from becoming Croats or Serbs. The task was made easier by the fact that the large majority of Bosnian Muslims considered themselves to be different from these two nations. Muslim leaders, however, opposed the creation of a Muslim nation with equal zeal. Not until the twentieth century did the transformation of Bosnian Muslims into a nation really begin.[15]

An important consequence of the Ottoman conquests was the creation of the Military Frontier (Vojna krajina). The Habsburgs invited the South Slav population, mostly Orthodox Serbs, from territories under Ottoman rule to inhabit the devastated and depopulated lands on the realm's southeastern borders. New settlers were given land to hold as free peasants, the Serbian Orthodox church became a legally recognized institution in the Habsburg monarchy, and Serbs preserved their patriarchal social organization, traditions, and historical memories.[16] They did not identify with the Croatian kingdom. By the end of the eighteenth century they made up around half of the 700,000 inhabitants of the Military Frontier.[17] Pressures to assimilate them were insignificant until the end of the nineteenth century.

The Military Frontier was the Habsburgs' *cordon sanitaire* between their Christian lands and the Muslim Ottoman Empire. As early as 1579, on a strategic position between Zagreb and the Adriatic Sea, the construction began of a large fortress town, Karlstadt (Karlovac), to serve as its headquarters. The crescent-shaped Military Frontier bordered the Muslim stronghold of Bosnia, from Slavonia in its northeast and north, and from inner Croatia in its northwest. In 1627 the Military Frontier was removed from the control of the Sabor and put under direct rule of the Habsburg military, which would have complete civilian and military authority over it until the Military Frontier's abolition in the early 1870s.[18] This loss of the territory considerably reduced the already small Croatian domain and further weakened the Croatian nobility. Croatia now occupied only 10,600 square kilometers, and its continued existence seemed doubtful. All higher command positions in the Military Frontier were initially held by foreign, mostly Austrian, officers, although over the centuries the number of Croats and Serbs in the highest ranks steadily increased. Inhabitants of the Military Frontier were expected to be unshakable in their loyalty to the emperor (*Kaisertreue*), and all able-bodied men were trained for military service.[19]

With victories over the Ottoman Empire, especially in the first half of the eighteenth century, Vienna added new territories to the Military Frontier and strove to increase its hold over it through administrative reforms and centralization. Around the middle of the century, the Military Frontier became a veritable garrison of the empire, completely incorporating the civilian administration into the military establishment. From that time on, the *Regimenten* from the Military Frontier were among the most important military forces of the Habsburg monarchy. Most Croatian and Serbian officers and many soldiers from the Military Frontier remained *kaisertreu* until the end of the First World War.

The loyalty of Croats and Serbs to the Habsburgs had its origin primarily in the destructiveness and despotism of the Ottoman Empire.[20] When fear of it diminished, demands for more independence grew. Most of the seventeenth century saw relative peace and security from the hitherto incessant raids from Bosnia. The Croatian nobles regained their self-confidence and began to demand the return of lost territories and more independence, in terms that were to become typical over the next few centuries: they insisted on the formal sovereignty of the kingdom of Croatia. Despite all the defeats, losses of territory, and dependence on the Hungarian diet and the Habsburgs over many centuries, the memory of the medieval kingdom, whose legal continuity was uninterrupted, remained strong.

The oppressed Croatian peasantry, that *misera plebs contribuens,* had some attachment to the memories and traditions of the Croatian kingdom but remained loyal to Vienna as long as the latter's reforms made life bearable and afforded protection from the Turks.[21] It was primarily the power of the old Croatian nobility and its roots in the traditions and rights of the Croatian state that presented an obstacle to the centralizing tendencies from Vienna or the attempts to incorporate Croatia into Hungary. However, by the end of the seventeenth century there survived only a few insignificant remnants of the old great noble families of Croatian blood. Closer contacts with Vienna, and its direct influence on Croatia's internal affairs, would often benefit Croatia in terms of economic prosperity, culture, civilization, and "progress" in general, but at the same time they weakened its independence.

The two most important social forces behind the creation of the modern state in western Europe were the urban middle class and the absolute monarchy. In Croatia toward the end of the eighteenth century the urban middle class was very small and consisted often of non-Croats; Vienna, the capital of the absolute monarchy from which modern reforms were emanating, was outside Croatia and was dominated by the German language. The creation of a modern Croatian national consciousness had to be achieved through a struggle on many fronts. As in western Europe, the Croats had to combat the traditional feudal forces: the nobility and the church. Croats, however, had additional obstacles, two of which were the carriers of modernity itself: the state "machinery" of the absolute monarchy, and the urban middle class. Both of these mostly used the German language and were a threat to Croatian identity. Finally, there was the growing Hungarian nationalism, which in the nineteenth century would become a powerful force trying to include Croatia in a greater Hungary and denationalize the Croats.

Around the middle of the nineteenth century both Croats and Serbs sought national emancipation and expansion, demanding the creation of certain national institutions (including a civil service, armed forces, basic industries, a national educational system, and safe access to international trade routes and markets). For the Serbs, this political awakening coincided with a cultural and linguistic national awakening. For the Croats, a cultural and linguistic awakening preceded the quest for political self-determination. The Habsburg monarchy never called the Croats a nation, since this term was associated with republicanism and the French revolution. But in the second half of the nineteenth century it officially recognized them as a "political people," which implied the right to political representation and political autonomy.

To become national ideologies, the national political programs of both Croats and Serbs had first to be accepted by their political and intellectual elites and then to penetrate to and be assimilated by the broadest segments of the population—that is, the peasantry. By the time Yugoslavia was created in 1918, both Croatian and Serbian national ideologies were fully formed and widely distributed.

The development of Croatian and Serbian national ideologies during the nineteenth century soon brought political disagreements and conflicts. One of these concerned the cultural and political rights of the Serbs in Croatia. Other disputes arose about territories: despite the fact that a large proportion of Croats and Serbs lived mixed together in the same regions, both groups demanded the inclusion of all their people in one state. Both nationalisms saw themselves as struggling in the first place for the restoration of their medieval kingdoms and romantically exaggerated the resemblance of those kingdoms to fully developed nation states. They were prone also to operate from selective memory, recalling the greatest territories possessed in the past and laying claim to them accordingly.

After the creation of the Kingdom of the Serbs, Croats, and Slovenes in 1918 (renamed the Kingdom of Yugoslavia in 1929), the Serbs' centralist conception of the state and their numerical preponderance caused a radical increase in Croatian nationalism. Between the two world wars the Serbian political, bureaucratic, and military elites, together with the monarchy, assumed a dominant, though not monopolistic, role in Yugoslav political life. The majority of Croatian political parties charged that Yugoslavia was under "Serbian hegemony." The support for a united Yugoslav state, which had been considerable among Croatian politicians since the beginning of the twentieth century, and had indeed become prevalent among young and educated Croats toward the end of the First World War, almost completely disappeared. Instead, during the interwar years Croats called for independence of some sort, ranging from limited autonomy to complete separation. They differed also about the size of territories claimed and the methods used, extending from peaceful protests to terrorism and plans for genocide.

In 1849 John Stuart Mill condemned nationalism for making men indifferent to the rights and interests of "any portion of the human species" except their own nation.[22] In the interwar years, Croatian and Serbian nationalists were oblivious even to the rights and liberties of their own conationals. Most Serbian politicians, for example, were willing to accept, at least temporarily, the establishment of King Aleksandar's dictatorship in 1929, because it preserved the unity of Yugoslavia. Likewise, the influential Croatian Peasant Party (CPP; Hrvatska seljačka stranka) made a deal in 1939 with the autocratic regime of Prince Regent Pavle, giving Croatia autonomy; the party's primary goal was Croatian independence rather than liberal-democratic institutions.

The Second World War brought the most violent conflicts between Croats and Serbs in their long history. Yugoslavia was invaded by Germany and its allies in April 1941 and was quickly defeated. The Axis victors divided the country among themselves and proclaimed their intention never to let it reunite. Italy shared Slovenia with Germany and took Montenegro and Dalmatia. Germany placed Serbia under direct military occupation and administration. Macedonia went to Bulgaria. Kosovo became part of a greater Albania under Italian control. Parts of Vojvodina were incorporated into greater Hungary, except for territories with a large German population, which went to the Reich. The Axis formed Croatia (minus Dalmatia) and Bosnia-Herzegovina into a puppet state, the Independent State of Croatia, and gave power to the Croatian extreme nationalist movement, the Ustashas. The scale and brutality of the Ustasha genocide against the Serbs (as well as the Jews and the Gypsies) has no parallel in the history of southeastern Europe. The subsequent nationalist civil war in the regions with mixed Croatian, Serbian, and South Slav Muslim populations claimed many victims. There, the Communist-led People's Liberation Army, better known as the Partisans, seemed to be the only force capable of bringing to an end the massacres by extremists. It was in these regions that the Communists won their largest following (at first mostly among the Serbs) and controlled the largest territories.

The Partisans' simultaneous campaign against occupiers, collaborators, and Croatian, Serbian, and other nationalist extremists made it possible after the war for the Communists to present themselves as the sole unifying force and to receive support even from many non-Communists. Their postwar federal system was an irreversible step toward national equality among the nations that compose Yugoslavia.[23]

one
———

From the Origins of Yugoslavism to Socialist Internationalism, 1740–1918

Examples of Yugoslavism (belief in the ethnic, linguistic, and cultural unity of the South Slavs, support for their unification, and/or the belief that the South Slavs are or should become one nation) were numerous before the creation of the Yugoslav Communist party in 1919.[1] Yugoslavism was closely correlated with "progressive" ideas—the eighteenth-century Enlightenment and its heirs, liberal democracy and revolutionary, mostly socialist, radicalism—at least from the time of the Napoleonic rule over parts of the South Slav lands until 1924, when the party temporarily abandoned its support for a united South Slav state.[2] The Communists' Yugoslavism, probably the most important single factor that from 1941 to 1945 helped it win the civil war in Yugoslavia and attain power, was not only an element in its revolutionary tactics but also a direct result of its "progressive" ideological makeup.[3]

The close relationship between Yugoslavism and "progressive" ideas began with its early association with the Enlightenment. Definitions of the Enlightenment often differed, but they always encompassed its belief in reason, understood sometimes as critical and scientific reason, but sometimes also as a pseudo-religious concept "Reason" that was considered capable of "perfect" social order.[4] In addition, most definitions of the Enlightenment included its faith in secular education and the demand for tolerance among different religions and confessions.[5] Perhaps there was more agreement on what the Enlightenment wanted to abolish than on what its program was. It was against the backwardness of the ignorant masses, against religious obscurantism and clericalism (the medieval "dark centuries"), against traditionalism, and against authority based on divine right and "noble blood." The duty and mission of the enlightened classes was to educate the masses and to free them from these "superstitions" of the past centuries.

The principal limitation of the Enlightenment was its failure to recognize the importance of tradition, history, and collective memory. But it did provide powerful insights into some of the foundations of national identity. Once it became possible to see the common South Slav characteristics of Croats, Bosnian Muslims, and Serbs independently of religion, individual traditions, and historical memories, and outside the existing structures of the Ottoman Empire and the Habsburg monarchy, an ethnic and linguistic homogeneity was discovered in the masses of the Croatian-Muslim-Serbian peasantry, and with it a potential for the creation of a new political community—a South Slav (Yugoslav) nation.

Whereas both Croatian and Serbian nationalisms were turned too much toward the past, the Enlightenment and Yugoslavism were excessively turned toward the future. Croatian and Serbian national consciousnesses were largely based on exactly those things that the Enlightenment was unable to see: history, tradition, religion. Moreover, the Enlightenment underestimated the propensity of the lower social classes to identify with the ruling class and to see its history as their own. The peasantry simply was not ahistorical to the degree that the Enlightenment and, especially, the Enlightenment's latterday partial heirs, the socialists and Communists, believed.

Yugoslavism was restricted mainly to the intelligentsia, which in the underdeveloped and semiliterate lands of the South Slavs included even those with only secondary education, since it presupposed an ability for abstract thinking about social and political matters, a way of thinking that was impossible without at least some systematic secularized education. The Croatian and Serbian national ideologies also were initially the creation and concern of the cultural and political elites, but in the second half of the nineteenth century they spread much faster than Yugoslavism, primarily because they corresponded to a premodern sense of identity based on the memories of medieval Croatian and Serbian polities. Not only was Yugoslavism from the very beginning primarily the concern of the educated, but it rarely reached the peasantry. When it did, the masses of Croats and Serbs did not accept it.[6] They preserved their Croatian or Serbian identity, or preferred regional or sometimes simply confessional appellations. Yugoslavism's greater influence among the masses of the population began only during the Second World War (after almost a century and a half of existence), when, in a Communist version, it appeared to many as the only way out of extreme denationalizing pressures and intranational massacres.

The "revolutionary youth" (mostly Serbs and Croats, but including some Bosnian Muslims) at the turn of the century combined a devotion to Yugoslavism with the romantic belief that one self-sacrificing revolutionary elite should lead the people in the struggle for the national and social liberation: an obvious similarity to the Communist attitudes during the Second World War. They also considered their own Yugoslavism as an example of a higher *nad-plemenska* (supratribal) national consciousness. For them Croats and Serbs were only "tribes," while Yugoslavs were a nation. The Yugoslavism of the "revolutionary youth," like that of the socialists, was strengthened also by their interest in social problems, that is, in Croatian and Serbian peasants and workers, whom they perceived as outside history, so that their common South Slav characteristics seemed much more important than their particular Croatian or Serbian heritages. Like the Communists before and during the Second World War, the "revolutionary youth" and socialists energetically and in a principled way opposed any form of nationalist conflict between Croats and Serbs.[7]

The Communist movement was elitist. Not only did Stalin state that Communists were "men made of special material"; Lenin also insisted that Communist parties should consist of "professional revolutionaries": dedicated and carefully selected cadres. Communist elitism was rooted in the ideas of Marx, which he inherited in part from Hegel, about the higher consciousness of those who comprehend the laws of history and know the inevitable development of mankind. Communist elitism became particularly attractive in underdeveloped Yugoslavia, where the Communists appeared not only as Marxist-Leninists, but also as the elite of the Enlightenment, that is, as radicals of the left struggling for the educational, social, and national emancipation of the masses.[8] The elitism of both the Enlightenment and Marxism-Leninism was antidemocratic. It left no space for the free political participation of the masses before these had been fully emancipated. However, there was a big difference between the two elitisms: the Enlightenment demanded as a precondition for political participation the achievement of concrete and practically possible goals, whereas Marxism-Leninism added utopian demands ("new man," "socialist consciousness," "withering away of the state," "creation of classless society," and so on) and therefore had a totalitarian potential. Its "dictatorship of the proletariat" was not self-limiting either in scope or in time. The Yugoslav Communist revolution was in part a negation and destruction of the ideas of the Enlightenment, especially those concerning individual liberty and political rights of citizens. But in another sense it was an affirmation of those ideas, especially concerning national emancipation and equality.

Absolutism and Enlightenment: The Reforms of Maria Theresa and Joseph II

During Maria Theresa's rule over the Habsburg lands in central Europe (1740–1780), Croatia ceased to be a medieval kingdom and took its first steps toward modernity. Using Enlightenment ideas in tandem with her own commitment to Catholicism, Maria Theresa introduced many important reforms in an effort to strengthen the monarchy and to make the apparatus of the state more efficient. She guaranteed a minimum of land to the serfs and limited the taxes imposed upon them. The legal system, courts, and state administration were modernized, and the number of schools, especially those for elementary education, increased. Maria Theresa also strengthened the state's control over the Catholic church, acquiring for herself decisive influence in the appointment of the higher clergy of her realm. Her reforms benefited the Croats, Slovenes, and Serbs within her monarchy. All these reforms laid the basis for the development of an educated and secularized middle class.

Joseph II, who ruled from 1780 to 1790, extended the religious reforms begun by his mother.[9] He also reformed the judicial system, banned torture as a method of extracting confessions, and reduced the application of the death penalty. He abolished the subordination of serfs to the will of their masters and imposed taxes on all social groups.[10] To protect their privileges and prevent these reforms, the Croatian nobility sought an alliance with the more powerful Hungarian nobility, which also opposed Joseph II. But the reaction of the Hungarian nobility to these reforms was different from the Croatian, reflecting a different level of involvement in the intellectual and social developments of western Europe.[11] The Croatian nobility had no political program but the preservation of the status quo. It reacted by rolling hedgehoglike into a prickly ball: it clung to traditionalism and invoked its medieval privileges. It resisted the use of German for state administration, not to promote the Croatian language, but to preserve Latin as the official language. Latin had been used for centuries in the multilingual Habsburg monarchy as the language of politics and administration and was used by the Hungarian and Croatian nobles in the Hungarian diet in Pozsony. Its use impeded the development of national cultures and of modern national consciousness. Nevertheless, Latin was still an important symbol and guarantor of the continuity of the medieval Croatian state. Thus, although Latin was supranational and therefore anational, the nobles saw it as a force protecting what remained of the individuality of the Croatian feudal state.

The Croatian nobility's opposition to the centralism of Vienna was largely inspired by prejudices against the modern state as such, including the selection of a civil service on the basis of merit and efficiency. At the same time the Hungarian diet began to develop a program of modern Hungarian nationalism. It aspired to the creation of a greater Hungary that would encompass territories from the Carpathian mountains to the Adriatic Sea and over which the Hungarian language would enjoy monopoly in public life, economic affairs, learning, and science.

Those few Croats who had benefited from intellectual developments in western Europe found eighteenth-century Croatia dominated by clerical-ism of the most conservative kind. The church hierarchy of Zagreb, for example, appeared to them as a "monstrum ignorantiae."[12] During the reign of Joseph II the dependence of the Roman Catholic church in Croatia on the policies of Vienna increased further. The power and auton-omy of the monasteries were severely limited by Joseph's reforms. Many were transformed into institutions with a medical or other utilitarian purpose. Yet the "progress" and Enlightenment, often achieved through coercive measures, inevitably had a darker side. The Pauline monastery of Lepoglava in Croatia, for example, an important and ancient center of Catholic learning, was closed and the monks expelled.

Joseph II had very limited success with his reforms, primarily because of opposition from the Hungarian and Croatian nobility. His projected reforms were fully implemented only after the revolution of 1848. Still, feudalism was retreating. A market economy was developing, and towns grew apace with the manufacturing industries. Maria Theresa and Joseph II considered a strong state apparatus centrally controlled from Vienna to be a necessary instrument for their reforms, as well as a successful mod-ern development of traditional powers of the throne. So, although the reforms of Maria Theresa and Joseph II did in general benefit Croatia, they involved an increase in centralism and thus further limitations to the independence of Croatia. Theresian and Josephinian reforms were resumed by the French administrators of the South Slav provinces after Napoleon's conquest of part of the Habsburg empire. The social, eco-nomic, legal, and above all else the educational basis was thus slowly being created for the appearance of the modern Croatian national con-sciousness, and to a certain extent also of the Serbian one, as well as for the appearance of the idea of cultural and, later, political unity of the South Slavs.

The Imperialists of the Enlightenment and the Unity of the South Slavs

The French revolution of 1789 aroused little attention in the South Slav lands of the Habsburg monarchy. Unlike most western and central Euro-pean countries, there was no revolutionary ferment in the towns, and the mood of the peasants did not become rebellious. In Croatia, remote from western European political and intellectual life, only the Sabor reacted to events in France, by moving closer to the Hungarian diet. It hoped that alliance with such a senior partner would guarantee the preservation of the political and social status quo. The ideas of the French revolution reached South Slav lands only with the arrival of Napoleon's troops. After their victories over the Habsburgs and the capture of Venice, the French marched into Dalmatia in 1805, into the city-republic of Dubrovnik (at that time better known by its Italian name, Ragusa) in 1806 (uniting it administratively with Dalmatia), and into inner Croatia and the Military Frontier in 1809.[13]

Many educated Europeans at that time regarded the South Slavs as descendants of the ancient Illyrians. In the same spirit, the French imperial administration considered the South Slavs to be one Illyrian people speaking one Illyrian language. (The individuality of the Slovenian language was only partly recognized.) The French called the conquered Croatian and Serbian lands (together with Slovenia, whose capital, Ljubljana, was made the administrative center) *les provinces illyriennes,* reviving the name from the time of the Roman Empire.

French rule, which could be described as a dictatorship of the Enlightenment, imposed on the South Slavs the political, social, and legal institutions of postrevolutionary France. The Illyrian provinces became a part of the French empire, though not a constitutional part of France; the Code Napoléon was only partly implemented in the region. However, all citizens of the conquered South Slav lands were equal before the law. Peasants were freed from their feudal obligations and made owners of the land they tilled. They were also released from *corvée,* obligatory labor on the estates of the nobles and the king and on roads and bridges. Nobles lost all political and legal privileges and were taxed along with all other citizens. (This reform, as well as some others, was partly a repetition of what Joseph II had tried but mostly failed to achieve.) The monopoly of craftsmen's guilds was abolished, and the learning and practice of crafts were made free. Modernization of agriculture, trade, and the region's nascent manufactures began. There was widespread construction of new roads and irrigation canals. In 1810 the French authorities decreed that children in elementary schools be taught *la langue du pays.* A population literate in its own language was regarded as essential for the development of trade and industry, of a modern administration, and of the taxation system. *Kraljski Dalmatin* (The Royal Dalmatian), published from 1806 to 1810, was the first journal to use the Croatian ("Illyrian") language (together with French).

Napoleon's empire collapsed before the reforms could be fully implemented. Nevertheless, enough traces survived to provide foundations for the South Slavs' development of their national culture. The perception of South Slavs as Illyrians was based on a poor knowledge of ethnology and history. But it was not ignorance alone that made French military and civilian officials see the South Slavs (both those recently under Habsburg rule and those still under the Ottoman Empire) as one people. The French civilian and military officials were, to be sure, above all else representatives of the French empire. But at the same time, by the nature of the reforms they were implementing they were veritable commissars of the Enlightenment and the French Revolution. They regarded both the Habsburg and the Ottoman empires as archaic political creations lacking any real legitimacy. Likewise, all crucial elements of the Croatian and Serbian individualities— their traditions, loyalties, historical memories, and their different confessions (Roman Catholicism and Serbian Orthodoxy)—also seemed irrelevant and archaic. In no way could, for example, the Sabor of the Croatian nobility, preserving the continuity with the Croatian medieval state, appear to the French officials as a parliament of *la nation*. To the French such phenomena were merely remnants of the feudal past, "reactionary" sediments deposited by history, and hence eminently unsuitable as a basis for any kind of modern national consciousness. The sooner they were eliminated, together with the social groups (nobility and clergy) that had sustained them, the sooner would appear the "real people," out of which a nation could be built. These "real people" were the peasants, and in the Croatian and Serbian lands they spoke one language and exhibited deep ethnic similarities. Precisely because of their abstract and rationalist method of thinking away history, tradition, and religion, the French were among the first to see the important unifying similarities among the South Slavs in general, and among Croats and Serbs in particular.

Illyrianism: The Croatian National Revival and the Yugoslav Idea

The Habsburg monarchy, for all its conservatism, was far from immune to the intellectual and political influences of western Europe. These influences were also penetrating its South Slav provinces. In the eighteenth and nineteenth centuries the Ottoman Empire was an archaic political structure in comparison with the Habsburg state. In terms of technological progress, economic development, and overall civilization, the "Austrian" ("western") South Slavs enjoyed a considerable advantage over their "Turkish" ("eastern") kin. Yet those under Ottoman rule enjoyed advantages of their own. In the eighteenth and nineteenth centuries the Ottoman Empire was not only inefficiently organized but also increasingly corrupt and militarily weak.[14] It was thus possible for Montenegro and Serbia to acquire self-rule, and later to emerge as internationally recognized sovereign states.

Moreover, Ottoman Turkey, as a Muslim empire, possessed none of the institutions of a modern nation state. Until the 1870s, when "Ottomanism" began to evolve into modern Turkish nationalism, it neither could nor sought to transform its subject peoples into Turks. On the other hand, the administrative, economic, cultural, and linguistic policies of the modern Hungarian, Italian, and Austrian-German nationalisms—the latter often using the imperial centralism of the Habsburg court—proved to be powerful and dangerous denationalizing forces for the western South Slavs. A high-ranking Habsburg military official who was also a Croatian patriot, remarked in 1861: "I would prefer to see my people under the Turkish yoke than to live under the complete control of one of its educated neighbors . . . Educated peoples demand from a people over whom they rule also their soul, that is to say, their nationality."[15]

The crucial difference for the Serbs in Serbia in relation to the Croats was the absence of a threat to their national identity. The Serbian peasant revolution of 1804 against Ottoman feudalism created conditions for their national cultural awakening, as well as for the development of an autonomous national political entity.[16] After the defeat of Napoleon and the Congress of Vienna in 1815, the Habsburg monarchy became increasingly centralized and imposed numerous antiliberal measures. Hungarian nationalism was gaining strength, as was Hungary's grip on Croatia. Probably at no other point in her history was Croatia so dependent on Hungary as after the Napoleonic War; nor was its political class (the high nobility and the clergy) ever so unquestioningly oriented toward it. Within the larger framework of the Habsburg monarchy, Hungary was undergoing transformation into a nation state. Hungarian was the sole language in the educational system and in the administration. In 1827 the Croatian Sabor introduced Hungarian as an obligatory subject in higher education. The *ban* (governor) of Croatia, appointed by Vienna, was often a Hungarian noble. Dalmatia was administered directly from Vienna; Slavonia was further integrated into Hungary. Croatia, it seemed, was more divided than ever. From that time until the dissolution of the Habsburg monarchy at the end of the First World War, the destiny of Croatia was largely determined by relations between Vienna and Budapest. Croatia received limited support from the emperor and his government when they wanted to exert pressure on the Hungarians. But when they preferred a policy of appeasing the Hungarians, the Habsburgs always found it wise to be conciliatory and to grant the Hungarians more and more power over Croatia.

Fear of Magyarization aroused patriotic resistance among the small Croatian intelligentsia. They launched a movement for national revival ("awakening") under the Illyrian name, which encompassed all the South Slavs (in some versions it included the Bulgarians also). The Illyrianist movement believed in the ethnic, linguistic, and cultural unity of all South Slavs.[17] Some of its proponents hoped for eventual political unification and even an independent South Slav state. Illyrianism was thus a proto-Yugoslav movement.

The three major nations surrounding the South Slavs of the Habsburg monarchy in the nineteenth century were the Austrians (Germans), the Italians, and the Hungarians. The ethnic and linguistic differences among the South Slavs were insignificant in comparison with their differences from those peoples. The nascent Croatian intelligentsia was much smaller than its neighboring Hungarian, Austrian (German), and Italian counterparts. Croatian cultural centers were small and underdeveloped. These facts increased the attractiveness of Illyrianism: as a concept encompassing all South Slavs it enlarged the number of people in whose name the Croatian educated elite sought to speak.

The ideas of the Illyrianist movement increased the self-confidence of the first Croatian promoters of the national awakening. The Croatian national identity, as purely "Croatian" (and not as South Slav or Illyrian), was based primarily on the memories and traditions of the medieval Croatian state. At the beginning of the nineteenth century those memories were fading. They would be resurrected in the second half of the nineteenth century by national, and often nationalistic, Croatian historians, and by the Party of Croatian Rights (Hrvatska stranka prava), which sought legitimacy for its program for Croatian independence in the surviving documents and treaties of the medieval Croatian state and the Sabor.[18]

In the 1820s and 1830s the Croatian appellation was applied mostly to the inhabitants of the central region of inner Croatia, mostly the territories around Zagreb and Varaždin, who spoke the *kajkavski* dialect. This dialect had its own independent literary tradition and was called at that time Croatian. Furthermore, the conservative petty nobility of this Croatian Vendée was Magyarophile (the so-called *madjaroni*), that is, pro-Hungarian. Ante Starčević, a Croatian nationalist and the founder of the Party of Croatian Rights, who supported Illyrianism in his youth, explained in 1870 that to call oneself a Croatian in the 1830s amounted to declaring oneself to be a Magyarophile.[19] The Croatian national revival, which centered mostly in Zagreb and inner Croatia, could transcend the confines of inner Croatia and encompass all Croatian lands only by using a more inclusive name—in this case, Illyrian.

In the 1830s, under the leadership of Ljudevit Gaj, the struggle for a national language began in earnest. Gaj, though a mediocre man of letters, had an exceptional talent for popularizing the ideas of the "awakening." The year 1835, which saw the launching of the journal *Danica ilirska* (The Illyrian Morning Star) under Gaj's editorship, is usually taken as the year of the birth of the movement.[20] The Illyrianists undertook a variety of cultural activities. They opened reading clubs in various Croatian towns, wrote didactic poems to awaken the national consciousness of the "Illyrians," and published journals, most of them literary. Some of this literature had to be written in German, since a good part of the Croatian middle class, especially in Zagreb, had become linguistically and culturally Germanized. A chair of "Illyrian" language and literature was established at Zagreb University, and the first Croatian opera was performed. Among the new literary works there appeared a masterpiece, Ivan Mažuranić's long poem *Smrt Smail-age Čengića* (The Death of Smail-aga Čengić), with a theme characteristic of the all-Yugoslav historical interests of the Illyrianists: the struggle of the Montenegrins against the Turks.

The Illyrianists had to decide which of the three dialects—*kajkavski, čakavski,* or *štokavski*—to take for the literary language. *Kajkavski* and *čakavski* were spoken only by Croats. *Štokavski* was used not only by the majority of the Croats but also by all Serbs.[21] Most of the first Illyrianists spoke *kajkavski*. Their decision to promote *štokavski* instead meant abandoning their own dialect, with its own well-developed literary tradition. Thus they sacrificed a large part of their regional cultural heritage to what they considered to be the true national interest.

It was difficult to call *štokavski hrvatski* (Croatian), as this appellation might have been understood at that time to mean *kajkavski*. Also, the Serbs spoke *štokavski* too, and called this common language Serbian. The Illyrianists hoped that the Illyrian name would prove acceptable to the Serbs, which the Croatian name could never be. Although the Illyrianists believed that the Illyrian name and the Illyrian idea encompassed and represented all South Slavs, the nexus of Illyrianism was in fact the cultural and linguistic heritage of the Croats and Serbs, especially those of the *štokavski* dialect. It was this dialect that was to be established as the literary language of both Croats and Serbs. In Croatia it was introduced into all aspects of public life despite opposition from the Magyarophile petty nobility of inner Croatia.

The Illyrianist movement was largely apolitical; its primary goal was the affirmation of the "Illyrian" language and culture. Most of its members appear to have been loyal to the Habsburg dynasty. The minority who had political aims merely hoped for a moderate improvement of Croatia's position in relation to Vienna and especially to Hungary. A few individuals formulated bolder plans. Count Janko Drašković was politically the most articulate Illyrianist. This educated and widely traveled Jacobin aristocrat argued for the creation of a South Slav kingdom— "greater Illyricum"—within the Habsburg monarchy. In 1832 his *Disertacija* (The Dissertation) was published—the first modern Croatian political treatise—in which he elaborated his proposals for enlightened and democratic political and social reforms.[22]

Metternich's Vienna initially supported the Illyrianist movement and even granted some financial help, since Illyrianism provided a useful counterforce to Hungarian nationalism. Politically moderate and even opportunistic and docile, the Illyrianists were ready to make compromises not only with Vienna, but also in internal Croatian politics. They were extremely cautious in proposing any reforms limiting the power and privileges of the clergy and nobles. Yet the Illyrianist movement, like other movements for national revival in central and southeastern Europe, did accomplish a major cultural revolution. In promoting the language and culture of the common people, Illyrianism implicitly challenged the political and social status quo, including the legitimacy of the Habsburg monarchy. For how could the ordinary people, the peasantry, be denied political rights if their language, literature, and traditions were proclaimed to possess great cultural and spiritual value? Journals, educational institutions, the use of the national language—all contributed to a "plebeian-democratic" national consciousness.[23]

The formation of the Magyarophile Croatian-Hungarian Party (Hrvatsko-ugarska stranka) was followed in 1841 by the formation of the Illyrian Party (Ilirska stranka), in a defensive reaction to the threat of linguistic and cultural Magyarization. The movement for a national language and culture thus acquired a political dimension. Yet the goals of the Illyrian Party were primarily cultural, rather than political in the exact sense. The party program demanded that the national language be taught in schools and that the educational system be reformed to reflect the national spirit.

The feeling of unease in the cautious Metternich administration at the relatively fast growth of the Illyrianist movement, and the strength of Hungarian influences in Vienna, are usually given by Croatian historians as causes for the banning of the use of the Illyrian name. In 1843 the Illyrian Party renamed itself the People's Party (Narodna stranka).[24] In the same year Ivan Kukuljević made the first speech in the history of the Sabor in the Croatian (that is, what has until recently been called "Illyrian") language. He demanded the introduction of the Croatian language into public life and the Croatian administration. The resistance of the nobility who defended the use of Latin, coupled with attempts to introduce German and Hungarian, delayed acceptance of Kukuljević's proposal until 1847. The People's Party was more political than the Illyrian Party had been. It demanded the unification of Croatian lands—that is, extension of the power of the Sabor to Slavonia and Dalmatia. Thus with the creation of the People's Party the Illyrianist movement, whose membership was from the very beginning almost exclusively Croatian, became primarily a Croatian national movement in its aspirations and ideology.

The necessary social precondition for the emergence of the Illyrianist movement had been a nascent social group of affluent and educated town-dwellers who had had contact with western European ideas. Their backgrounds ranged from peasant stock to the nobility. What they had in common was a relatively high level of formal or informal education, and a standard of living high enough to enable them to acquire such an education. Some had lived and worked in the capitals of western and central Europe. A few had been students at Austrian universities, where they had met promoters of the Czech and other national revivals. Their intellectual influences were the Enlightenment in general and German, central European, and Italian romanticism in particular. Illyrianism did not develop on the basis of any concrete political tradition or through established political institutions and practices. Most Illyrianists were outsiders to the existing political structures of Croatia and the Habsburg monarchy. Their approach to the social reality was, therefore, abstract and rationalistic.[25] All this accounts for the Illyrianists' frequent lack of political realism, the unstable and even irresponsible conduct of some of their leaders, and their attraction to utopian ideas and fantastic plans.

But the abstract and rationalistic character of Illyrianism was what assured its main achievement: the Croatian national awakening. At the time of its appearance, Croatia's three main provinces—inner Croatia, Dalmatia, and Slavonia—were "submerged" in separate, largely alien cultural and political traditions. Croatian identity was hidden under separate influences and loyalties. Any cultural movement that might have sprung from a concrete institutional framework and existing political institutions would have failed to get beyond the boundaries of any of the three provinces. Through the political practice and experience then prevailing, Croatia as a whole could never have been reached, nor would the common Croatian and South Slav linguistic and cultural values have emerged.[26]

The Serbian Rejection of Illyrianism

The Illyrianist movement did have some support among educated Habsburg Serbs, especially in Vojvodina, which was prosperous and culturally advanced. But the Serbs in Serbia simply did not need it. They had already begun to develop their own national identity. The *štokavski* dialect had already been accepted in Serbia as the literary language and was called Serbian. Vuk Stefanović Karadžić, a Serbian scholar, was collecting Serbian epic poetry, stories, and proverbs; compiling a dictionary; and writing on history and ethnology. Serbia was in fact already on its way to becoming an independent sovereign state.

The Illyrianists never avoided using the name *Serb*. (However, for them this appellation—like the appellation *Croat*—did not stand for the name of a separate nation. It was more a "tribal" and regional name.) They also showed no prejudice against use of the Cyrillic alphabet, and indeed advocated its use together with the dominant Latin alphabet in the Croatian administration and educational institutions. Illyrianism did promote contacts and cooperation between Croatian Zagreb and Serbian Belgrade. But at the same time—with the incipient political national consciousness—significant sections of the political and cultural elites of Zagreb and Belgrade were already beginning to confront each other with different ideas and programs about the political and cultural organization of the South Slavs.[27] Serbian critics of Illyrianism rightly objected that the name *Illyrian* was artificial and alien, but the main reason for their rejection of Illyrianism was the fear that Illyrianism would strengthen Habsburg and Catholic influence among the South Slavs and the cultural prestige and political power of Zagreb, at the expense of Belgrade and the Orthodox church. They also feared that it would advance Croatian influence in Bosnia, thereby undercutting Serbian influence in that province. Because it was led by Croats and its center was in Zagreb, many Serbs perceived Illyrianism (Yugoslavism) as a movement for Croatian national expansion. (The same applied in reverse after the creation of Yugoslavia in 1918: Croats perceived Yugoslavism led by Serbs and with its center in Belgrade as primarily furthering Serbian interests. Thus, the Illyrianist movement remained confined to its Croatian membership. Although its aspirations were Yugoslav, its lack of attraction for the other South Slavs reduced it to a Croatian national revival. Still, Illyrianism was to survive in a changed and developed form, as the idea of close cultural and political cooperation between Croats and Serbs and among South Slavs in general.

Croatian and Serbian Pan-Slavism

Pan-Slavism during the nineteenth century was an incoherent set of often sentimental and vague pronouncements about cultural affinities and political sympathies among Slav peoples. It was not an ideology with any clear-cut political goals (except when it was used by Russian imperialism), nor did it exert a decisive influence on any major political movement. Few pan-Slavists envisaged some future "melting" of all Slavs into one supernation; pan-Slavism presupposed the existence of individual Slav nations. Pan-Slavism was, therefore, a supranational ideology. However, it was not a universalist ideology like, say, liberalism, Roman Catholicism, or Communism. It did not address itself to humanity as a whole or to human beings as individuals. It consisted of ideas about ethnic characteristics, language, history, tradition, and so on—all the typical elements of a nationalist ideology. In other words, its scope was supranational, but its content was deeply national, and even nationalist. These apparently incompatible characteristics were well suited to the Croatian national awakening.[28]

At the beginning of the nineteenth century the Croatian people were exposed to denationalizing pressures from their non-Slav neighbors: Austrians-Germans, Hungarians, and Italians. Pan-Slavism spread the knowledge of the numerical strength of Slavs, their cultural achievements, their history and traditions. It was thus a source of inspiration and self-confidence for those early small groups in Croatia—mostly members of the Illyrianist movement—who were involved in promoting the national language and culture. Croatian pan-Slavism, like pan-Slavism in general, exaggerated the similarities among the Slav peoples.[29] Nevertheless, in underlining their common ethnic and linguistic characteristics, it not only showed them to be similar to each other but also differentiated them as a group from non-Slav peoples. Pan-Slavism could thus help Croats develop a consciousness of their individuality in relation to their non-Slav neighbors. Like its Czech counterpart, Croatian pan-Slavism was primarily anti-German. Also, Croatian pan-Slavism advocated the unity of South Slavs; that is, it was Yugoslavist.[30]

In Serbia and Montenegro pan-Slavism was primarily anti-Turkish. The Christian Slav world and Russia in particular were seen as fraternal allies in the struggle against the Muslim Turks. Fear of Austro-Hungarian and German expansion became widespread in Serbia only after Austria-Hungary's formal annexation of Bosnia-Herzegovina in 1908.[31] At that time Serbia pursued close links with Russia, not from any romantic interest in Slav unity and solidarity, but in order to protect its independence.[32] Among both Croats and Serbs, pan-Slavism was accepted only by members of the cultural and political elite. It had no influence on the majority of the population, the peasantry. It was more widespread in Montenegro, but interpreted in a Russophile way, since Russia had been for centuries that region's protector—more illusory than real—from the Turks.

Serbia and the Unification of the South Slavs

Serbia and Montenegro were more distant than Croatia from central and western European influences. This geographic isolation hindered cultural and economic development but allowed greater opportunities for the creation of independent states. Two great peasant uprisings in 1804 and 1815 launched the process that ultimately led to Serbia's independence from the Ottoman Empire. Throughout the nineteenth century, despite periods of stagnation and even regressions, Serbia was gradually developing the institutions of a modern European state. At least from the middle of the century, Serbia's educated elite looked to England and, especially, France rather than to central Europe for political ideas. This would influence aspects of Serbia's political life and make it in some respects more "western" than that of Croatia.

Around the middle of the nineteenth century Serbia's political elite and intelligentsia increasingly viewed Serbia as the leader of the Serbian and South Slav struggle for unification. Often they equated unification with the territorial expansion of Serbia. This outlook was condensed in a secret document called Načertanije, a draft of a program for Serbia's foreign policy. It was prepared in 1844 by Ilija Garašanin, a conservative states-man with Bismarckian aspirations.[33] (He was helped in his work by a Polish exile, Prince Adam Czartoryski, and his Czech employee and col-laborator František Zach.) His principal aim was to transform Serbia into a strong state with an efficient centralized administration and a standing army. Garašanin's belief in centralism was typical of many nineteenth-century European statesmen, who identified regionalism, autonomy, and federalism with the feudal anarchy of the European nobility and believed that a modern state, in the Jacobin mold, should not allow any such devolution of power.

In Garašanin's view, the strengthening of Serbia was a prerequisite for an assertive foreign policy. The first goal of such a policy would be to achieve complete independence from the Ottoman Empire without allow-ing any great power to take its place. Garašanin showed no pan-Slavist sentimentality about Russia. He held that alliances should be based on a realistic appraisal of power and be guided solely by the interest of the Serbian state and the Serbian nation. (For Garašanin, of course, there could never be any conflict between the interests of the nation and the interests of the state.) The second goal was the unification of all Serbs and South Slavs. For Garašanin this goal was simply a continuation of the first. There was no qualitative difference between them: Serbia as a state was to achieve independence, and then expand. Garašanin showed little understanding of the individuality and traditions of either the Serbs out-side Serbia or the other South Slavs.

Načertanije crystallized the attitudes of the intellectual and political elites, which would remain dominant in Serbia until the creation of Yugoslavia in 1918 and would also decisively influence the policies of Serbian political parties between the two world wars.

Garašanin was a pronouncedly conservative statesman. Hierarchy and order, he believed, rather than freedom of the press and political parties were of the highest importance for an illiterate Balkan country. Garašanin's brand of conservatism, as far as internal politics were con-cerned, was to encounter many opponents in the years after 1844. Demands for the increase in political liberties and for popular participa-tion were to dominate political life in Serbia in the second half of the nineteenth century. On the other hand, Garašanin's ideas about foreign policy for Serbia—or rather, the ideas that he summarized in his program—were seldom challenged. His equation of the interests of all South Slavs with the interests of the Serbian state, and his idea of Serbian and South Slav unification as an extension *tout court* of the Serbian state found almost universal acceptance in Serbia.[34]

Serbia and Montenegro were finally recognized as sovereign states in 1878 at the Congress of Berlin, although their subordination to the Sublime Porte had long been only formal. The last Ottoman troops had left the Belgrade citadel in 1867, leaving only the Ottoman flag as a symbol of Ottoman sovereignty—an object of passionate, almost obsessive, hatred by Serbian patriotic youth. Montenegro had not acknowledged Ottoman suzerainty since the beginning of the eighteenth century. Serbia became a kingdom in 1882, Montenegro in 1910. Serbia continued its territorial expansion through the second half of the nineteenth century until after the Balkan wars of 1912 (against Turkey) and 1913 (against Bulgaria) it encompassed the territories of what are today Serbia and Macedonia, but without Vojvodina, which remained under Austria-Hungary until 1918.[35] In 1903 the pro-Austrian and autocratic Aleksandar Obrenović was overthrown. The grandson of Karadjordje, who ninety-nine years earlier had led the first Serbian uprising against the Turks, ascended the throne and became King Petar I. The small kingdom became a constitutional monarchy with liberal-democratic political institutions such as an uncensored press, political parties, and democratic elections. Nevertheless, the military and the monarchy (the latter only from 1914, when Crown Prince Aleksandar became the regent) exerted considerable influence on Serbia's political life.[36]

In the late nineteenth century Austria-Hungary sought to prevent Serbia and Montenegro from achieving political unity. The monarchy was even more eager to prevent the Serbs from Croatia and Bosnia-Herzegovina from developing common policies with Serbia. These efforts intensified after 1903, when Serbian foreign policy freed itself from the influence of the Habsburg monarchy. The increase in the number of protective barriers erected by Austria-Hungary against the cultural and economic influences emanating from the Serbian state aroused powerful fears among Serbian politicians and intellectuals everywhere that Serbs would remain permanently divided. The creation of the Kingdom of the Serbs, Croats, and Slovenes in 1918 was therefore seen by the majority of Serbs as a form of unification of the Serbian nation, as well as a just reward for the high loss of life and other Serbian sacrifices during the First World War.[37]

Since the middle of the nineteenth century until today the Serbs have been internally divided, not about the need for and desirability of a union of Serbs alone or of Serbs and other South Slavs, but about the constitutional framework and political content of such a state. The conservatives promoted centralism and Serbian primacy over other Serbian and Yugoslav provinces, and of Serbs in general over non-Serbian nations, while the small but vocal and influential left advocated national equality and cultural polycentrism.[38] Only a few believed that Serbs should not or could not exist with other South Slavs in one united state. The ideals and ambitions of socialists were even greater than those of the conservatives, for they also aimed at the creation of a Balkan federation. They considered the creation both of Yugoslavia and of a greater Balkan federation not only a prerequisite for the integration of all South Slavs (including the Bulgarians), but also a step toward a future socialist Europe.[39]

The Serbian left characteristically insisted that the policies it favored were intrinsically good. They promoted the rights of individuals and tolerance among nations. Thus they satisfied some crucial criteria for an enlightened and humanitarian political morality on the national question. Moreover, such policies were the only way in which a true and lasting unity of Serbs with other South Slavs and other peoples of the Balkans might be achieved. Hegemony and great-Serbian domination over others would only cause nationalistic hatreds and conflicts. National equality and polycentrism would be the weapon with which to subdue Serbian hegemonistic nationalism and at the same time the "preventive medicine" against all separatist nationalisms of the other South Slavs.[40]

Conflict and Cooperation between Croats and Serbs

During the last quarter of the nineteenth century Croatia's economic development was accompanied by more intense conflicts with Hungary. The Croatian railways were being constructed as an integral part of the Hungarian railway system, and Hungarian was the only language used on them. Also, Hungarian flags, emblems, coats of arms, and inscriptions were being erected everywhere. The penetration of the Hungarian language, however, inspired the greatest resentment.[41] Yet the Croatian intellectual and political elite, most of them from the small middle class, was too weak to resist. This fact was demonstrated clearly when Vienna appointed as the *ban* of Croatia Károly Khuen-Héderváry, who was to rule over Croatia from 1883 until 1903. A resourceful politician, Khuen-Héderváry approached Croatia in the way a governor appointed by an imperial power would approach a backward but not unruly colony. Khuen-Héderváry's achievements as an administrator and organizer were darkened by his style of rule, which combined cunning and ruthlessness with an ingenious feeling for the weaknesses of a society with an undeveloped political life, whose inexperienced political elites lacked self-confidence. Khuen-Héderváry soon achieved full control over the Croatian Sabor and the dominant People's Party. The opposition of the Party of Croatian Rights and of the Independent People's Party (Neodvisna narodna stranka) was ineffective, primarily because their middle-class constituency was rather small. The masses of peasants were still not politicized.[42]

Even a less perceptive "colonial governor" than Khuen-Héderváry would have noticed the increasing split between Croats and Serbs in Croatia, and in particular the Serbs' fear of the nationalist extremism of the Party of Croatian Rights. (Its founder and leader, Ante Starčević, sometimes even threatened the Serbs with extermination.)[43] Khuen-Héderváry quickly applied the well-known precept that it is easier to rule over a province when one increases its internal divisions. Minor concessions to the Serbian minority with respect to the Orthodox religion, use of the Cyrillic alphabet, and participation in local government gained him a degree of loyalty and support from a section of the Serbian middle class. So began a long period of bitter nationalist polemics and confrontations between parts of the Croatian and Serbian intelligentsia. This conflict culminated in anti-Serbian demonstrations in Zagreb in 1902, during which there were violent attacks on Serbs and destruction of their property.[44]

During Khuen-Héderváry's rule two nascent political movements tried to address constituencies outside the middle class. The social democrats focused on the small working class, the liberal nationalist intelligentsia on the peasantry, which made up the majority of the population. In 1904 the latter formed the Croatian People's Peasant Party (Hrvatska pučka seljačka stranka) under the leadership of brothers Antun and Stjepan Radić.[45] Both movements were "progressive," that is, they addressed the lower social classes and were anticlerical and antitraditionalist. The social democrats, however, were internationalists, whereas the Peasant Party was patriotic (or, perhaps, nationalist). Nevertheless, intellectuals of the Peasant party (Antun Radić in particular) asserted that the Croatian people, whom they identified with the peasantry, had no history, since their ruling nobility, who were the creators of history, were of non-Croatian origin or were unpatriotic and dependent on foreign powers and interests.

Once the social democratic and peasant party intellectuals had begun to "see" the Croatian people quite apart from their history, tradition, and Roman Catholic religion, and then "saw" the Serbs with the same eyes, it was inevitable that the ethnically and linguistically homogeneous Croatian and Serbian peasantry would appear to them as close to each other and even as one nation. The Pravaši, the supporters of the Party of Croatian Rights, based their claim for a sovereign Croatian state on the legal documents, sometimes centuries old, of the Sabor, with which they tried to prove the continuity of the Croatian state from medieval times. For them this state was a reality, on the basis of a legal existence, even if it existed only on paper. The new young democratic forces, on the other hand, demanded Croatian independence and political rights for the peasants in terms of liberal-democratic principles and ideas about the rights of man.

The Croatian-Serbian Coalition of 1905

Toward the end of the nineteenth century western European political influences began to make themselves felt in Dalmatian towns, especially Split, Zadar, and Rijeka. Politicians of vision appeared who considered the future of Croats and Serbs within the broader context of European politics. Unlike the politicians of inner Croatia and Slavonia, who were almost exclusively concerned with resisting Hungary, the Dalmatian politicians Ante Trumbić and, especially, Frano Supilo perceived German expansionism—the *Drang nach Osten* ("drive to the east"), with its influential allies among politicians and the military of the Habsburg monarchy—as the greatest threat to South Slav aspirations for independence.[46]

Freedom of the press and assembly was greater in Hungary than in Croatia. Therefore, the city of Rijeka, then under direct Hungarian administration from Budapest, was chosen for a meeting of Dalmatian political leaders in October 1905. The ensuing resolution of Rijeka was much more broadly conceived than any previous Croatian political document. It showed that Croatian politics could go beyond mere resistance to external pressures from Vienna or Budapest. At that time political developments in Hungary seemed to be leading toward claims for that nation's complete independence. Traditionally, this would have prompted Croatian politicians to seek protection from Vienna. But the resolution of Rijeka did the very opposite—it declared support for the Hungarians.[47]

The resolution was the sign of a newfound confidence and a new maturity in an important section of the Croatian political elite, and a sign that the Croats were developing a modern political national consciousness. The Hungarians' aspirations were accepted and supported on the grounds that every nation had the right to self-determination. The same right to an independent political, cultural, and economic development was claimed for the Croats, coupled with a demand that Dalmatia be incorporated into Croatia. The resolution demanded freedom of the press and assembly, an independent judiciary, and free elections.

The resolution of Rijeka was the first expression of support by a major Croatian political group for the idea of a South Slav state.[48] It was particularly influential in Dalmatia, but it was also accepted by several political groups in inner Croatia and Slavonia. In addition, it was supported by many Serbian politicians, both in inner Croatia and Slavonia, and in Dalmatia (in the resolution of Zadar of October 1905). These Serbian politicians, however, added their demand that Serbs be recognized as a nation, and not merely as a religious group belonging to the Serbian Orthodox church.

The liberal-democratic ideas of the resolution of Rijeka promoted cooperation between Croatian and Serbian politicians. Factions within the Party of Croatian Rights, for example, developed a liberal version of its ideology: the resolution of Rijeka asserted that the rights of the Croatian nation were founded on the rights of man; thus, the claims based on the legal continuity of the Croatian state, which had been paramount in the Party of Croatian Rights, were reduced to secondary importance. The new concept that the claims of the individual citizen and voter had priority over claims based on the legal traditions of the state also made it possible to involve other citizens of a different national consciousness— that is, Serbs—in the Croatian political process.

The creation of the Croatian-Serbian Coalition (Hrvatsko-srpska koalicija) in Croatia in December 1905 was a crucial event in the history of Croatian-Serbian relations.[49] This was an alliance between Croatian political parties—the Party of Croatian Rights and the Croatian Progressive Party (Hrvatska napredna stranka)—and Serbian ones—the Serbian People's Independent Party (Srpska narodna samostalna stranka) and Serbian People's Radical Party (Srpska narodna radikalna stranka). The Social Democratic Party of Croatia and Slavonia (Socijal-demokratska stranka Hrvatske i Slavonije), which had mixed Croatian and Serbian membership, was a member of the coalition until April 1906. The coalition held power in Croatia only briefly in 1906, when after winning the elections it dominated the Sabor, but there were other intervals of coalitional rule when it held power in local administration. Until the end of the First World War its influence on the Croatian and, at least within Austria-Hungary, on South Slav politics was greater than that of any other South Slav political party.[50]

For the first time, large and representative groups of Croatian and Serbian politicians were united in one political body around a common national program that proclaimed as its ultimate goal the unification of the South Slavs. The coalition also fully acknowledged the danger to all South Slavs from German-Austrian nationalism and imperialism. At that time both Vienna and Berlin considered independent Serbia as an obstacle to their goal of *Drang nach Osten*. As a result, Serbs living in Austria-Hungary were often suspected of being a subversive and secessionist national element. Yet most of the Viennese government's pressures and intrigues against the coalition were unsuccessful; they merely served to compromise the monarchy in Europe, and helped present and popularize the idea of South Slav unification to European public opinion.

The Yugoslavism of the Croatian-Serbian Coalition was made possible by its emphasis on liberal-democratic political institutions and on the universal right of nations to self-determination. Arguments for political legitimacy had moved away from the irreconcilable Croatian and Serbian national ideologies based on historical memories. The coalition opposed the participation of clergy in political affairs and held that religious beliefs and values were the private concern of the individual. This separation of the churches from politics helped to remove an important obstacle to Croatian and Serbian cooperation and unity.

"Revolutionary Youth"

Toward the end of the nineteenth century a generation of young revolutionaries arose among the Croats and Serbs of the Habsburg monarchy, inspired by radical "progressive"—populist, anarchist, and socialist—ideas. Most of them hoped for the destruction of Austria-Hungary; many also favored the unification of South Slavs in one sovereign state with a republican form of government, democratic political institutions, and some form of socialist economic organization. Known in Yugoslav historiography as the "revolutionary youth," this group professed no coherent or developed ideology. Their ideas were rarely Marxist. There were other influences, such as that of Proudhon, but probably the strongest was the influence of the nineteenth-century Russian revolutionaries. With romantic enthusiasm, these young revolutionaries believed in the inevitability of a national and social revolution in which the masses would participate. To inspire and move the people to revolutionary action, deeds by heroic and self-sacrificing individuals were indispensable. Such ideas, and the example of the nineteenth-century revolutionaries, led almost inevitably not only to the formation of small revolutionary groups and secret societies, but also to amateurish assassination attempts on high-ranking Austro-Hungarian civilian and military officials. Many of the perpetrators became popular and even legendary figures in the eyes of the young and occasionally also among broader segments of the population.[51]

Most of the "revolutionary youth" were students at universities or secondary schools, and many came from illiterate or semiliterate peasant families. Typically they were intelligent, courageous, and honest, loved their people passionately, lacked any systematic education, held naively romantic political views, and were attracted to revolutionary violence. Their militancy was in part a reaction to the increased oppressive measures of the Austro-Hungarian regime. The failure of moderates and reformists to improve significantly the status of South Slavs in the Habsburg monarchy inflamed them further.

The "revolutionary youth" included Croats, Serbs, and some Bosnian Muslims. Their tightly knit societies with mixed membership were often permeated by a spirit of fraternity, which made them even more Yugoslav.

The best example was Young Bosnia, the organization of young Croats, Muslims, and Serbs in Bosnia-Herzegovina. One of its members was Gavrilo Princip, who assassinated the Archduke Franz Ferdinand in Sarajevo on 28 June 1914.[52]

There was an important connection between radicalism on social questions and radicalism on the national question. Most revolutionary South Slav socialists were national revolutionaries struggling both for the destruction of Austria-Hungary and for the unity of all South Slavs and an independent South Slav state. This intertwining of "progressive" and national radicalism stemmed from the tendency to seek radical solutions in all spheres of political and social life. The choice of Yugoslavism, however, requires some explanation. Why did so many radicals believe in the national unity of the South Slavs and in the need to create an independent and united South Slav state? Other forms of radical nationalism were also possible. One could have combined one's "progressive" revolutionary passion with an equally passionate belief in, say, the creation of a greater Croatia or a greater Serbia. Indeed, since most left-wing radicals were also internationalists, why was it necessary to add to this revolutionary cosmopolitanism the belief in Yugoslavism?

Yugoslavism was the preferred national choice of a large number of radicals for four reasons.

First, no form of internationalism or cosmopolitanism could of itself promote the idea of Yugoslav unity, since they were all by definition void of any national, ethnic, cultural, or linguistic content. Yet, when sincerely held, such values could help to foster cooperation, unity, and solidarity among members of different nations. When cooperation, unity, and solidarity were fostered in revolutionary groups with mixed Croatian, Muslim, and Serbian membership, at least partial transformation and merging of their identities occurred and a new Yugoslav identity began to develop.

Second, "progressive" revolutionaries were anticlerical and, in many cases, atheistic. Among Croats, Muslims, and Serbs, for whom confessional or religious differences were an important element of national identity and a source of cultural dissimilarity (and, in the case of the Serbs, also the preservers of the memory of the Serbian medieval state), atheistic and anticlerical views tended to obliterate these differences and to make unity much easier to achieve. With regard to the idea of Yugoslav unity, there was no perceptible difference between the South Slav liberal democrats and the progressive revolutionaries. At least as far as religion and the church were concerned, the ideas and values of both were founded on the heritage of the Enlightenment and the traditions of European critical rationalism. In the case of the revolutionary socialists, however, atheism and anticlericalism were radical and total.

Third, though sometimes enamored with epic poetry and the memories of medieval states, revolutionary socialists were, on the whole, hostile to history and critical of tradition. They saw history in terms of class struggle, oppression, and exploitation. Through their radicalism, "progressive" revolutionary socialists lost a part of their national consciousness—in their view, a backward-looking and reactionary part. This elimination of extremely important distinctions based on historical memories between Croats and Serbs brought them closer.

Fourth, "progressive" revolutionaries' concentration on social problems tended to diminish the political importance of national bonds and of national identity. Here again there was an affinity with the liberal-democratic ideology espoused by the Croatian-Serbian Coalition. Concentration on social problems meant primarily focusing on the peasantry, since the working class was diminutive. The revolutionaries saw the peasantry as an exploited proletarian group that was living outside time and history—except, of course, when it was its victim—and as an eternal prey to unpatriotic elites (feudal, clerical, monarchical, bureaucratic, and capitalist). For the progressive revolutionaries there was little difference between Croatian and Serbian peasants. And for them, the peasants alone were the true people and the true nation.

The Socialist Movement in Croatia, 1860–1914

The socialist movement began later in Croatia than in western and central Europe, primarily as a result of its comparative economic underdevelopment. In general, during the whole period 1860–1914, socialist ideas and the socialist movement closely followed and reflected the development of the country. There were, however, some short periods when foreign, primarily Hungarian, domination kept the socialist movement below the level at which it could have been expected to operate given the growth of industry and the number of workers. In the late 1860s and early 1870s small groups of workers, employed primarily in handicrafts, began demanding shorter working hours and higher wages. This first struggle for workers' rights was limited to occasional and spontaneous protests. At that time Croatia was primarily a peasant country, with 13.3 percent of the population literate. Its largest center, Zagreb, had around 20,000 inhabitants, of whom 13 percent were workers, employed mostly in small handicraft workshops. There were only a few factories with more than a hundred workers.[53]

The socialist movement in this early period consisted almost completely of workers, with no support from intellectuals. There were no attempts to formulate a broader political program; demands were limited to subsistence matters. Its ephemeral leadership was recruited primarily from the ranks of those craftsmen who had come into contact with

German and Austrian socialist movements and accepted their political programs and ideas. Some were foreigners themselves, mostly from Germany and Austria. These craftsmen had come to Croatia because the lack of a qualified workforce increased the price of their labor. Most machinery and tools, together with manuals for their use and repair, were imported from Germany and Austria, which were also the only available centers of advanced technical education. (In inner Croatia and Slavonia, and to a certain extent in other parts of Yugoslavia, many technical terms and names for tools and machine elements remain German to this day.)

Even workers who had never been outside Croatia and were not of German origin often used the German language. Lack of Croatian terminology was one reason, but another was the guildlike style of organization of the skilled workers; erecting the barrier of a foreign language was one way to protect their profession from competition. The first socialist terminology used in Croatia was also German. Indeed, German socialist vocabulary became a symbol of the higher status of skilled workers. Foreign leadership, the use of German, and the influence of Austro-German socialist ideas, few of which applied to the local circumstances, contributed to the perception that socialism was something alien to Croats and Croatia. The working-class movement in Croatia was too weak and the influences of the economically more developed neighboring central European countries too overpowering for it to avoid becoming attached to centers abroad.[54] This attachment was therefore not the consequence of ideological internationalism, although some individuals established contacts with the First International and read and circulated its publications.

The abolition of guilds in 1872 stimulated the formation of permanent workers' associations. Their first aims were rather modest, simply providing the welfare functions earlier performed by the guilds: help for the sick (and a decent burial for the dead) and some scholarships for the education of younger workers.[55]

The first socialist press was bilingual (in Croatian and German) and ideologically dominated by German and Austrian social democracy. These journals and newspapers had a small circulation and in many cases a brief existence. Most workers were still apolitical, and their interest in the "problems of socialism" and in general social and political issues could not be aroused by borrowings of political propaganda aimed at the working class of central Europe, which had different social and economic problems. The bilingual political weekly *Radnički prijatelj/Der Arbeiterfreund*, which was published in 1874 and 1875, propagated internationalism but asserted that it should be combined with the love of one's own native land.[56] The concepts of native land and native people, however, were ambiguous; it was not clear if they meant Croatia and the

Croatian nation at large, or just individual regions and their populations. The journal at first defined itself as a voice of the Croatian working class, but soon claimed to speak for the Yugoslav working class. Its central political demand was universal franchise, which European socialists were demanding at the time. The journal also defended freedom of the press and demanded an eight-hour working day, free Sundays, and a citizens' militia (the German term was *Volkswehr*) instead of a standing army. Working men were to have a "decent wage" and their children free compulsory education. Most of these demands were simply a translation into the Croatian language of demands of the European working-class movement, and Croatian workers did not identify with them.

In Croatia there was no class struggle in the European sense until the early 1890s. The greatest conflicts in the 1870s and 1880s were between small craftsmen and workers on one side, and their more prosperous colleagues on the other. Something resembling class struggle existed on large estates, primarily in Slavonia, where owners of large estates employed peasants. In industry, owners worked in their firms themselves, often with members of their extended family. In 1890, under the aegis of the Second International the First of May was celebrated for the first time.[57] The event marked the beginning of a new period for the Croatian working-class movement, characterized by more activity and better organization. A small, semilegal trade union movement was created and achieved some initial successes in increasing workers' wages. These first trade unionists were interested primarily in the welfare of the workers, and very little in general economic, political, and social questions. Austro-Hungarian authorities were often willing to make concessions in the realm of purely working-class problems, in order to keep the workers apathetic toward general political problems. The trade unionists did, however, make two political demands with national significance: universal franchise and full legal status for trade unions. In the 1890s Croatia was the only European country with a constitution where trade unions did not have full legal recognition.

Trade unionists usually dismissed the national question as a "bourgeois ideology," of no interest to the working class. Under the influence of Austrian social democrats and the Second International, trade unionists argued that the liquidation of capitalism would solve, or rather, abolish, the national question. This attitude had the full approval of all who opposed Croatian national emancipation, since it implied the nonparticipation of the Croatian working-class movement in the struggle for that emancipation. In the conflict between Croatian and Serbian nationalisms in Croatia, socialists also refused to take sides and favored peace and cooperation among the two nations. In general, socialists in Croatia considered the working class as completely immune to nationalism, and this a priori established "fact" was then propagated as an example to other social groups.[58]

Toward the end of the nineteenth century national political parties often accused socialists of being the servants of Vienna and Budapest, and of betraying the interests of the nation while defending the interests of the working class. The only element the socialists' program had in common with the program of these "bourgeois" Croatian parties—whom socialists frequently accused of protecting selfish class interests under the mask of patriotism—was a demand for universal franchise. Only 2 percent of the population of Croatia had the right to vote. These voters tended to be dependent on the government; they included owners of enterprises that received commissions from the government, civil servants, and other government employees. From 1883 to 1903 the regime of Károly Khuen-Héderváry skillfully manipulated the elections and prevented its political opponents—both "bourgeois" and "socialist"—from achieving any real influence. The national parties believed that universal suffrage would be the most efficient weapon in their struggle for more independence for Croatia, while the socialists wanted it in order to implement social and economic reforms.

Further growth of the socialist movement led to the creation of the Social Democratic Party of Croatia and Slavonia (Socijal-demokratska stranka Hrvatske i Slavonije) in 1894. This first South Slav socialist party quickly established links with Slovenian socialists, who in 1896 founded the Yugoslav Social Democratic Party (Jugoslovenska socijal-demokratska stranka). The Croatian social democrats rejected revolutionary struggle and confirmed their acceptance of constitutional and reformist methods of political struggle. As a political party with a general political program, socialists had to take a stand on most political issues. In relation to the Croatian national question their demands were moderate: a widening of autonomy without fundamental alterations in the existing relations with Vienna and Budapest. The social democrats were convinced that the greatest obstacles to the successful struggle of the working class were religious and national intolerance and hatred. They were also sincere in their belief that Croats and Serbs in Croatia should live and work together in an atmosphere of tolerance and that the workers of all South Slav nations should cooperate in the common class struggle. The attitude of the Croatian social democrats to the national problem was, then, enlightened, moderately reformist, and somewhat naively idealistic.[59]

Socialist propaganda found acceptance in some agricultural regions. In Croatian Zagorje, the region surrounding Zagreb and Varaždin, for example, where poor soil and overpopulation contributed to emigration, the social-democratic demand for general franchise found a favorable reception among impoverished peasants who did not have the right to vote. The socialists' opposition to the wealthy landowners was clear, but their attitude to land ownership was not. For land-hungry peasants private ownership would have been an attractive idea. Socialist ideology, however, which considered collective ownership of all "means of production" to be a superior form of social and economic organization, prevented socialists from demanding it. At its second congress, in 1896, the Social Democratic Party discussed this problem but reached no conclusion. It did, however, decide to create political clubs in the countryside, and by means of education and propaganda to mobilize peasants and arouse their interest in broader social and political issues. The party repeated its demand for the general right to vote.[60]

Apathy more than oppression remained the main enemy of the socialist movement. It was often as difficult to persuade workers to demand universal franchise as it was to avoid being persecuted by the authorities for making such demands. At the turn of the century the socialist movement was still weak and incapable of leading larger protests or strikes. For the authorities it was often enough to arrest or even just threaten a few of its leaders, and the whole movement would be removed from the political scene for a considerable time. Khuen-Héderváry's persistent and sophisticated methods of political intimidation were in general more than a match for all opposition parties and groups in Croatia.

The traditional lack of interest in the struggle for Croatian independence among the working class and the social democrats was paralleled by an almost complete disregard for workers' welfare by other Croatian political parties, which were preoccupied with the national question. But the turn of the century brought a certain change in the attitude of the educated classes to the socialist movement. The Progressive Youth (Napredna omladina), a group of young Croatian intellectuals, developed a program under the influence of Czech national liberals and their leader, Tomáš Garrigue Masaryk.[61] Though opposed to the ideology of socialism, they accepted the necessity of cooperation with the social democrats.[62] The Progressive Youth advocated popular democracy and the general right to vote, and for them the socialist movement represented an increasingly important segment of the population. On their part, the socialists appeared for the first time on the political scene in Croatia as a party whose program and activities were of national importance.[63]

At the all-Yugoslav socialist conference held in Zagreb in 1902, Croatian socialists enthusiastically supported the proposal for cooperation with the socialists in Serbia. In Croatia itself, they firmly opposed attacks from some Croatian politicians and the press against Serbs in Croatia and the kingdom of Serbia. The anti-Serbian demonstrations in Zagreb that year also encountered their opposition. But the socialist movement was too small to counter successfully this massive outburst of extreme Croatian nationalism.[64]

The socialist movement began to develop in Dalmatia in the 1890s and had little contact with inner Croatia and Slavonia. It was still not national, because of the influence of the much more powerful and better-organized Italian socialist movement. The first socialist organizations appeared among Italian workers who had come to Dalmatia because there was no qualified workforce. The Trieste socialist organization had great influence in that industrial region and close contacts with the Social Democratic Party of Italy. The latter, however, was a national Italian party. Though internationalist in its ideology, engaged in pacifist propaganda and opposed to any form of expansion and conquest, it showed very little understanding of the national individuality of Dalmatian workers. The Croatian workers in Dalmatia, though generally successful in resisting the assimilating Italian influences, were primarily Dalmatian—that is, regional rather than Croatian—patriots.[65]

In the 1890s inner Croatia industrialized with great speed. In 1890 there were 270,457 workers, making up 12.28 percent of the population; only ten years later there were 428,367 workers, forming 17.73 percent of the population.[66] The changes in the composition of the working class were even greater. Industry developed considerably faster than handicrafts, so there was an increase in the number of industrial workers, as well as an increase in the number of enterprises with more than a hundred workers. At the turn of the century the number of industrial workers equaled the number of those employed in handicrafts. The highest rate of growth was in food, building, and wood processing—industries that did not require a large number of skilled resident workers: they were closely tied to the sources of the raw material, much of the work was seasonal, and many workers were still peasants.

At the turn of the century an increasing number of intellectuals were joining the socialist movement.[67] This development necessarily brought with it theoretical discussions, debates, and conflicts with other political parties over major issues. With regard to the national question, intellectuals on the left both in the Social Democratic Party or in the socialist movement in general, opposed collaboration with "bourgeois" parties in their struggle for Croatian independence. The right, however, favored cooperation. In their view, the social democrats should be the party of all groups that considered themselves to be oppressed, and not just of the working class. Since Croats were oppressed as a nation, it was natural for a social democratic party to show interest in the struggle for Croatia's greater autonomy. Moreover, they pointed out that the development of the working class and of its movement was linked with the increase in national independence, especially in the economic sphere.[68]

Dogmatically adhering to the principles of internationalism and the noninvolvement of the working class and its movement in any form of nationalist conflict, the left insisted instead on pursuing a "pure class struggle." They even opposed the participation of the Social Democratic Party in public protests against Hungarian domination, although almost all Croatian political groups took part in these. After the end of Khuen-Héderváry's oppressive regime in 1903, freedom of the press increased, and trade unions became legal. In 1906 about 13,000 industrial workers and 2,500 agricultural laborers belonged to the Social Democratic Party. Many strikes were successful too—in 1911 as many as four-fifths. The working day was limited for most workers to eight hours. Nevertheless, the socialist movement was still small, and its influence limited almost completely to a section of the working class. The Social Democratic Party of Croatia and Slavonia had only one member in the Sabor before the outbreak of the Great War in 1914.[69]

South Slav Socialists and the Unification of the South Slavs

Socialists throughout Europe believed that complete solution of the national question would be possible only after the revolution and the overthrow of the "bourgeois class."[70] Some, however, believed that partial reform was possible even within the "capitalist order." The more dissatisfied and radical ones held either that the working-class movement should leave any form of nationalist struggle to the bourgeoisie, avoiding contamination by nationalist ideologies and concentrating on the pure "class struggle" (this was, for example, the view of Rosa Luxemburg); or that, on the contrary, it must develop policies on the national question in order to attract the oppressed nations to the revolutionary struggle.[71] In essence, the latter, smaller group wanted the internationalist revolution to use the national question and nationalist passions for its own goals. Such views gained influence after Lenin and the Bolsheviks successfully implemented policies based on them during the civil war in Russia.

At the congress of Austrian social democrats in Brno in 1899, dominated by the "right-wing centrism" of Eduard Bernstein and Karl Kautsky, the idea was forwarded of solving the national question through giving every nation the right to cultural, linguistic, and educational autonomy. Such a program was antirevolutionary: it demanded reforms that would lead to the depoliticization of the national question and implied the preservation of Austria-Hungary.[72]

For the South Slav (Yugoslav) social democrats, as for other socialists influenced by Marxism, nationalism was a derivative phenomenon. It could be understood only through analysis of the economic and social relations ("basis" in Marxist terminology). Often it was simplistically described as a patriotic mask behind which the bourgeoisie hid its selfish interests. Sometimes it was more astutely perceived as an aggressive and expansionist collective myth born of the "evils of the capitalist order." The South Slav socialists were internationalists; they believed that global unification of all nations into one stateless society was possible in a postrevolutionary world. For them the national question was subordinate to the demands of the class struggle. Yet nationalism sometimes prevailed even among the socialists.[73]

In the view of the South Slav socialists, the South Slavs spoke a common language (Slovenian was mostly recognized as separate but was considered very similar and closely related), had a common origin, and were ethnically similar. Many socialists saw the South Slav peoples as tribes—usually Croats, Serbs, and Slovenes—that ought to be unified into one modern Yugoslav nation. Differences among the South Slavs—connected with religion, memories of medieval states, historical traditions—were considered either artificial (created through conquests by foreign powers) or irrelevant to modernity.[74] The Serbian Social Democratic Party (Srpska socijal-demokratska stranka), founded in August 1903, was readier than other South Slav social-democratic parties to acknowledge the existence of differences among the South Slavs; as citizens of an independent state, Serbian socialists were more aware than their counterparts elsewhere in the region of the importance of individual political and historical traditions.

Socialists interpreted the history of the South Slavs as tragic, in ways that resembled the Marxist understanding of the history of the exploited and oppressed classes. For them, unification of the South Slavs was therefore also an act of revolutionary justice and liberation. Before the First World War the socialists presented four proposals for some degree of unification: (1) South Slav lands of Austria-Hungary would become an autonomous unit in a decentralized and liberal-democratic Habsburg monarchy. (2) Austria-Hungary would be transformed into a Danubian federation, and the South Slav lands, with or without Serbia and Montenegro, would become an autonomous unit within this federation. This solution presupposed a radical restructuring of Austria-Hungary and was expected to come from below, through "revolutionary action by the masses." (3) A federation of Balkan countries would be created, with or without inclusion of the South Slav lands of Austria-Hungary. This proposal was most common in Serbia. (4) An independent multicentral Yugoslav state would be created.

In general Croats and Slovenes were oriented more to solutions within Austria-Hungary and the Danube basin, and the Serbs more to those in the Balkans. (The Serbian socialists argued, for example, that federation between Serbia and Bulgaria was the only lasting solution to the rivalry and conflict between them.) Yet the Yugoslav idea was omnipresent, and the more educated and younger socialists defended it with particular intensity. It appealed to them partly because of its radicalism: it presupposed the destruction of Austria-Hungary.

Those who favored the creation of Yugoslavia were usually denounced as nationalists by the proponents of reforms within the framework of Austria-Hungary and in alliance with the Austrian social democrats. The latter described themselves as internationalists who sought unity with other nations, and not just with the South Slav "tribes." In reality, the internationalists were moderates, whereas the nationalists advocated radical transformation of both the international and the social order. These nationalists, intensely dissatisfied with social conditions and national relations in Austria-Hungary, and convinced that change could come only through revolutionary struggle, were the predecessors and founders of the Communist Party of Yugoslavia.

The internationalists had achieved some improvements in working conditions and wages, and these successes tied them even more to the Austrian trade-union movement. They had no interest in revolutionary action or the destruction of the Habsburg state. Nor did many workers, until the last phase of the First World War. The internationalists almost completely dominated the Slovenian socialist party and were strongly represented in the Croatian socialist party and the socialist groups in Bosnia-Herzegovina.

The first conflict between Croatian and Serbian socialists occurred in 1908, after the Habsburg annexation of Bosnia-Herzegovina. The Croatian and Slovenian socialists believed that the annexation would strengthen the South Slav element in the Habsburg monarchy, move South Slavs closer to becoming equal partners with Austrians and Hungarians, and increase the South Slav working class. Serbian socialists viewed the annexation as imperialist aggression by the Austro-Hungarian bourgeoisie. They protested, criticized Austrian socialists for their lack of energetic opposition to the monarchy's expansionism, and sided briefly with Serbian nationalists.[75]

In spite of all this the Croatian socialists soon came out with a proposal for the creation of a Yugoslav nation. Croatian and Slovenian theoreticians of the national question considered the creation of a Yugoslav nation (which sometimes was meant to include Bulgarians also) a prerequisite for the triumph of socialism in the South Slav lands. The division of South Slavs into regions, religions, "tribes," and ethnic groups obstructed the modern social-democratic movement. Socialists should work toward the creation of one South Slav nation with one language and one culture.

The all-Yugoslav socialist conference in Ljubljana in 1909 developed a program for the solution of the "Yugoslav question." This term did not refer to relations among Croats, Serbs, and Slovenes. All of these were considered to be one nation (or at least suitable material for a future nation), and it was assumed that relations among them would pose no real problem. Rather, the Yugoslav question concerned the relations of all the South Slavs with the Austro-Hungarian monarchy in general, and with Austro-German and Hungarian nationalism. The socialists at the Ljubljana conference did not call for destruction of the Austro-Hungarian monarchy, but they demanded political as well as linguistic and cultural autonomy.

For the first time the idea appeared that socialism could unify the South Slavs. (This belief persisted until the early 1950s among the Yugoslav Communists, including Tito.) Only the workers and the working-class party (that is, socialists and, later, Communists) could be the creators of

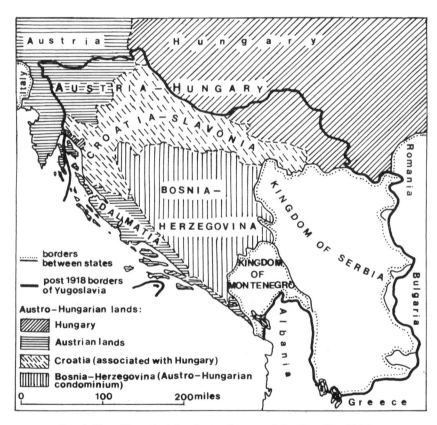

South Slav (Yugoslav) lands on the eve of the First World War

the Yugoslav nation. This was a new idea. Before, when Yugoslavism had been promoted by the intelligentsia, it had been expected (like, for example, literacy) to permeate the lower classes from above. Few socialists, however, necessarily connected this transformation with the creation of a Yugoslav national state. Croatian social democrats continued to advocate primarily cultural unity for the South Slavs within the monarchy. Most Croatian and Slovenian socialists believed in Yugoslav unity but regarded the idea of an independent Yugoslav state with suspicion. They feared the destruction of Austria-Hungary because it would also mean the destruction of the powerful social-democratic movement there and an end to its considerable successes in achieving improvements in the standard of living of the working class. In short, not being revolutionaries, they feared upheaval, changes of borders, and the destruction of states.

The Tivoli resolution, drafted at the end of the all-Yugoslav socialist conference in Ljubljana, presented a program to address the national question: Austria-Hungary should, through constitutional changes and reform of the electoral law, become a confederation, with democratically elected political parties that would represent the nations rather than the sovereign states.[76] Sovereignty was within the nations, it argued, and the unity of the South Slavs should first be achieved through one literary language. The Tivoli resolution stated that the main task for socialists was to resist the "imperialist efforts" of European capitalism. Also, socialists should work for international working-class unity not only for humanitarian reasons and reasons of equality, but also because bigger territories meant a more efficient class struggle.[77] Dimitrije Tucović, the leader of the Serbian Social Democratic Party and their representative at the Ljubljana conference, had a more revolutionary approach; he insisted that southeastern Europe was in a position of colonial subservience to the Habsburg monarchy. His stance seemed sectarian to Croats, while Tucović regarded the Croats as opportunistic. Tucović was not only against Austro-Hungarian imperialism and aggression. A man of high internationalist principles, he later bitterly criticized the annexations made by Serbia in 1912 and 1913, especially the oppression of the Albanians. He also argued for the rights of Macedonians to autonomy and even to constitute themselves as a nation.

The Ljubljana conference and the Tivoli resolution showed on the eve of the First World War that socialists of the different Yugoslav nations had no great difficulty in working together in the spirit of Yugoslavism. Differences arose, often about the way to achieve the unification of the South Slavs, but they were caused primarily by the fact that some social democrats were moderates (reformists), while others were radicals (revolutionaries). Their membership in the Croatian, Serbian, or Slovenian nation played only a secondary role. After the First World War the Communist

Party of Yugoslavia was one of the successors of the prewar socialist parties. The division between moderates (right) and radicals (left) would reemerge within it. Association with one of these two groups would influence the attitudes of the Communists to the national question much more than their belonging to a particular nation.

two
___

The Yugoslavism and Separatism of the Communist Party of Yugoslavia, 1918–1925

Bolshevism and Nationalism

Soon after the two 1917 revolutions in Russia—the abolition of czarist autocracy in February and the Bolsheviks' seizure of power in October—a third revolution began in the non-Russian lands of the former Russian empire. Though organized and led by groups with different political views, it had a common goal: a struggle against the Russian state for national independence. The hegemonistic Russian state had created a united opposition (though rarely in the sense of a direct alliance) among the most divergent political movements. This unity, though only temporary, played an important role in the destruction of the ancien régime. Lenin and the Bolsheviks skillfully exploited these anti-Russian sentiments.[1] Although the Bolsheviks reconquered most czarist lands during the civil war of 1918–1922, their propaganda concentrated on the right of nations to self-determination and severely censured greater-Russian chauvinism.[2] Initially they allowed some independence to non-Russian peoples, except in major matters such as military and foreign policy. Also, when non-Russian Bolsheviks protested the decisions of the center, they were often successful. But by 1922 centralism had already become stronger. The Soviet federation began to resemble the Russian Communist state, and it was in turn to be a model for a future worldwide Soviet federation. The further increase in centralism, ideological uniformity, and monolithism and domination by a small group in the Politburo over the Russian Communist party caused similar developments throughout the Soviet federation. However, the domination exercised by Moscow and the Politburo at that time still did not mean domination by the Russian nation over non-Russians.

Lenin soon recognized that the disappearance of bourgeois society had not brought about the withering away of nationalism, that indeed centralism was strengthening it. But his perceptions were not followed by action. Lenin, the great activist and ruthless realist, was somehow transformed toward the end of his life—he died in 1924—into a vague and confused preacher for ethnic tolerance, a more internationalist education, and legal and constitutional reforms that would allow more autonomy to the non-Russian nations. However, he did not try to limit the power of the party or to change its centralist character.[3]

During the civil war the Bolsheviks fought for the right of small nations to their own languages and cultures, and this revolutionary idealism retained a firm place in Soviet policy until the early 1930s. After 1922 Moscow supported the cultures and languages of small nations by subsidizing school textbooks and fostering their national educational systems. The Russian language and culture were not forced upon any nation, and attempts were made to create literary languages where these had not previously existed. Help given to "small" cultures was also motivated by Communist ideas about the educational prerequisites for industrialization and the "building of socialism." Furthermore, the existence of an ideological one-party state such as the Soviet Union presupposed the active collaboration of its people—that is, mass mobilization; it could not function solely on the basis of passive obedience, and illiterate and totally uneducated masses could not be reached by propaganda.

By the end of the 1920s Soviet leaders realized that the new political, technical, and economic elites being created in non-Russian lands held strong national loyalties. Yet Soviet rulers continued to suppose that in the future a supranational Soviet man would be created. They assumed that national identity would continue to exist but would gradually lose its political potential. In Stalin's view, national culture should by form be national, but by essence socialist. This meant that language and some customs should be preserved, but political loyalty and political identity should be "socialist," that is, reflect acceptance of Marxism-Leninism and of the Soviet state.[4]

In the 1930s, however, Stalin concluded that Communism alone could not unify and strengthen the Soviet Union. He therefore began to Russify it, believing that the Russian language and culture, once they were censored and "adapted" by the Bolsheviks, would provide a more powerful cohesive force than pure Marxism-Leninism. For Stalin, just as for the czarist regime, Russification was primarily an instrument to achieve homogeneity in the state. His Russification program penetrated all layers of society. The Cyrillic alphabet was made official, and so was the Russian language. A whole new history was invented, one that stressed the "traditional" fraternity between Russian and non-Russian peoples. Opponents of czarist hegemonism, who during the civil war had been hailed by the Bolsheviks as progressive patriots, became villains again; the "servants" of czarism and autocracy, as they had been called under Lenin, were now heroes. The Second World War revealed the weaknesses of the Russification program. The Russians fought almost alone against the Germans; the war between National Socialism and Communism was primarily a war between Germans and Russians. Stalin exploited Russian patriotism and national traditions and after the war continued the Russification of non-Russian nations with increasing intensity.

The Comintern and the National Question

From its foundation in March 1919 the Third Communist International (Comintern) was controlled by the Russian Bolsheviks, who justified their dominance by the fact that they were then the only Communist movement in the world to have brought about a revolution.[5] In the late 1920s and early 1930s their confidence was further increased by what they considered to be their successes in the "building of socialism." The Soviet Union began to resemble an imperial power, and Moscow became the Communist metropolis. The Comintern easily displayed a tendency to generalize uncritically the Russian Communist experiences in revolutionary tactics and organization and to demand that other Communist parties imitate them. It was often ignorant of the political, social, and economic problems facing Communist parties in other countries. It also showed little concern for the degree of authority and popularity of particular Communists in their own countries and in their own parties, appointing party cadres to the leading positions in their parties and proclaiming them the "true representatives of the working people" of their respective countries primarily on the basis of its own criteria.

Under Stalin (at least from the late 1920s), the Comintern increased its efforts, through purges and other forms of control, to transform the world Communist movement into a centralized organization whose main task would be to serve the interests of the Soviet Union.[6] The Soviet-dominated Comintern saw itself as a kind of general headquarters of a world-encompassing movement, on which it wanted to impose a discipline similar to that of military organizations. It tended to demand that individual national Communist movements undertake political actions that were incompatible with the political, social, and economic context of their countries and with their national interests.

In the first few years after the October Revolution the Bolshevik leadership expected a world revolution, while at the same time fearing the victory of the anti-Communist forces in Russia itself. In the autumn of 1919, for example, Lenin believed that never before had the Bolsheviks been so near the world workers' revolution, and yet never before had they been in such a perilous position. In spite of its precarious hold on power,

Lenin's party was confident that it was witnessing the fulfillment of Marx's cataclysmic prophecies about the end of capitalism, and expected that the conflicts among social groups in post-1918 Europe would soon reach their culmination and lead to the final and liberating conflict: the Communist "proletarian" revolution.

It was primarily under the influence of Lenin's ideas that the Comintern saw the coming world revolution not only as an intranational conflict between the proletariat and capitalists, but also as the product of international conflicts. Global revolution was to be preceded by global war, and the ideologies of the combatants would inevitably be nationalist.[7] Communists had to distinguish between the nationalism of the oppressors (and fight against them) and the nationalism of the oppressed (and fight for and with them). A supranational Communist internationalism should not make Communists abstain from conflicts among nations. Lenin considered such "purity" dangerous for a revolutionary movement; he believed that it would isolate revolutionary leaders from the masses, which often harbored strong nationalist sentiments. Grigori Zinoviev, one of the Comintern's leaders and perhaps its greatest demagogue, was voicing the views of Lenin when, at the September 1920 Baku congress (a continuation of the second congress of the Comintern, held in Moscow in July 1920), he addressed himself to the peoples of the Near East and central Asia:

> Seventy years ago, our common teacher, Karl Marx, issued his appeal: "Proletarians of all countries, unite!" We, the disciples of Karl Marx, continuers of his work, have the opportunity to develop his formula, broaden it, and say: "Proletarians of all countries and oppressed peoples of the entire world, unite!"[8]

The Bolshevik leadership displayed its contempt for the advocacy of "pure" working-class revolution when it stated that many oppressed nations of the world, as well as those in Europe who had been defeated in the First World War and felt unjustly punished and humiliated by the peace treaties of post-1918 Europe, could be attracted to the cause of revolution and Communism.[9] In order to form such alliances the Leninist type of party must be ideologically united, purged from outside intellectual influences and from internal dissent and disunity, yet capable of flexible tactics.[10] It had to be well organized, disciplined, and have a tight hierarchical chain of command. The principles of conspiracy and secrecy were to be applied not only in outside activities but also in relations among party members. Lenin demanded, with characteristic bluntness, that his Bolsheviks be a combination of Young Turks and Jesuits.

The Leninist idea of a revolutionary party that would be firm in its ideology and organization but ready to make compromises and tactical alliances, prepared even to take over ideas and slogans from ideological opponents if these were popular with the masses, had a great appeal for many educated and semieducated young people with socialist leanings from underdeveloped countries.[11] They were attracted by the energy, radicalism, and seeming efficiency of Communism in transforming Russia from an underdeveloped, primarily agrarian, country into an industrial one. The Comintern's Executive Committee was quick to notice that relative youth and education distinguished those European socialists who were moving toward revolution and Communism from those who were moving toward reformism and social democracy. These two factors were much more important than social origin, since socialists of working-class origin were not more likely to embrace Communism than were those with a middle-class background.[12]

The leadership and the delegates of the Comintern were mostly middle-class intellectuals, predominantly teachers, journalists, and lawyers. Very few workers and peasants attended the first congresses of the Comintern. Yet these were the very social groups that the Comintern wanted to represent and lead. The Comintern believed that revolution would be possible in nonindustrialized countries with a small working class only if the support of the peasantry could be gained first. In order to achieve this, the Communists had to make good use of slogans and promises that were popular with the masses of peasants, such as those promising distribution of large estates to peasants and farm laborers and liberation from national and colonial oppression.

The problem of designing party tactics for the national question in underdeveloped agrarian countries with a small working class and a peasant majority was considerable. The party had to use slogans that appealed to the peasant masses and make temporary and tactical alliances with other political parties while keeping itself "uncontaminated" and devoted to its revolutionary goals. This was accomplished through careful selection of cadres and through Marxist-Leninist indoctrination. Moreover, the party must avoid becoming a mere follower of the masses and their demands. Lenin and his followers considered "surrendering" to the "spontaneity" of the masses or falling under the domination of usually much larger "bourgeois" allies—that is, social-democratic, peasant, or national-liberal parties—to be among the gravest political sins.[13] One of the best critical summaries of Lenin's ideas concerning the tactics that should be employed in agrarian countries with colonial status or an unresolved national question was given by Professor Antonio Graziadei, the Italian delegate at the second congress of the Comintern: "One notes a striking similarity between Comrade Lenin's theses on the national and colonial question, and those on the agrarian question . . . It is the same method that has been used with regard to other issues; it consists in sizing up one's opponents, then making them such concessions as they or the moment may demand."[14]

Comintern policies and tactics for handling the national question were in general better suited to conditions in the colonies of western European countries, especially those in Asia. There, tactical flexibility required an alliance with national anti-imperialist forces—such as the Kuomintang in China—which had the support of the majority of the people in their struggle against the colonial power.[15] But the Comintern was not aware that the existence of national oppression and peasants in both cases did not make the colonial question identical with the national question. The weakness of the Comintern's policies concerning the national question in Yugoslavia during the entire interwar period were largely a result of uncritical application of the colonial-imperialist model to the Yugoslav situation: by the reduction of extreme complexity—ethnic similarities among the South Slavs, territories with mixed populations, cultural affinities, long traditions of a struggle for a Yugoslav unification, and so on—to Serbian "expansionism" and "hegemony."

As soon as national independence had been achieved through cooperation with "bourgeois" democratic parties, the Comintern expected the Communists to follow up with revolutionary action, without waiting for capitalism to develop and for the working class to increase in numbers and become organized. Independence should be followed immediately by the proletarian Communist revolution. Once such a revolution was in progress or had succeeded, the principles of national self-determination, independence, and sovereignty would immediately and radically change their meaning and become "reactionary": the unity of the "international working-class movement" (that is, the Communist parties) must always transcend national borders; and the relations among Communist movements and Communist states should be based on "internationalist" principles.[16]

The Russian Bolsheviks and the Comintern showed a tendency early on to judge the need for national independence in other countries according to their own interpretation of the interests of the proletariat there; they identified these interests with those of the Russian Bolshevik party. As early as the Russian civil war, Stalin, Lenin's trusted expert on the national question, demonstrated this attitude clearly.[17] The right of nations to self-determination, Stalin insisted, belonged only to the working people. But for him only the Bolsheviks really represented those "toiling masses." The implication was that there could be national independence only for those Russian borderlands in which a Bolshevik party was in power.[18] According to the internal logic of this argument, if a particular Bolshevik party did not decide to unite with the first country of socialism, it could not be recognized as internationalist, and therefore was not truly Bolshevik. And if they were not Bolsheviks, they were not the true representatives of the workers. It was then the duty of Soviet Bolsheviks to fight against them and to free the lands where these "false" Bolsheviks were in power.[19] The Comintern approached the national question in a functional way, analyzing it in general as well as in particular cases from the point of view of world revolution and Communism. It applied the attributes "reactionary" and "progressive" to national movements almost solely according to these criteria. Very little attention was paid to analysis of the actual programs, organizational structure, and methods of a particular movement to establish whether it was in fact progressive or reactionary. Thus, for example, a social-democratic movement could be pronounced reactionary if it was opposed to Soviet power, and a conservative Muslim one progressive if it was combating Western "imperialists."[20]

While the Russian Bolsheviks and the Comintern were expecting the international proletarian revolution to begin in western Europe (especially in 1918, 1919 and 1920), they were also planning for this revolution to spread to the colonies. A country in Asia or Africa was, therefore, expected to "receive" its revolution from its former colonial power. (This colonial power would, needless to say, at that time already be firmly in the hands of the "true representatives of the toiling masses," that is, the Communist party.) The "bourgeois-democratic" forces of the colonies struggling for independence would then have to be defeated. Their struggle for independence would immediately be proclaimed "reactionary." If, however, the revolution in Europe failed, and "capitalists" succeeded in stabilizing their states, then nationalist movements in the colonies would immediately become "progressive," since they were weakening the "capitalist" and "imperialist" countries.

When Stalin and the Soviet Communists in the late 1920s and in the 1930s directly identified the interests of the world's workers and of the Communist revolution with those of the Soviet state, such modes of thought were to become little more than a rationalization and a legitimation of Soviet imperialism. The Comintern under Stalin tried to transform national Communist parties into mere instruments of Soviet foreign policy. The policies of these parties concerning the national question, as well as all other important questions, would be expected to conform to the momentary interests of the Soviet Union and its appraisals of the international situation.

The Comintern and the Kingdom of the Serbs, Croats, and Slovenes

To the Comintern's Executive Committee the creation of the Kingdom of the Serbs, Croats, and Slovenes in 1918 appeared to be just another territorial enlargement after the "imperialist" Great War: one of the victors

(Serbia) had appropriated some of the territories of a defeated and dissolved country (Austria-Hungary). Although Lenin had written at the beginning of the First World War that Serbia was fighting a just war, since it was defending itself against Austro-Hungarian military aggression, the Kingdom of the Serbs, Croats, and Slovenes was perceived by him, the Bolshevik leadership, and the Comintern as a hegemonic expansion carried out by the political and military elites of Serbia.

The pre-1918 kingdom of Serbia, whose politicians, generals, and civil servants ruled the new state, had been an ally of czarist Russia. The prime minister of Serbia, Nikola Pašić, had enjoyed the czar's trust, and he and his cabinet had based their foreign policy, both before and during the First World War, on close relations with Russia, which they had seen as their protector against Austro-Hungarian and German military expansionism.[21] After the Bolshevik revolution and the civil war in Russia, many "white" counterrevolutionaries emigrated to the Kingdom of the Serbs, Croats, and Slovenes. The Comintern's animosity toward the new state was further increased by its friendly relations with the "imperialist" states of Great Britain and France. These two countries, which dominated what Moscow regarded as the "unjust" Versailles peace conference in 1919, also played a crucial part in the creation of the new state. The Comintern considered the Serbian nation to have little revolutionary potential, since its national aspirations had been satisfied; it was therefore expected to have a vested interest in the preservation of the status quo.

The Comintern regarded the new state as an heir to Austria-Hungary, and thus as a new "prison of the peoples." It was seen as the creation of British and French "imperialists" and as itself a kind of Serbian mini-empire. The obvious strategy for the Comintern was to look for allies among the non-Serbian nations that felt oppressed and to support their demands for national rights, including the right to secede and create independent states. And if the demand for complete dissolution of the Kingdom of the Serbs, Croats, and Slovenes would increase the influence of the Comintern, then its Executive Committee had no doubts that the Communists there should make that demand. Croatian nationalism, with its mass popular basis and its separatist character, seemed an important potential ally.

The Comintern's Executive Committee knew little of the nineteenth-century struggle for South Slav unification or of the fact that many leading Croatian, Serbian, and Slovenian politicians from Austria-Hungary and from Serbia had made plans for unification during the First World War, before the leaders of Great Britain, France, and the United States had entertained any idea concerning the dissolution of Austria-Hungary, and long before the 1919 Versailles peace conference.[22] The Comintern also seemed unaware of other reasons for a common Yugoslav state: ethnic and linguistic similarities and the mixture of different populations in many regions, which would make the drawing of borders difficult if the country was not left unified.

At the first congress of the Comintern in 1919, Christian Rakovski claimed to speak for the Balkan socialists in analyzing the possibilities for a revolution in that region. Yet he was not an elected or authorized delegate from any of the socialist parties of Bulgaria, Greece, Romania, or Serbia. He had no firsthand knowledge of Serbia. Rakovski was of Bulgarian origin and had been a militant member of the Romanian socialist movement before 1917. He became the head of the Bolshevik government in the Ukraine and a member of the Central Committee of the Communist Party.[23] When, after the first congress, the Comintern decided to devote its attention to central and southeastern Europe, it created its Southern Bureau in Kiev, and Rakovski became one of its leaders.[24]

From 1919 to 1921 the Comintern saw the Kingdom of the Serbs, Croats, and Slovenes as an arbitrary combination of different regions, with nothing more to hold them together than the armed forces and police of the victorious kingdom of Serbia. In 1919 Bolshevik power was still weak, and the Comintern probably could not have prevented the creation of a united Yugoslav Communist party. Nevertheless, it considered the country to be so unintegrated that it could never be an autonomous, independent element in the imminent European and world revolution. The Comintern believed that there could be, among others, a German, French, or Hungarian Communist revolution as part of the world revolution, with partly independent national leadership, but that there could never be a Yugoslav revolution. Yugoslavia could participate in the world revolution only as part of a wider, all-Balkan and southeastern European revolutionary upheaval.

The regions of Yugoslavia should be connected directly and independently (not via an all-Yugoslav revolutionary center) to a command center somewhere in southeastern Europe. Such a center would be established when successes of the revolutionary forces in the region and the advances of the Red Army created the conditions for the Communist seizure of power. Some leaders of the Comintern, in particular Karl Radek, believed that the Red Army should advance through Romania and Hungary (both countries were considered "powderkegs" because of their agrarian problems), promising the abolition of large estates and the distribution of land to the peasants.[25] In this scenario Bucharest or Budapest would have been the headquarters to which regional revolutionary committees in Yugoslavia would have been instructed to attach themselves.

From the point of view of world revolution and the victory of Communism—and this was how the Comintern tried to evaluate all political events—the establishment of the Kingdom of the Serbs, Croats, and Slovenes was a good thing, since the country was riddled with nationalist conflicts that created revolutionary situations. But this "positive" evaluation of the unification of the South Slavs was completely different from the also positive one given by the new Communist Party of Yugoslavia, which saw the new country as a framework within which the South Slavs could overcome their centuries-old semicolonial status and become one modern nation.

The Two Unifications

All Communist parties in the interwar period believed that cumulatively the ideas of Marx, Engels, and Lenin—Stalin's name was added in the 1930s—explained all basic laws of history and were universally valid. It was the primary task of Communists to apply these ideas to the analysis of political, social, and economic conditions in their own countries. The CPY always insisted that its whole revolutionary activity, including its policies toward the national question in Yugoslavia, was founded upon just such an application of "scientific socialism." Party leaders would therefore have great difficulty in justifying any changes in their views on the national question to CPY members and followers, whether such changes occurred as a result of the pressure of circumstances or the influence of the Comintern.

The Kingdom of the Serbs, Croats, and Slovenes, proclaimed on 1 December 1918, consisted of the prewar kingdoms of Montenegro and Serbia and the South Slav parts of Austria-Hungary: Slovenia, Croatia, Dalmatia, Bosnia-Herzegovina, and Vojvodina. Soon after, in April 1919 in Belgrade, the congress of the revolutionary factions of the prewar social-democratic parties took place—the first Yugoslav Communist congress. The new party, named the United Socialist Workers' Party of Yugoslavia (Communists) (Ujedinjena socijalistička radnička partija Jugoslavije—komunista), decided to join the Third Communist International (Comintern) but reached its resolution on the national question in Yugoslavia independently of the Russian Bolsheviks and the Comintern. The resolution was, however, Marxist and conformed to the internationalist and pro-Yugoslav tradition of the prewar South Slav socialists: it called for a unified national state with a great deal of self-government in the regions, districts, and communes. A large majority of South Slav Communists at that time believed in the necessity of establishing a unitary Yugoslav state. Such beliefs were particularly strong among the Croats and Serbs, who represented the overwhelming majority of delegates. Unification was also welcomed because it was expected to provide a framework for a large economic market; this would create conditions for the development of a modern industrial working class and its revolutionary movement, which, in turn, would bring the Communist revolution nearer.[26] The Communists also favored centralism: Yugoslavia as a centralized republic. They considered centralism as something positive and progressive, even though the forces that were at that time the agents of centralism were seen as reactionary. Centralism for them meant primarily opposition to separatism and to the creation of federal units; at the same time they favored local autonomy.

August Cesarec, a leading Croatian Communist intellectual, proclaimed unification to be a "national revolution"—the highest compliment a Marxist can pay to a historical event.[27] Indeed, Yugoslav Communists saw no contradiction between their devotion to the Yugoslav idea, which was "national," and their general ideological opposition to nationalism and belief in internationalism. The South Slavs had until recently been subjugated by foreign nations and empires, and Yugoslav patriotism therefore represented the emancipation of the oppressed; it could not be compared with the oppressive nationalisms of large European nations.

Communist Yugoslavism implied the necessity for the creation of a unified Yugoslav Communist organization, and the congress created such a party. It remained united, with considerable ups and downs as far as the actual unity of structure was concerned, until the reform of the Yugoslav federation in the late 1960s, when both the party and Yugoslavia began a transformation along "confederalist" lines. The inclusion of "Yugoslavia" in the party's name rather than "of the Serbs, Croats, and Slovenes" reflected the unitarist nature of the party. The united Yugoslav Communist youth organization—the Alliance of the Communist Youth of Yugoslavia (Savez komunističke omladine Jugoslavije)—was also created in October 1919 in Zagreb.

Centralism versus Nationalism

The Yugoslav idea found considerable support among the Croatian and Serbian intelligentsia toward the end of the First World War, but this soon declined after unification as conflict between Croatian and Serbian nationalism increased.[28] The Serbian military, civil service, monarchy, and many politicians identified with the larger state, but their Yugoslavism was largely influenced by Serbian traditions, historical memories, and loyalties. Most Serbs accepted the new state primarily because they perceived it as a Serbian creation, led by the Serbian monarchy, in which the Serbs were finally united. But Serbs never became Yugoslavs in the sense of developing a new national consciousness, either political or cultural. Yugoslav Communists mostly spoke about "greater-Serbian hegemony" in the interwar period, but this "hegemony" was actually predominance by the political, military, and administrative elites of Serbia proper, that is, the pre–Balkan Wars kingdom of Serbia. Although in the central government and state bodies in Belgrade Serbs from other parts of Yugoslavia had a share in political power, they were in a small minority in relation to Serbs from Serbia. Also, Vojvodina and Montenegro, which had a tradition of self-rule independent from Serbia, had no autonomous institutions or political influence. It would be wrong to say that they were nationally "oppressed," but from the standpoint of political power they had become marginal.

Nationalism in Yugoslavia in the interwar period was not fundamentally different from nationalism elsewhere in Europe. National mythologies and aspirations more often than not overcame class divisions and class loyalty. Both those in power and those in opposition exploited this for their purposes. In Croatia, as in many other smaller nations of central and southeastern Europe, the fear was widespread that Croats would lose their identity and disappear. The opposition movements to Belgrade centralism therefore emphasized the need for Croatian national unity: social harmony was considered necessary for national survival. The ideas of the state and of sovereign political power as protectors of the nation's existence played a dominant role in both Croatian and Serbian interwar politics; liberal-democratic institutions were neither sufficiently developed nor rooted deeply enough to curb the cult of the state that accompanied nationalist ideologies and their demands.

The main reason for the malfunctioning of parliamentarism after the unification and in the whole interwar period was the conflict between Croatian and Serbian national ideologies. The majority of Croats did not identify with the new state, and most major Croatian political groups began to demand concessions from the central government toward more autonomy or even independence. The degree of radicalism of their demands largely depended on their perception of Belgrade's ability to resist them. The centralist Vidovdan Constitution of 28 June 1921, primarily the creation of leading Serbian parties, brought an open rupture between centralists and (primarily Croatian) anticentralists.[29] The largest and most influential political party in the anticentralist camp was the Croatian Republican Peasant Party (Hrvatska republikanska seljačka stranka). In November 1920 (at that time still called the Croatian People's Peasant Party—Hrvatska pučka seljačka stranka) this party had won 230,590 votes and 50 seats in parliament. In March 1923 it won 473,733 votes and 70 seats. In February 1925 it would win 532,872 votes and 67 seats.[30]

Communist Unitarism

In the early 1920s, unitarist Yugoslavism was not official policy, even though the country was being governed in a centralist way.[31] Unitarist Yugoslavism was to be introduced only after the establishment of the royal dictatorship in 1929. Communists, however, were unitarists from the very foundation of Yugoslavia. For them, as for some "bourgeois" unitarist politicians, the differences among Serbs, Croats, and Slovenes were negligible and transient, soon to disappear as the result of the development of industry, capitalism, and market forces and of a unified legal system, administration, and educational system. In a similar vein, some Communists even believed that Yugoslavia was now embarking on a socioeconomic, cultural, and "national" transformation similar to the one that had occurred in Germany after the unification of 1871. There were, however, important differences in relation to "bourgeois" unitarists. Cesarec, for example, claimed that Yugoslavism could create peace, solidarity, and unity among Serbs, Croats, and Slovenes, but that only social revolution (the triumph of Communism), which would abolish social classes, would unite the people and create a harmonious society. In this way he rightly criticized those romantic Yugoslav unitarists who believed that unification would not only solve the national question but also create a harmonious society; he exchanged, however, their nationalist utopianism for the Communist utopia.[32]

Communists expected the proletariat of Yugoslavia to overcome regional differences and become a national—that is, Yugoslav—political class. They stressed the importance of combatting the influence of religion, which was not only a "reactionary" force and the "opiate of the masses" but also the divisive force for the working class of Yugoslavia, since Roman Catholicism and Eastern Orthodoxy were among the major causes of national differences between Croats and Serbs. Unitarist Yugoslavism was so strong among the Communists that many did not even consider Slovenian an independent language, but merely a branch of Serbo-Croatian. The population of Macedonia was considered to be mostly south Serbian, while Montenegrins were simply Serbs. Bosnian Muslims were not even mentioned as a national group; they were regarded as simply a religious group. Many leading Communist intellectuals in Croatia—such as August Cesarec, Miroslav Krleža, Djuro Cvijić, Lovro Klemenčić, and Kamilo Horvatin—who had been members of the pro-Yugoslav "revolutionary youth" before 1914 believed, together with most other members of the CPY, that Serbs, Croats, and Slovenes were nothing more than three tribes (*plemena*) of one South Slav nation. In this respect they seemed to be in agreement with those few radically unitarist "bourgeois" politicians, and in Croatia Communists were sometimes mockingly called "red Pribićevićs." (Svetozar Pribićević, a Serbian politician from Croatia, was at that time an extreme proponent of both Yugoslav centralism and unitarism. He persecuted Croatian nationalists while he was minister of the interior from 1918 to 1920.)[33]

Just as social democrats had often been perceived as unpatriotic in nineteenth-century Croatia, many Croats considered Communists to be an anational force, even to be traitors. Yet they were actually very different in their ideology from the ruling Serbian elite. They opposed Croatian separatism because they considered the ideology on which it was based to be reactionary, not because they had any sympathy for Serbian-style centralism or for the Serbian monarchy. In July 1919 the Croatian Communist paper *Istina* (The Truth), published in Zagreb, pronounced both the Croatian and Serbian national consciousnesses to be "feudal" and "medieval," since they were rooted in the memories of the medieval states. In this context, of course, the terms *feudal* and *medieval* had a purely pejorative meaning, which in itself was a prejudice that the Communists inherited from the Enlightenment. *Istina* further announced: "Tribal chauvinisms are becoming more and more open . . . Raise your voice against all these tribal chauvinisms, which were possibly suited to medieval times, but today—today in the epoch of social revolution—we believe are misplaced."[34]

The April 1919 Congress of Unification completely underestimated the importance of the national question for Yugoslav politics and for the future of the country, as well as for Communist revolutionary action. The majority of delegates did not even seem to be aware that the national question existed as a genuine problem, since it was believed that Serbs, Croats, and Slovenes were one nation. The party's Program for Practical Action described Yugoslavia as a one-nation (*jednonacionalna*) state. But although the congress did not acknowledge that Yugoslavia was multinational, it strongly opposed any form of national oppression, protesting sharply against the central government's discriminatory policies toward non–South Slav minorities (especially Albanians and Hungarians, but also Germans).

The same "party line" continued during the second congress of the party (when the party officially changed its name to the Communist Party of Yugoslavia—Komunistička partija Jugoslavije), held in Vukovar in June 1920. The party proclaimed as its main revolutionary goal—and revolution was expected to occur in the near future—the establishment of a Soviet Yugoslavia. It accepted the Kingdom of the Serbs, Croats, and Slovenes as one unitary state, rejecting it only to the extent that it was a "bourgeois" state and thus an instrument of capitalist exploitation and oppression. The party defined itself as a "pure" working-class party and still saw no need to develop a program concerning the national and peasant question. The struggle for the national Yugoslav unity of the working people was stressed as one of the most important immediate tasks for Communists. However, the congress did again demand for persecuted minorities the same civil and political rights as those enjoyed by the South Slav citizens of Yugoslavia.[35]

In November 1920, fifty-nine Communists were elected to the Constituent Assembly. The CPY became the fourth largest party in Yugoslavia, after two predominantly Serbian groups—the People's Radical Party (Naradna radikalna stranka) and the Democratic Party (Demokratska stranka)—and the Croatian Republican Peasant Party.[36] The CPY received 198,736 votes. At the time it had 65,000 members, while the trade unions under its control numbered 208,000 members.[37] The party was staunchly Yugoslavist, and in Croatia the Communist proclamation for the November elections for the Constituent Assembly attacked Croatian nationalism and separatism:

> The Communist proletariat does not have and can never have anything in common with patriotic, today counterrevolutionary phrases about the independence of Croatia and about the "Croatian fatherland." For the struggle of the proletariat is elevated above such old-fashioned naïveté. It is a part of the struggle of the international proletariat and its goal is: the Soviet Republic of Workers and Peasants not only of Croatia, but of the whole of Yugoslavia within the Balkan Federative Soviet Republic.[38]

Although the Communists were in favor of centralism, they were supported by masses of people in some regions where national dissatisfaction was considerable, including Montenegro and Macedonia. The term *national dissatisfaction* in these two cases should not be understood literally. Most Montenegrins did not consider themselves a separate nation from Serbs, and they supported the creation of Yugoslavia. They were, however, dissatisfied with the complete loss of Montenegrin state traditions and symbols and with the predominance of the political and military elites from Serbia proper and their coercive methods of rule. Macedonians at that time lacked a widely distributed national consciousness but were primarily an ethnic group different from Bulgarians and Serbs. The transformation of Macedonians into a modern nation began only after 1945. What is, however, essential is that since Montenegrins and Macedonians did not have national political movements, they saw the Communists, in spite of the fact that these supported both centralism and unitarism, as their defenders because the CPY opposed Serbian nationalism and "hegemony" and advocated fundamental changes. Hence, from the beginning the party was perceived, in matters relating to the national question, as the defender of the oppressed. As a radical opponent of the status quo, it was for many a "protest party" for all kinds of dissatisfactions, including national discontents.

In Croatia in September 1920 there had been peasant rebellions that were not inspired or led by any political party.[39] The CPY, blinded by its interest only in the "pure" class struggle and the mobilization of the industrial proletariat for social revolution, failed to use this revolutionary potential. Yet the working class of the newly created state, which the party considered as the only truly revolutionary social group, was still small. The agrarian reform, begun in February 1919, distributed land from large estates to peasants and increased the number of small and medium-sized peasant landholders. In 1921 agriculture consisted mostly of extensive farming; 78.9 percent of the population were peasants. Most of these were small and medium-sized landholders, and thus suspicious of collective land ownership. Only a minority of peasants were without any land. Even ten years later 33.8 percent of estates were under two hectares, 34 percent were two to five hectares, and 29.3 percent were five to twenty hectares.[40]

The anti-Communist regulations of the so-called Obznana (Pronouncement) in December 1920 and Zakon o zaštiti države (Law for the Defense of the State) in August 1921 outlawed the CPY. Mass arrests of Yugoslav Communists followed, and many went into exile. The party was unprepared for underground struggle, and it almost ceased its activities with trade unions and other workers' organizations. At the time of the third party conference in January 1924, the party had fewer than 1,000 active members.

In the first Comintern debates, optimism about the Balkan revolutionary situation had no limits. The revolutionary potential of demonstrations, strikes, and peasant upheavals that were taking place at the time was wildly overestimated. The Comintern seemed particularly ignorant of the situation in the Kingdom of the Serbs, Croats, and Slovenes. For example, although the large majority of Serbs in Bosnia-Herzegovina, which had a mixed Croatian, Muslim, and Serbian population, accepted the unification of the South Slavs with enthusiasm, the Comintern announced that "Bosnians" were rising against "Serbian hegemony" and their Muslim landowners. Yet the Comintern's mistaken perceptions of the national problems of the South Slavs had little effect on the policies of the CPY. The Comintern's influence at that time was still very limited; it was more a symbol of Communist internationalism than the center of an organized world movement.

In those early years Yugoslav Communists identified both federalism and separatist nationalism as dangerous enemies of national unity: a further proof of their unitarism and centralist orientation.[41] For example, the first conference of the CPY, held in Vienna in July 1922, insisted that the Communists' main task was to reveal to the proletariat the "class interests" concealed in the nationalism of both the Croatian and the Serbian "bourgeoisie." Yet some Communists perceived that the "nationalist psychosis" in Croatia was at least temporarily unifying most social groups and classes. The first conference acknowledged Serbia's predominance in a resolution stating that Yugoslavia was under the "hegemony" of the "great-Serbian bourgeoisie," which had allied itself with the monarchy. The "Croatian bloc" (the coalition of Croatian parties, largely dominated by the Croatian Republican Peasant Party), was described as the most important force opposing that hegemony.[42] Yet the Communists, blinded by Marxism, believed that the essence of the national conflict was the struggle of the "tribal bourgeoisies" for the largest share of the economic market. To the Communists who adopted this resolution, the fact that the "Croatian bloc" had succeeded in uniting capitalists, small businessmen, the majority of peasants, and even part of the proletariat was merely further proof that there was a "nationalist psychosis" in Croatia, rather than evidence that the Croatian nation was, at least in some respects, oppressed. The "nationalist psychosis" was then blamed for the weakening of the class struggle, since it temporarily united all social classes and prevented social differentiation.

The CPY's Left versus Right

The persistent strength of nationalism, especially in Croatia, was proving to the Communists that the Yugoslav "bourgeoisie" was unable to perform the task of national unification. This was blamed on the "backwardness" of the Yugoslav bourgeoisie, and disappointment with its poor performance made some Communists believe that only a Communist revolution could perform such a task. The variety of proposals on the national question in the 1920s, as well as the groups in the CPY that advocated them, are divided in official party documents and by Yugoslav historians into two main groups, described as the right wing and the left wing.

The most influential proponent of the party's right was the leading Serbian Communist intellectual Sima Marković. He was elected secretary of the CPY at the party's first congress in April 1919 and at the third party congress in May 1926. In two books in 1923, *The National Question in the Light of Marxism* and *The Constitutional Question and the Working Class of Yugoslavia,* he applied the prerevolutionary ideas of Lenin and Stalin on the national and colonial question to the Yugoslav situation.[43]

Like many other idealistic supporters of Yugoslav unity, Marković was astonished by the persistence of national feeling—which was still considered by Communists as "tribal" and "regional"—and especially by the strength of Croatian nationalism and the mass support it enjoyed. He set out to explain why a single Yugoslav nation had not been created since the establishment of a centralized Yugoslav state. He recognized the existence of three South Slav national identities—Serbs, Croats, and Slovenes—although he continued to believe that in the future they would be transformed into one Yugoslav national consciousness. For him the national question was caused by the struggle among the Serbian, Croatian, and Slovenian bourgeoisies for the control and exploitation of one economic market: the three capitalist classes were fighting against each other and trying to gain the support of their peoples through nationalist propaganda. Nationalism was, then, an ideological expression of this hidden economic motive; and its function was to legitimate capitalist aspirations and to seduce workers and peasants into serving capitalist interests.[44] It was the Communists' duty to help the working people recognize the economic interests concealed behind the mask of ideology.

Marković was wrong. The Croatian masses, for example, who supported Stjepan Radić's Croatian Republican Peasant Party, were moved by very complex political motives and were not simply seduced by "bourgeois propaganda." For one thing, there was much truth in the Croatian nationalist claim that Yugoslavia was dominated by the Serbian political and military elite. Moreover, the claim that the essence of the national conflict was the struggle among "bourgeoisies" for economic predominance failed to explain why large masses participated in the conflict; why the supposed interests of the capitalists correlated so highly with the national grievances experienced by the masses; why so many wealthy merchants and industrialists in both Croatia and Slovenia actually supported the centralist Belgrade regime; why there was so little solidarity between the Croatian and Slovenian bourgeoisie even though both opposed the politically dominant Belgrade bourgeoisie; and why, if the only motive for capitalists was profit, they were organizing on a national basis, and not on a religious, provincial, party, or other basis.[45]

In reducing the national question in Yugoslavia to an economic basis, Marković implicitly proclaimed all nationalisms of Yugoslavia to be identical. He ignored or simply did not see the crucial difference between Serbian nationalism, whose concept of the state had triumphed in Yugoslavia, and, say, Croatian nationalism, whose aspirations were largely unfulfilled. Also, Marković's simplistic Marxist categories did not take account of the deep and very real feeling of oppression among most non-Serbs in Yugoslavia. Marković's monocausal and reductionist explanations—given the fact that Communists saw themselves as completely opposed to every form of bourgeois interest and ideology—implied a policy of passivity in the national conflicts in Yugoslavia. For why should a party which defined itself as the "conscious avant-garde of the exploited" bother to get involved at all, let alone take sides, when the "exploiters," motivated by desire for more profit, were quarreling and fighting with each other?

And, indeed, Marković opposed Communist cooperation with the most powerful parties in Croatia and Slovenia, the CRPP and the Slovenian People's Party (Slovenska ljudska stranka).[46] The danger was that in this way the CPY would isolate itself from the national demands of the Slovenes and Croats who supported these parties. Neither party, however, would have sought or welcomed such cooperation. The CRPP was ready to seek support from the Soviet Union for its national demands, but it was also careful to preserve its distance from Communists. The Catholic-based SPP was aggressively anti-Communist and anti-Soviet. Its primary interests lay in sharing power in the government in Belgrade and extracting concessions for greater independence for Slovenia.

Most Communists saw themselves as radical leftists committed to a struggle against all forms of oppression. They therefore found it difficult to accept Marković's views and to treat certain widespread feelings of oppression as not founded in reality. Also, a sense of being nationally oppressed obviously motivated people to political and revolutionary action, and it was useful for the party to create programs that would channel and guide these considerable energies toward Communist revolutionary goals.

Marković's Marxism was doctrinally pure and even doctrinaire. He argued for the orientation of the party to the working class, for him the only truly revolutionary social group, and against any attempts to mobilize a "backward" and "nationalist" peasantry. He advocated pure internationalism and a pure class struggle. Nevertheless, the party's more radical and activist left attacked his views as right-wing, opportunistic, and social democratic. Marković was even accused of being a Serbian crypto-nationalist, since his neutralism was seen as helping to preserve the status quo of "Serbian hegemony." Although Marković's explanation of the causes of national conflicts may seem simplistic, many other of his ideas show a deep understanding of the dangers of nationalist passions. For example, he interpreted the principle of national equality as implying, among other things, that every nation is sovereign. The corollary was that the Yugoslav constitution should recognize an unlimited right to self-determination, including separation from Yugoslavia and the creation of independent states.[47] The party's left opposed this approach as opportunistic and unrevolutionary, since it attempted to solve the national question within the framework of a capitalist state.

Although Marković believed that his views were mostly influenced by the prerevolutionary ideas of Lenin and Stalin, his demand for recognition of the right to self-determination was derived from what those two theoreticians had adopted from nineteenth-century European liberalism. In fact, his "formula"—national equality means sovereignty of nations, which in turn implies their right to create separate states—was attractive exactly because of its lack of originality, that is, because it was merely a concise expression of that liberalism. The application of the right to self-determination and to the creation of separate national states was also one of the proclaimed goals of the liberal democracies toward the end of the First World War and was the essence of President Wilson's Fourteen Points in his January 1918 proposal for the postwar peace.[48] Marković's solution was, therefore, very similar to the principles on the basis of which Austria-Hungary was dissolved at the end of the First World War; in a way, it was an application of these principles to the Yugoslav situation. In spite of all this indisputable and well-known evidence supporting such an illustrious pedigree of the principle that a nation is truly free only when it has the right to create its own state, Sima Marković, an erudite man who wrote essays on the philosophy of science, considered the principle to be uniquely Marxist and Communist. This view was shared by most Yugoslav Communists, even when they disputed the applicability of this principle to the Yugoslav situation.

Communists in general believed that there could be no real solution to any fundamental social, political, or economic problems without the revolutionary application of Marxism. They then "forgot" the liberal lineage of some of their ideas, since they considered them realizable only through Communism. Liberalism was proclaimed a "bourgeois" ideology of the past, both "reactionary" and irrelevant to contemporary problems. This is, however, only part of the explanation. The Communists' refusal to acknowledge their expropriation of liberal views on the national question was not solely a result of their ideological fervor. The social and political context of post-1918 Europe played a crucial role in making Communists believe that national self-determination was their idea alone. The right to self-determination ceased to be a generally recognized principle granted for nations of Yugoslavia as well as most other European countries once the postwar borders and states had been established. Separatists and sometimes even moderate nationalists were persecuted. Separatists themselves formulated their demands using non-liberal nationalist arguments. In Croatia, for example, the demands were mostly based on the historical rights and the legal continuity of Croatia, rather than on liberal principles of the rights of nations to self-determination. And when such principles were invoked it was mostly to support one's own demands rather than apply them as general rules to other nations all over Yugoslavia.

The right of separation, Marković further argued, should be exercised not through "bourgeois" parties, but through a referendum. He seemed unaware of the complexity of using the referendum as a method of creating new state borders within a country where there was no universal agreement about political borders or historical rights and where, in many regions, the population was mixed. Marković did not exclude the possibility that different nations might decide to live together in the same state. He used Lenin's view of 1921, that the right to self-determination did not mean that nations should in all cases form separate states, to support his thesis that the "Marxist proletariat" of Yugoslavia should recognize for Croats and Slovenes the unlimited right to self-determination, but not itself demand that Croats and Slovenes make use of that right and separate from the Serbs. Finally, Marković believed that in order to help bring about favorable political conditions for the solution of the national question, Communists should struggle for radical changes in the 1921 constitution and for a general democratization of political life.

The constitution of 1921 was in the tradition of nineteenth-century Serbian nationalism that believed, in the Jacobin tradition, that the appropriate form of government was a centralized one that abolished all regional individualities, autonomies, and traditions. These were considered "feudal" and "reactionary" (obstacles to progress, democracy, and citizenship) as well as perilous, since they would supposedly foster disunity and render the new South Slav kingdom vulnerable to its many external enemies. To paraphrase Clausewitz's dictum, the politics of Yugoslavism were, for the Serbian ruling elite, the continuation of the war for Serbian unification by other means. Also, many ordinary Serbs identified with the Yugoslav state and began to develop a cult of the state that often proved stronger than other social or political loyalties. Although many Serbs were ready to abandon specific Serbian traditions and historical memories in the name of a new Yugoslav idea, the majority still interpreted Yugoslavia in a Serbian key.

Yet it was not Serbian nationalism that made Marković insist that the separation of Croatia or Slovenia was neither inevitable nor necessary. He considered the right of separation to be primarily a kind of safety valve against national oppression, not a first step toward the dissolution of Yugoslavia. Precisely because he was against Serbian nationalism and national oppression Marković wanted a permanent guarantee of the right of separation and argued that the country should consist of autonomous units. Through these measures he hoped ultimately to promote the unity of Yugoslavia, that is, to prevent nationalist conflicts that were detrimental to it, and to create a unified Yugoslav national consciousness on a voluntary basis.[49] Although he did not think that they needed separate states, Marković argued that sovereignty was inherent in the Croatian, Slovenian, and Serbian nations. Marković defined Yugoslavia as a union of sovereign nations but not of sovereign states: something more than a federation, but still not a confederation.[50] His imprecision became a permanent characteristic of Yugoslav Communists when discussing (con)federal arrangements. If confederation meant a union of already existing states, then Marković could not have been for confederation, for the simple reason that at that time there existed only one state: the Kingdom of the Serbs, Croats, and Slovenes. If, on the other hand, confederation meant a union in which the common central government had only certain limited rights over its constituent national units but none over their citizens, then it was possible to argue that Marković was a confederalist.

Marković seemed unaware that placing sovereignty permanently inside Croatian, Slovenian, and Serbian nations did not imply a need for either federal or confederal arrangements. It was possible to argue for a Yugoslavia in which constituent nations would be sovereign and have a right to secede, but at the same time to favor a centralist and even unitarist organization of Yugoslavia. Also, there could be a federation or confederation inside a one-nation state (such as the United States). Marković did not specify which state institutions and ministries the three autonomous units should share and which they should possess separately, but he was clearly opposed to independent military forces and in favor of a united economic market. He envisaged Yugoslavia (before the final triumph of the Communist revolution) as a liberal-democratic state on the European model.[51] Liberal-democratic political institutions were to serve, among other things, as a guarantee that the rights of national minorities would be respected; they would prevent the tyranny of the majority over the minority. This was an important safeguard, because even if there was a division into autonomous units (or a complete separation), both the Croatian and Serbian units of Serbian-Croatian-Slovenian Yugoslavia would, because of territories with mixed populations, inevitably have sizable minorities.

Marković's solution to the national question was probably better suited to a country with greater democratic traditions, and the left was correct in accusing him of naïveté in believing that there was much room for democratic reforms or that Belgrade centralists were ready to make great concessions. He was, however, right in his assessment that Yugoslavia was not ripe for revolution. While there was much truth in the left's accusation that the right was not revolutionary but reformist, the right's comparatively cautious approach to the national question was based in part on clearer perceptions of the dangers of nationalist extremism in Yugoslavia. Given the nationalist massacres of the Second World War, such caution seems to have been justified.

The left in the party favored a more radical approach to the national question: Communists should struggle not only for constitutional recognition of the right of self-determination but also for its realization; there could never be a just solution to the national question within the Yugoslav "bourgeois" state. Fighting Serbian nationalism should have priority, and considerable tolerance should be shown toward separatist nationalisms. The party should not struggle for the Yugoslav unity of the workers of different component nations, since such a struggle at that time could only strengthen Belgrade centralism and alienate the non-Serbian working class nations from the Communist movement.

Official postwar party history presented the prevalence in the mid-1920s of the views of the left over those of the right as a sign of the maturation of the party and as a victory of the truly Marxist approach to the national question.[52] Yet it would perhaps be better to describe these views as truly Leninist rather than truly Marxist, since the left wanted to unite the struggle for the solution of the national question with the Communist struggle against the capitalist system. It was also more revolutionary than the right, which searched for solutions within the "bourgeois society." The Bolshevism of the left was also manifest in its demand for the creation of a strong and disciplined illegal party. The left asserted that only such an organization would be able to carry out revolutionary policies on the national question.[53]

As early as its second conference, held in May 1923 in Vienna, the CPY was under considerable pressure from the party's rank and file to change its policies toward the national question in Yugoslavia. The electoral successes of the non-Serbian national parties (in particular of the CRPP) were a clear warning that Communists must take a more energetic and involved attitude toward national conflicts.[54] The conference acknowledged that the CRPP had become the representative of the Croatian nation, and that the chief culprit of the national conflicts was "greater-Serbian hegemony" and centralism. The CPY was slowly abandoning its dogmatic Marxism, which reduced the whole national question in Yugoslavia to the competition for the economic market by three equally greedy "tribal" bourgeoisies. In order to attract the masses of the "oppressed nations" and use the national question for revolutionary purposes, the party decided to demand for the nations of Yugoslavia the right of self-determination, including the creation of separate states. Nothing was said, however, about the territories that would be encompassed and the location of the new borders—further proof that the Communists treated self-determination and separation primarily as tactical expedients.

The Third Party Conference of January 1924

A crucial event in the search for new policies toward the national question was the third party conference, held in Belgrade in January 1924.[55] Although the national question had already provoked bitter polemics and begun to dominate the party's press, only then did the party officially acknowledge the importance of the national question in Yugoslavia and, especially, of the conflict between Croats and Serbs. Disagreement immediately arose about the nature and causes of the national problem, as well as about the methods of solving it, and for more than a decade this disagreement was the most important cause of disunity among the Yugoslav Communists. Yet even as late as 1924 no one in the Yugoslav party or in the Comintern seemed to be aware that there might be more than three nations in Yugoslavia. The process of "discovering" Montenegrins, Macedonians, and Bosnian Muslims was to be a slow one.

Although the conflict between the right and the left was increasing at that time, the third conference produced a common resolution. The conference was in one sense a compromise, but in another sense a victory for the left. It resolutely rejected all slogans about "national peace" among the working masses of different nations and stated that there was no possibility of achieving national equality through a reform of the Yugoslav constitution. The nations of Yugoslavia (except the Serbs, who were not nationally oppressed) should be urged toward revolutionary national action. They should strive to achieve a united front of workers and peasants and to create revolutionary governments of the workers and peasants of Croatia, Slovenia, Macedonia, and other nations. These should be united into a socialist republic of Yugoslavia, which should then join the Balkan federation. The dominant left further insisted that one of the priorities for the party was the struggle against Serbian chauvinism. This was an important change, since in previous years the enemy had been the "bourgeois chauvinism" of all nations. The party's right continued to oppose such policies, and some of its members maintained the original party view, claiming that there was simply no national question in Yugoslavia, since it was a one-nation country. But even on the right most members were already aware that Yugoslavia was not a one-nation state. The right held that, in general, the struggle against greater-Serbian chauvinism should be paralleled by an equally committed struggle against separatism, irredentism, and nationalism of the oppressed nations. To the left this approach seemed not only advocacy of the status quo but also an unjustified identification between the feelings, reactions, and beliefs of the oppressors and the oppressed.

The third conference decided that the process of assimilation of Serbs, Croats, and Slovenes into one nation had been halted at the very beginning, because the Serbian "bourgeoisie" was "exploiting" and "oppressing" the other South Slav nations, the non-Slav national minorities, and the movements for regional autonomy in Montenegro, Macedonia, and Bosnia. The Kingdom of the Serbs, Croats, and Slovenes could not be considered a homogeneous national state with few minorities. It was a state in which a ruling class of one (Serbian) nation oppressed other nations. The resolution of the third party conference stated, among other things, that the hegemony of the "greater-Serbian bourgeoisie" interrupted the process of the creation of one Yugoslav nation. Instead, three independent nations—Serbian, Croatian, and Slovenian—were being formed.[56] The conference endorsed the right of self-determination but insisted that it did not consider it desirable or necessary in all circumstances. The party decided to keep its options open and to argue for or against separation depending on the concrete circumstances and on its interpretation of the interests of the proletariat and revolution. The party's resolution was directed primarily toward solution of the conflict between Croats and Serbs, Croatian nationalism being recognized as by far the most vocal and the most powerful in Yugoslavia. Its strong separatist tendencies were capable of endangering the whole of Yugoslavia, something no other nationalism could achieve.

Although the third conference supported the continuation of a common South Slav political entity, it did not consider the decisions of the 1919 Versailles peace conference as sacrosanct, nor the borders of the Kingdom of the Serbs, Croats, and Slovenes as unchangeable.[57] For example, the conference expressed its support for unification of the Macedonian part of Yugoslavia (Vardar Macedonia) with the Macedonian parts of Bulgaria (Pirin Macedonia) and of Greece (Aegean Macedonia) into one independent political unit. Although the Macedonians were not considered to be a nation (Macedonia being described as a land with mixed population), it was believed that only Macedonia's autonomous status could provide a guarantee for the national rights of the Macedonian South Slavs, as well as of the non–South Slav groups on its territory. After the revolution this Macedonian unit was to become part of a larger federation of workers' and peasants' republics in the Balkans and in the Danube basin. The exact names and size of the units that were to form this Balkan-Danubian Communist superstate (itself to be a part of the world union of Soviet republics) were not stated, but the inclusion of Bulgaria, Greece, Albania, Romania, Hungary, and the Kingdom of the Serbs, Croats, and Slovenes was envisaged.[58] The important feature of this viewpoint was that although Yugoslavia was to consist of separate units, it was still meant to join the Balkan federation as a single unit, just like other units that, though containing sizable minorities, were basically one-nation states. Thus, although the CPY had abandoned its uncritical belief in the national unity of Yugoslavia, it still did not consider Serbs, Croats, and Slovenes to be as different from one another as they were from neighboring nations.

Certain views that were accepted at the third conference remained embedded in the party's policy toward the national question until it came to power in Yugoslavia in 1945: (1) the ruling elite (the "bourgeoisie") had not succeeded in creating a common Yugoslav national consciousness; (2) there was Serbian predominance ("hegemony and oppression") in

Yugoslavia; (3) every nation should have an inalienable right to secede; and (4) the struggle for solution of the national question should be part of the Communists' revolutionary struggle for the liberation of the proletariat— in other words, the national question was connected with the social question and, in that way, with the revolution. There was nothing particularly Marxist or Communist about these four points. Point 3 was a statement of faith or, perhaps, of intention, but definitely not an observation, let alone a deep analysis; it was also a part of a European liberal tradition, which Communism inherited. Point 4 was simply a decision about tactics in connection with the national question. Points 1 and 2 were accurate observations but unoriginal. They were simply a Communist acceptance of what many non-Serbian nationalist politicians had been saying since the creation of Yugoslavia. It is, however, crucial to remember that no other political organization in Yugoslavia at that time, including those with a liberal-democratic approach to the organization of the political system (that is, advocating parliamentarism, a free press, an independent judiciary, and so on) had argued in such a principled way and with such passion for the application of liberal-democratic principles to the national question.

The third conference of the CPY is hailed in the party's history as a great step forward toward a better understanding of the national question in Yugoslavia, achieved by the supposed application of Marxist principles. It would, however, be more accurate to describe it as a great step toward designing policies relating to the revolutionary potential of the national question based on general liberal-democratic principles and on Lenin's tactics, which would help the party win the support of the masses.

The Influence of the Comintern

The Comintern was more cognizant than the Yugoslav Communists of how important and deeply rooted nationalism was, especially among the peasants. The Comintern believed that the national question in Yugoslavia had enormous revolutionary potential. At the same time it did not believe that there were any serious chances for a revolution in this underdeveloped country with a small working class if the Communists addressed themselves only to the industrial proletariat. Although the left in the CPY also subscribed to radical solutions, it never saw Yugoslavia the way the Comintern did, as the pure creation of imperialism. Even when it agreed with the Comintern that Yugoslavia was an ally of the "imperialists" (Great Britain and France), it was aware that the struggle for the creation of Yugoslavia had preceded the Versailles peace conference and that the Yugoslav idea had deep roots in the history of the South Slavs. Moreover, although according to Marxist criteria the political leaders from the kingdom of Serbia and from the South Slav lands of the Austro-Hungarian monarchy, who had fought together for unification during the First World War, could be regarded as "bourgeois" politicians, they could not simply be proclaimed the agents of the "imperialists." The left agreed with the Comintern that Yugoslavia was under "Serbian hegemony" and that this could be considered as a form of "imperialism," but it was still aware—unlike the Comintern—of the great similarities among the Yugoslav peoples.

In 1922 there had been a decrease in strikes and revolutionary turmoil in western Europe. During 1923 the Comintern began to take greater interest in southeastern Europe, and especially in the "peasant question." This most numerous social group in the region was considered a potential ally of the international Communist movement. In 1923 the Comintern formed the International Peasant Union, also known as the Peasant (or "Green") International, in an attempt to gather around itself dissatisfied and persecuted peasant parties, especially those of the oppressed nations. After the national conflicts in Yugoslavia intensified in the early 1920s, the Comintern quickly realized that the most important one was between Croats and Serbs. Stjepan Radić's visit to Moscow in the summer of 1924—the CRPP joined the Peasant International in July—further influenced them in supporting separatist nationalisms in Yugoslavia.[59] The fifth congress of the Communist International, held in Moscow in June and July 1924, passed the following resolution on the national question in Yugoslavia: "the general slogan of the Communist Party of Yugoslavia about the right of nations to self-determination must be expressed in the form of separation of Croatia, Slovenia, and Macedonia from Yugoslavia and their establishment as independent republics."[60]

The fifth congress gave support to the views of the party's left but was more radical, especially in relation to the question of the dissolution of Yugoslavia. Stalin also supported the views of the left. But the subsequent victory of the left in the CPY was only partly the result of his and the Comintern's support. The main reason was that the radicalism of the left was simply more attractive to most party members. Yugoslav Communists were, therefore, not primarily obeying the decisions of the Comintern. (In any case, at that time Stalin and the Comintern had little means of coercion to enforce their views on the CPY. Their influence was based primarily on the perceived authority of the Comintern as the center of world Communism.)

In June 1925 Stalin criticized "Semić" (the pseudonym Marković used in many of his publications), insisting that the national question was closely connected to the peasant question and could not be solved (except in a few rare and exceptional cases) without a revolution.[61] Stalin also accused Marković of not seeing the national question in Yugoslavia in the context of international relations, in which "Versailles Yugoslavia" was an ally of the imperialists and a threat to the Soviet Union. Stalin claimed that a constitutional solution was impossible, since the national question could not be solved within a "bourgeois society." Thus it was the duty of Communists to support the separatists, since the latter's activities were likely to create a revolutionary situation. Nevertheless, alliance with the separatists should always be treated only as a tactical move. Stalin did not openly advocate the dissolution of Yugoslavia but mentioned that this possibility should be also taken into account as a necessary tactic.[62] Stalin stated that "under certain conditions after the victory of the Soviet revolution in Yugoslavia, it is quite possible that certain nationalities would not want to secede, for the same reasons for which they did not want to secede in Russia."[63]

In reality there were simply no conditions under which the nationalities would ever be allowed to secede if the party decided that they should not.

In the late 1920s the CPY accepted most of the views of the left, and the right came to be considered as the "opposition." The left pronounced the views of the right to be similar to those of the social democrats and of the Second International, and its own as "revolutionary," "Marxist," "proletarian," and "internationalist." Yugoslavia was proclaimed an "imperialist creation" and was called "Versailles Yugoslavia." The Communists would abandon this attitude toward Yugoslavia only during the Second World War.[64]

The Non-Nationalist Conflict over the National Question

Until the mid-1930s the CPY was, though formally centralized, an agglomeration of unassimilated regional (but neither national nor nationalist) working-class movements, which were themselves not well organized. In its structure and organization the party bore less resemblance to the Leninist type of party (ideologically monolithic, hierarchical, disciplined, active in the masses) than to a social-democratic one. The result was factionalism, which had been a chronic problem since the party's foundation in 1919. Prominent Communists created groups of personal followers who pursued policies and maintained independent organizational and hierarchical structures, disregarding the decisions of the central party bodies. The conflict over the national question increased this factionalism and even became its main cause.

From the time the CPY was outlawed in August 1921 until the mid-1930s, it had little influence on Yugoslav politics. It lacked proper organization and was unprepared for illegal struggle.[65] Despite the existence of a left-wing Communist intelligentsia, Communist trade unions, and a Communist press, there were no effective policies and tactics even when there was revolutionary turmoil in the country. The party lived partly in a world of fantasy, dreaming about the Communist society of a distant future, and partly in expectation of an immediate world revolution. The leadership of the CPY at that time was in the hands of middle-class intellectuals. In the 1920s the party was oriented chiefly to theory, debate, and polemics, whereas in the 1930s its primary interests were the creation of revolutionary organizations and the tactical adaptation of established views. The spirit of the party was more democratic in the 1920s, but there was more disunity and much less ability to organize political action.

Internal disagreements on the national question often escalated into conflicts of such intensity that they threatened to destroy the party. However, no Croatian or Serbian faction ever formed about any fundamental issue, including the national question; factions remained mixed in their composition. Therefore, although the dispute about the national question seriously disrupted the unity of the party on a number of occasions, it never turned into a conflict between Croats and Serbs.

Yet, the still-scarce historical evidence seems to suggest that there was a certain difference in approach to the national question between the Belgrade and the Zagreb party organizations, that Croatian and Serbian Communists were not quite free from the influence of their own national ideologies.[66] Among the leaders of the CPY there were, for example, some intellectuals from the prewar Serbian Social Democratic Party. These Communists were not Serbian nationalists, and they consistently and passionately opposed any form of persecution on national or religious grounds. Sima Marković, for example, was definitely not a Serbian nationalist. Yet his development into a socialist and Marxist occurred in ethnically homogeneous Serbia, and as in the case of other Serbian Communists, this background contributed to his lack of sensitivity to and understanding of the problems of a nationally heterogeneous country.[67] At the same time, the victory of the party's left made the CPY somewhat more permeable by the nationalism of non-Serbs. Expulsion came more swiftly for the "sin" of Serbian nationalism than for the display of non-Serbian nationalist attitudes.

With rare exceptions, members of the CPY were primarily Communist internationalists, and their major goal was the revolution. They judged all political questions and social problems primarily according to the function these played in the preparation of revolution. The national question was, therefore, largely a tactical question for both the left and the right: how to use it to further the cause of revolution. This distance from the various nationalist sentiments of Yugoslavia represented a Yugoslavist potential; that is, tactics could change, and the party could come to favor a united Yugoslav state. If the party cadres had been deeply immersed in the ideologies of their nations, this would not have been possible.

Yugoslav communists were sincerely opposed to national persecution and were genuinely sympathetic to the struggle of oppressed nations for their emancipation and liberation. And they supported them whenever they believed that in this way they were also furthering the cause of revolution. But no Communist worth his salt, either in Yugoslavia or in the Comintern, ever believed in the fundamental need for national independence after the revolution.[68] In general, the trend of the postrevolutionary world was expected to be one of integration and unification into a global union of Communist nations. The party's policy, which in the late 1920s demanded the dissolution of Yugoslavia (at that time increasingly called the "prison of the peoples"), thus did not commit the Communists to giving national independence, or the right to create independent states, to the non-Serbian nations and provinces of Yugoslavia after the Communist accession to power. It was primarily a tactical expedient and a propaganda slogan designed to arouse the support of dissatisfied nations.

At its third conference in 1924 the CPY abandoned its previous Yugoslavism; this was the first time in the history of the South Slavs that a major left-wing group had done so. Yet even after 1924 the party continued to be the only political organization in Yugoslavia to have members distributed among all nations of Yugoslavia. It could still be regarded as the only genuinely Yugoslav political party in the history of the South Slavs. Although a detailed political inventory of interwar Yugoslavia shows that there were other political groups and parties with Serbian and non-Serbian members and with Yugoslavist aspirations, several factors make it impossible to describe them as genuinely Yugoslav: their small size, making them almost irrelevant; Serbian numerical superiority in these parties; their disproportionately smaller influence outside Serbian regions (where it was also diminutive); their antireformist attitude to the national problem; and their support for or lack of genuine opposition to oppressive measures against dissatisfied nations.[69]

From 1919 to 1941 the CPY frequently changed its views in relation to Yugoslavia. It is, however, wrong to state with the Croatian historian Jozo Ivićević that "the CPY programmatically tested all the viewpoints that are at all possible about Yugoslavia and about the national question in Yugoslavia."[70] The party was always opposed to national oppression and intracommunal violence, and it severely censured the traditional nationalist ideologies even when it accepted some of their demands for tactical reasons.

three

The Communist Party
of Yugoslavia and the
Popular Front, 1925–1941

Smoldering Nationalism

In January 1925 the leaders of the Croatian Republican Peasant Party—
Stjepan Radić, Vladko Maček, Juraj Krnjević, Josip Predavec, August
Košutić, and Stjepan Košutić—were arrested.[1] Two months later the representatives of the CRPP in the Belgrade parliament accepted the centralist Vidovdan Constitution and the Karadjordjević dynasty and changed
the party's name to the Croatian Peasant Party (Hrvatska seljačka
stranka; CPP). Later in 1925 four members of the CPP joined the People's
Radical Party in the cabinet of Prime Minister Nikola Pašić, but they
returned to opposition in 1927.

Stjepan Radić, the leader of the CPP, had no original political ideas or
developed political program. Yet it was through him and his party that
the Croatian peasantry became an active force in politics for the first
time.[2] The CPP was the first party to reach large numbers of the Croatian
population with the idea that the Croats should be a sovereign entity, and
as a result it helped develop a Croatian national consciousness. In a sense,
this was the final stage in the transformation of the Croats into a modern
European nation.

Changes of government and the formation of coalition cabinets were
frequent during the unstable parliamentarism of interwar Yugoslavia,
although Serbs were always dominant.[3] The mortal wounding of Stjepan
Radić and the assassination and wounding of several other leading members of the CPP in the parliament in June 1928 provided King Aleksandar
with a pretext to dissolve parliament, suspend the constitution, and
severely limit the activities of political parties.[4] Even before this, there had
been serious violations of democratic procedures and manipulations of
elections.[5] The Communist Party of Yugoslavia had been outlawed since

1921. The establishment of a dictatorship was merely the final episode in the decline of parliament and of liberal-democratic institutions from 1918 to 1929. Under the dictatorship the press was censored, opponents of the regime persecuted, and the number of political prisoners increased.[6] The masses, however, did not resist. Parliament had lost its authority with Serbs primarily because it seemed unable to find a solution to the national conflict. At the same time, the Croats saw it as an institution dominated by Serbian nationalism. From 1929 until the disintegration of Yugoslavia in the Second World War, the CPP considered its main duty to be the struggle for Croatian national autonomy and independence, rather than for the restoration of parliament. The party's interest in liberal-democratic political institutions rested largely on the extent to which such institutions were considered useful for the achievement of Croatian national goals.[7]

King Aleksandar chose as his ministers politicians from banned political parties. His dictatorship was directed against parliamentarism as a system of government rather than against individual politicians (even when they were corrupt and nationalist). Many political leaders (mostly Serbs, but also some Slovenes, Bosnian Muslims, and Croats) joined the government or accepted lucrative posts in the civil or diplomatic service or in state-controlled enterprises. Few new political names appeared during the dictatorship, that is, before King Aleksandar's death in 1934. The fact that so many politicians agreed to serve in governments that were not elected and to which there could be little effective opposition showed a lack of support for liberal democracy both among politicians and among the general population. National conflicts weakened any resistance from political parties and prevented the creation of a permanent, united all-Yugoslav front against the dictatorship.[8]

The constitution of September 1931, granted by King Aleksandar, made the crown the primary constitutional factor and fulcrum of all political life.[9] The centralization of Yugoslavia begun by the 1921 Vidovdan Constitution was carried through with new ardor and persistence. The 1931 constitution was intended not only to strengthen centralism but also to generate a unitary Yugoslav national consciousness. The existence of a Croatian or any other national question was simply not admitted; only Yugoslav nationality was recognized. The king hoped to solve the national question by simply abolishing it. One of his many measures to effect this was the division of Yugoslavia into nine provinces called *banovine,* which were named after rivers, except one, which encompassed a large part of the coast and was named Primorska banovina (Coastal Banovina).[10] The borders of these provinces were established with intentional disregard for the national aspirations of Croats and Serbs. The administrative reorganization of Yugoslavia, the suppression of political parties that had defended particular national interests, and the reform of the educational system in order to promote Yugoslavism were expected to create a new Yugoslav nation. Although some supporters of the dictatorship were genuine Yugoslavists, including, as some evidence suggests, the king himself, Croats inevitably considered the dictatorship as thinly disguised "Serbian hegemony." Indeed, the dictatorship was bitterly resented in Croatia. Instead of dissolving traditional Croatian nationalism, the dictatorship strengthened the extremists.

The 1931 constitution curtailed civil liberties, institutionalized nonparliamentary monarchical rule, and gave the monarchy enormous political rights.[11] For example, all ministers were appointed by the king, and the government was accountable solely to him. King Aleksandar promoted the idea of one Yugoslav nation but made no fundamental changes in the method of rule or in the personnel of the government, police, and army. The large majority of ministers, officers, policemen, and civil servants were still Serbs. King Aleksandar's dictatorship lasted, albeit in a constitutional dress, until his death in 1934 and continued in a somewhat milder form under his successor, Prince Pavle. Although its procedures were considerably amended and softened in political practice, the constitution formally remained in effect until the Communists proclaimed a new one in January 1946. During the Second World War, for example, King Petar II, though still only in his teens, dismissed and appointed members of the Yugoslav cabinet at will.[12]

The pressure of the royal dictatorship speeded up the transformation of Croatian nationalism into a closed and often aggressive ideology. Many Croatian nationalists in the 1930s considered Croatia to be an occupied territory.[13] They regarded their Serbian rulers, a group of people whom they considered culturally, psychologically, and in every other respect alien, as having taken political power thanks to use of force, Serbian numerical superiority, and historical circumstances, but without the consent of the Croatian people. This attitude was more extreme than the simple claim that the "national rights" of the Croatian people were not being respected. It increased the inclination of nationalists to blame all bad features of the contemporary political scene (and often of the nation's history as well) on "aliens." A weak economy, biased judiciary, or corrupt administration tended to be explained away solely as the consequence of this alien interference. The propensity to think in those terms had characterized southeastern European nationalisms since the nineteenth century.[14] But from the 1930s onward, Croatian nationalists tended to think of their nation as a body politic with "inborn" political institutions. It only had to free itself from external forces, and its naturally good political "self" would come to life.

A dearth of political ideas was another inevitable consequence of this reduction of Croatian politics to the cause of national independence. Everything was subordinated to the nation's "foreign policy," or (since some Croatian nationalists had an inclination to political violence and terrorism) to "war." This pseudo-romantic revolutionary spirit echoed Rousseau's argument that freedom could be achieved simply by breaking the chains of a corrupt sociopolitical order that enslaved naturally free human beings. Since for Croatian nationalists Croatia was by its nature free, liberation from the "alien" simply meant the restoration of that natural former freedom. This was why some nationalists suggested that a liberated Croatia should be called "Croatia Restituta."[15]

In some ways Croatian nationalism in the 1930s resembled Marxist-Leninist theory—with Serbs as the "exploiters" and Croats as the "exploited." The "colonialist" and "oppressing" Serbs, it was often claimed, depended on the exploitation of the "proletarian" Croats. The Serbian national consciousness, like the "superstructure" of the Marxist scheme, was determined by this "economic basis." The Serbs were then seen as solely interested in power and exploitation, and the whole of Serbian history as little more than a conspiracy to enslave other nations, especially the Croats. Important figures of the Serbian cultural heritage were included in this perception.

Marxists tend to see all non-Communist political groups as basically the same, that is, as different expressions of the same or very similar class interests. So for them, political conflict among non-Communists is not really a conflict at all; real history is only the conflict between the exploiters and the exploited. Likewise, for Croatian nationalists the differences among the Serbian political parties were irrelevant. To these Croats the Serbs seemed a completely united political group whose sole purpose was oppressing Croats. In fact the Serbs were not at all ideologically united. Although the majority favored the preservation of Yugoslavia, they were not one political party (much less a secret organization), but a nation with a variety of political groups and ideas.

After the murder of King Aleksandar at the beginning of his state visit to France in October 1934, nationalist tensions increased.[16] Relations between Croats and Serbs went through a particularly difficult phase, since the assassination had been organized by the exiled members of the Croatian Ustasha movement, who in turn were supported by Fascist Italy. Prince Pavle, a cousin of the king, became regent for his eleven-year-old nephew, King Petar II, and retained the same autocratic powers that the constitution had conferred on King Aleksandar.[17] In June 1935 he appointed Milan Stojadinović, the minister of finance, as prime minister. Stojadinović, a financial expert and a former prominent politician of the People's Radical Party, had built up his own following within the government party. A new political party with a Yugoslav orientation, the Yugoslav Radical Union

(Jugoslovenska radikalna zajednica), was formed. The party united in a loose alliance a fragment of the People's Radical Party, the Slovenian People's Party, and the Yugoslav Muslim Organization (Jugoslovenska muslim-anska organizacija), the party of Muslims from Bosnia-Herzegovina, led by Mehmed Spaho.[18] The latter two parties were purely Slovenian and Muslim, and joined the government with the primary goal of protecting and furthering their own national interests rather than trying to develop some all-Yugoslav national consciousness.[19]

The new government abandoned the dogmatic unitarism and Yugoslavism King Aleksandar had imposed on Yugoslavia after January 1929, which had denied the existence of any national question. The existence of differences in the historical traditions of Serbs, Croats, and Slovenes was recognized although they were still considered one people. At the same time this was partly an anti-Croatian coalition, and was perceived as such. Croatian nationalism was seen as the greatest danger to the Yugoslav state, and Prince Pavle tried to isolate it by making concessions to the Slovenes and Bosnian Muslims. Yet the Serbs were not united in one political party. Stojadinović's Yugoslav Radical Union was not even completely representative of the People's Radical Party, nor were the Radicals representative of the Serbian people in the sense in which the Croats were almost completely united behind the Croatian Peasant Party, the Slovenes behind their "clericalists" (Slovenian People's Party), and the Muslims behind their Yugoslav Muslim Organization. Stojadinović's attempts to shape the Yugoslav Radical Union into a monolithic party were unsuccessful. It remained a coalition until the end of its existence (and Stojadinović's rule) in February 1939.

The Comintern's Support for Separatism in Yugoslavia

The Comintern's policy toward the national question in the period 1918–1925 was to "support the rebellious." To further its aim of world revolution, the Comintern engaged in propaganda for national emancipation, distribution of land, and peace. During the Russian civil war (1918–1922), similar slogans had proved attractive to the dissatisfied peasants and non-Russian nations. They were expected to be as effective on the central and southeastern European revolutionary front. The period 1925–1935 was a time of "rallying the separatists." The Comintern recognized the rapid growth of nationalist peasant parties in central and southeastern Europe and often instructed the Communists to support many of their demands. The Communists incorporated some nationalist (and even separatist) slogans into their programs; on occasion they even supported the right wing and militant groups in the peasant parties. The period 1935–1945 (except when the Molotov-Ribbentrop Pact was in effect, from August 1939 to June 1941) was one of "uniting against fascism" and represented a radical change in Communist policy. The Soviet Union was dismayed by the successes of fascism in western Europe. The Comintern therefore began to advocate Communist alliances with all antifascist movements and political parties and to create the so-called Popular Front. For Communists, opposition to fascism now became an almost sufficient reason to proclaim any particular movement "progressive." Such generosity was in stark contrast to the previous Communist attitude according to which even social democrats had been labeled "social fascists."[20]

The Comintern's radicalism of the 1920s had done great harm to the left everywhere in Europe. Through their campaign against social democrats, for example, the Communists assisted the triumph of National Socialism in Germany. Instead of helping the Communist revolution, national antagonisms tended to help right-wing and fascist movements that were friendly to Hitler, or Mussolini, or both.[21] The Soviet Union particularly feared Hitler, who had come to power in Germany in January 1933, and the Comintern began to see the countries of central and southeastern Europe as a useful barrier between the Soviet Union and German expansion and aggression.[22] The dissolution of Yugoslavia or Czechoslovakia into smaller states would have weakened this barrier. In the 1920s, of course, this same barrier had been considered a hindrance to the Comintern's revolutionary expansion in Europe.

Toward the Radical Rejection of Yugoslavia

The resolution of the fifth plenum of the Comintern's Executive Committee in April 1925 was radical in its demands.[23] It called for the dissolution of Yugoslavia and the creation of a revolutionary Balkan federation.[24] The spontaneous nationalism of the Croatian masses was to be supported by Yugoslav Communists. The Comintern instructed them to criticize only "bourgeois" Croatian nationalism, but every form of Serbian nationalism was to be censured. The Comintern had in fact encouraged these policies even before the fifth plenum, disregarding the possibility that Communist support for dissatisfied nationalists might fan passions. (The intracommunal massacres in Yugoslavia during the Second World War amply demonstrated their destructive, genocidal power.) Echoes of Comintern radicalism were also evident in the theses of the Central Committee of the CPY, prepared in 1925 for debate in the Executive Council of the Comintern. For example, Serbian domination in Yugoslavia and the "imperialism" of Great Britain and France were referred to as if they were the same thing, with the implication that the non-Serbian lands of Yugoslavia were simply Serbian colonies. One party decision of 1925 went as far as to speak of the need to increase the struggle against "chauvinism and nationalism of the ruling nation and great-Serbian prejudices among Serbian workers and peasants."[25]

The third congress of the CPY, held in Vienna in May 1926, accepted the Comintern's line to support separatism and to propagate the idea of a revolutionary Balkan federation.[26] During this congress there was a reconciliation between the left and right factions of the party; Sima Marković, the leader of the right, was elected party secretary.[27] But soon afterward conflict over the national question revived with new strength. The party's organizational structure had already been much weakened by persecution, and the party was becoming increasingly passive. The renewed conflict threatened to destroy it. After numerous interventions by the Comintern, the fourth congress of the CPY was convened—the last party congress of the interwar period. A small group of delegates (representing a party of only 2,034 not very active members) met in Dresden in October 1928.[28] The fourth congress agreed that in Yugoslavia the national question had greater revolutionary potential than social and economic questions, and that without considerable national content in its ideology the party would not be able to influence and lead the masses. The congress also agreed that organizing an uprising of the oppressed nations would be a much more efficient method of defending the Soviet Union, were it to be threatened by western "imperialists" approaching via Yugoslav territory, than would an uprising of the "oppressed" working class. All Communists at that time considered the defense of the Soviet Union to be their highest moral duty. The Comintern and, under its influence, the Yugoslav party overestimated both the threat from the west to the Soviet Union and the revolutionary potential of the national question in Yugoslavia. Although nationalism was widespread and dissatisfaction enormous, the possibility of a national uprising against the Belgrade centralists was small.

All political groups in the countries of southeastern Europe, which had large peasant populations, had to design strategies that would motivate them for political action. It was therefore simply impossible to achieve legitimacy without reference to the national problem. The CPY could not successfully demand loyalty from anyone if it did not show that it was itself loyal to national interests and aspirations. Yet the CPY's indiscriminate antagonism to the Yugoslav state, as proclaimed by the fourth congress, was out of harmony with the feelings of many cadres. Nor was the party likely to increase its following simply by repeating the slogans of the traditional nationalist parties. It needed to design its own strategies. But this process would take some time. The party had to mature and reorganize; and above all else it needed new cadres.

During the fourth congress Yugoslavia was described as an "imperialist creation"—a country based on a violent and unjust imperialist conquest that had put Croats, Macedonians, Montenegrins, and Slovenes under the rule of the "great-Serbian bourgeoisie." Should a new "imperialist" war take place, it would be the duty of Communists to transform it into civil war (national liberation and revolutionary war), which would have as one of its aims the dissolution of Yugoslavia.[29] Any attempt at a constitutional solution was rejected as opportunism, and dubbed a "petit-bourgeois illusion." For Yugoslavia could never be reformed within its present borders; it must be broken up into smaller states. The congress was a clear victory for the revolutionary as opposed to the constitutional approach to the national question. But it was an extreme version of the revolutionary approach, partly imposed by the Comintern.

The fourth congress also decided that the party should support the activities of political groups in Croatia that were demanding an independent state: it was wrong to identify the Serbian "bourgeoisie" with the "bourgeoisie" of the oppressed nations, since the Serbian was a ruling group. This was a big concession for Communists, who normally considered all "bourgeoisies" equally evil.[30] The creation of an independent Croatia was viewed as a highly important element of party policy, and the Communists were expected to struggle for that goal without any reservations or conditions. The right to self-determination was no longer to be considered the exclusive prerogative of workers' and peasants' representatives, implying that the struggle of "bourgeois" parties for that goal should also be supported. However, neither the method of establishing the Croatian state nor the territories it would encompass were specified. There was no mention, for example, of a referendum. The party simply expressed its support for Croatian nationalism, even when it took a militant and separatist form. Although the party continued to reject in principle any summary condemnation of an entire nation, and this remained also its policy in regard to the "ruling" Serbian nation, it did not state at what point the non-Serbian nations' struggle for liberation would itself become a form of chauvinistic oppression, either in the sense of territorial demands or of persecution of Serbian "oppressors."

The party further supported independence for Slovenia and Montenegro, and in the case of Macedonia proposed not only independence but also amalgamation with Aegean Macedonia in Greece and Pirin Macedonia in Bulgaria. Even an "independent Vojvodina" was mentioned.[31] National minorities—Albanians in Kosovo and Hungarians in northern Vojvodina—were also to have the right to separate. Yet these two minorities were to join Hungary and Albania only when these two states had themselves undergone a revolution and become part of the federation of Balkan workers' and peasants' republics.[32]

The fourth congress was an extreme and bitter reaction to the erstwhile strong unitarism in the party and to the general underestimation of the national question. National dissatisfaction in the country was great, and the party wanted to purge itself of any Yugoslavist views that could alienate the masses from the party. Equally important was the party's zeal to show the Comintern that it had completely abandoned all supposed social-democratic weaknesses and compromises. (After January 1929, when the royal dictatorship was established, the party wanted to challenge as radically as possible the ruling unitarist concepts.) Yet support for separatism was in the long run contrary to the CPY's interests, ideology, and structure; evolution toward federalism was preferable. The party, was after all, Yugoslav in its structure and opposed to national extremism, and it could not gain any real influence by imitating the policies of other parties; it would only lose its own identity.

After the proclamation of the 1929 dictatorship, the Central Committee of the CPY called upon the people to revolt against the dictatorship.[33] The party had misinterpreted the mood of the country, but it had also been misled by the sixth congress of the Comintern, held in August 1928 in Moscow, which predicted a new cycle of wars and revolutions in Europe and adopted a policy of "extreme leftism" set forth by Stalin. There was no response from the masses to the party's call. It was in this atmosphere that the party misinterpreted certain conflicts between Croatian nationalists (partly connected with the exiled Ustasha leadership) and the Yugoslav police, such as the attack on the police station near Gospić in Lika, a central mountain region of Croatia. The party momentarily believed that the Croatian nation was rising in arms against the oppression of "great-Serbian imperialism."[34]

At the beginning of the dictatorship the official organ of the party's Central Committee, *Proleter,* seems to have believed that there was some support for the dictatorship among the Serbian peasantry. There was some foundation for this inference, since King Aleksandar enjoyed personal popularity among some Serbian peasants as a military leader from the First World War. Also, the will to preserve Yugoslavia as a state (for which the Serbs had paid a heavy price during the First World War and in which they were finally united) was strong among the Serbian peasantry. Nevertheless, the party had never identified the "oppressed classes" of a nation with the actions of their "ruling classes," and now in the case of the Serbs it appeared to be making an exception and setting a precedent.

On 1 December 1929 *Proleter* denounced the dictatorship:

The proclamation of "Yugoslavia" in place of the "Kingdom of the Serbs, Croats, and Slovenes" and the simultaneous administrative division of the country into nine *banovine,* represent the culmination of the hegemonist-imperialist policies of the bloody rule of great-Serbian fascism. By proclaiming the military-fascist dictatorship, the coup d'état of 6 January set itself among other things a goal of creating national "unity" through merging all peoples of Yugoslavia into one single nation. What the Balkan "parliament" was unable to achieve, the great-Serbian bourgeoisie, with the support of the bourgeoisie of the oppressed nations, intends to achieve with the open force of the military-fascist dictatorship. The ten-month balance sheet of the bloody rule of the Belgrade hangmen clearly shows and proves what is meant by national unity, and how this "unity" is being realized. This new division of the country basically means the division of oppressed nations, their even greater and more ruthless oppression and exploitation.

The "Belgrade tyrants" led by "Aleksandar the Last" were further accused of continuing the "ruthless, brutal, barbarous policies of the great-Serbian bourgeoisie." For they had also "oppressed without any limits, economically and culturally, the non-Serbian nations, depriving them of all political rights," while the revolutionary cadres of the national-liberation movements were "terrorized, persecuted, arrested, and, while in prison, monstrously tortured and murdered." *Proleter* was radical in its demands:

> Down with the military-fascist dictatorship! Down with the bloody Serbian monarchy! Down with the great-Serbian policy of national oppression! Long live the union of workers, peasants, and oppressed nations! Long live independent Croatia, Macedonia, Montenegro, Slovenia, Bosnia, Vojvodina, and Serbia! Long live the worker-peasant government! Long live the federation of worker-peasant republics of the Balkans!

In June 1933 the CPY repeated its call for workers' and peasants' power and for a voluntary alliance of the worker-peasant republics of Serbia, Croatia, Slovenia, Macedonia, and Montenegro. This alliance was to be created on the ruins of the "imperialist" Yugoslavia of "Versailles" by way of a revolutionary struggle of workers and peasants of the oppressed nations along with the working class and peasantry of the ruling Serbian nation.[35]

The fourth conference of the CPY, held in Ljubljana in December 1934, by and large continued the party line of the 1928 fourth congress.[36] Under the blows of the January 1929 dictatorship the party had disintegrated and could not evolve any new policies.[37] It repeatedly rejected any idea of transforming Yugoslavia into a federation, even one with a republican constitution. This latter idea, which came from the left-wing Agrarians, a small but vocal political group led by Dragoljub Jovanović within the Union of the Agrarians (Savez zemljoradnika), was considered just a way of preserving "Versailles Yugoslavia" and as the expression of fear of a workers' and peasants' revolution. The fourth conference decided to create within the CPY the Communist Party of Croatia and the Communist Party of Slovenia, and, as soon as there were enough cadres, the Communist Party of Macedonia. It asserted that all nations should have the right to self-determination and demanded the establishment of worker-peasant governments in Serbia, Croatia, Slovenia, Macedonia, Kosovo, Montenegro, Bosnia, and Vojvodina. An important problem remained unnoticed by the party. Serbia did not include almost half of the Serbian population. A worker-peasant government in Slovenia, for example, would have been a national Slovenian government, since there were very few Slovenes living outside Slovenia in other parts of Yugoslavia. (There was, however, a Slovenian minority in Austria and in Italy, and the Slovenian Communists demanded that it should join Slovenia.)[38] Also, worker-peasant government in Croatia would have represented most Croats, with the exception of a sizable Croatian group in Bosnia-Herzegovina and Vojvodina. Such a government in Serbia, however, would have ruled over only slightly more than half of all Serbs.

The conference also insisted on the use of the national languages in the schools, courts, and even the army, and opposed mandatory learning of the Serbian language in non-Serbian regions. Croats, Slovenes, Montenegrins, and Macedonians should not do their military service outside their regions, and the same should apply to the Albanian, Hungarian, and German minorities—almost a demand for the creation of separate national armies. The conference further demanded the expulsion of Serbian "occupiers" (troops, civil servants, and police) from Croatia, Slovenia, Dalmatia, Bosnia, Montenegro, Macedonia, and Kosovo. However, unlike the nationalist extremists, it did not ask for the actual expulsion of Serbs (or Serbian settlers) from these regions.

A New Party

In the mid-1930s the CPY underwent a fundamental transformation that was an important precondition for the subsequent development of the policies of the Popular Front (including those related to the national question). There was an influx of new cadres. The organizational structure was strengthened, and the struggle among factions ceased. The "new" party was partly a result of purges and terror by two dictators: Stalin and King Aleksandar. (In comparison with Stalin, King Aleksandar was an "ordinary" autocrat; he imprisoned his most active political opponents and perhaps ordered the assassination of some, but he was not a totalitarian despot responsible for the deaths of millions of people.)[39] In the Comintern's purges, more than a hundred members of the CPY (including some leaders and founders of the party) were either executed or sent to concentration camps, most of them never to return. Stalin's political police made no national distinctions: Croats and Serbs perished together.[40]

Stalin's terror, along with the dictatorship of King Aleksandar, all but destroyed the party. And yet both enormously helped the cause of Communism in Yugoslavia. The older generation of Yugoslav Communists, unprepared for clandestine struggle and paralyzed by factional conflict, was succeeded by younger Communists who were much more united and active among the masses. Also, King Aleksandar's dictatorship radicalized the young, especially in secondary schools and universities.[41] They became contemptuous of political parties that appeared mostly conservative and nationalist and failed to offer a determined opposition to the dictatorship; the young advocated revolutionary change. From then until the end of the Second World War, Communism held enormous attraction for the young intelligentsia. For example, of the 212 awarded the medal "hero of the people" before 1952 and who had been killed during the war, 109 were from the intelligentsia, and most were in their twenties when killed.[42]

The new generation of Communists was at least as indoctrinated as the previous one, yet less involved in theoretical disputes and more activist. Although they considered theory important, they were also convinced that Marxism-Leninism had already answered all key problems of society and politics; thus, they believed, direct political action and influencing the masses should be the Communists' main concern. It was precisely this mixture of dogmatism and pragmatism that made the Communists of the new generation so successful.[43] There was an obvious connection between Communist revolutionary beliefs (that is, the certainty that one's ideological convictions were universally true) and the creation of a united and strictly organized party. The young Communist revolutionaries of the 1930s were not just rebels fighting against injustices and oppression, but participants in what appeared to them to be a global struggle. They believed that their actions were based on an understanding of historical processes and society that offered solutions to the whole of humankind. Such a universalist world view could not accept limitations or divisions either in the realm of political ideas or in the realm of party organization. It was by definition (since it was universalist) also applicable to all nations of the world and, needless to say, to all nations of Yugoslavia.

In many respects the young Yugoslav Communists of the 1930s, though active in arousing the masses, were psychologically outside society. In this sense they were not integrated in their own nation. They lived for prolonged periods in close-knit groups that became not only their political and ideological universe but also a kind of family. For many revolutionaries this ideological-political family was more important than attachment to their nation. These Communists defined themselves as people of the future and their revolutionary family (the party) as the organization of the future. For them, the idea that one day all people could feel an international political loyalty stronger and emotionally deeper than the loyalty to one's nation was based on personal experience and not simply on theory. For since all today's real Communists were internationalists, then tomorrow, when everyone became a Communist, everyone would also be an internationalist.

The difficulty of reconciling traditional patriotism with revolutionary radicalism had been apparent since the nineteenth century. Radicalism meant internationalism. In his writings on revolutionary organization, Mikhail Bakunin had argued in favor of the creation of an "international family," which would be a kind of European central committee.[44] The use of the concept of family was significant. It was a closed, tightly knit, psychologically "intensive" unit, with a strong loyalty among members; a unit that stood largely outside the bounds of rational analysis and was difficult for its members to challenge. National central committees were to be nominated by this international family, and then closely and constantly controlled and supervised by it. (This concept had obvious similarities not only to the later role of the Comintern but also—in the late 1930s, after the foundation of the Communist parties of Croatia and Slovenia—to the relations between the Central Committee of the CPY and the central committees of these two parties.) Bakunin had used the word *brother* and not *comrade* for a fellow revolutionary. This usage never came to be accepted, but it was a better description of the relationships among revolutionaries. Of course, revolutionaries often did treat each other in a less than brotherly way, but even this conduct demonstrated the emotional intensity characteristic of a conflict inside a family. An analysis of the concepts of brother and family makes it easier to understand why the Yugoslav Communists accepted with such zeal the Comintern's puritanical line on sexual matters in the 1930s.[45] Inside a close-knit revolutionary party, free relationships tended to cause bitter conflicts and sometimes even to be psychologically experienced as incest.

The Communist Utopian ideal seemed real and realizable for the new generation of Yugoslav revolutionaries. The egalitarianism and fraternity within the organization made the new activists feel that they were living in an already-realized Communist society. Since the party was multinational, and instead of national conflicts there was one revolutionary Yugoslav national consciousness, their commitment to Yugoslavism was strengthened. The mixed national composition of many Communist cells increased the sense of Yugoslav solidarity and the feeling of a common destiny for all the Yugoslav peoples.[46] This Communist experience was, in a sense, a large-scale and more intensive repetition of the pre-1914 multinational Young Bosnia. Also, Yugoslav Communists saw the Comintern as an established Communist microcosm that the forthcoming explosion of world revolution would expand until it became a macrocosm. The Comintern defined itself not just as an instrument for revolution but as a prototype of a Communist society. Its anthem stated, and Yugoslav Communists believed, "L'Internationale sera la genre humain."

In the late 1930s Croatian and Serbian Communists were equally unshakable in their devotion to the Soviet Union and Stalin, and therefore also to the Comintern's policies, including those on the national question. Until the Yugoslav break with Moscow in 1948, the Soviet Union was praised as a model of a justly solved national question. For example, in August 1940 at the first conference of the Communist Party of Croatia (Komunistička partija Hrvatske) the participants sent the following message to Stalin:

> These dear words "Comrade Stalin" are a program for us. The working people of Croatia see in You the realization of an unswaying proletarian fighter, leader, and teacher who, through difficult times and bloody struggle against all exploiters, leads the working people of the Soviet Union along the path which the working people of Croatia would also like to take.[47]

During the Second World War the Partisan movement was characterized by "holy devotion, unbending austerity, rigid discipline and lugubrious puritanism";[48] this was exactly what the CPY began to look like in the mid-1930s. These characteristics were combined with powerful collectivist sentiments and a system of internal sanctions, the strictest being expulsion.

The Comintern appointed Tito the general secretary of the CPY probably in December 1937 and gave him the right to veto any decision by the Central Committee. By now there were few factional struggles, and the firmly united party increasingly saw itself as the advance guard of the popular democratic demands of the masses, overcoming the isolation into which it had been pushed by persecution as well as by its dogmatism and sectarianism. This unity made the Communists a force for Yugoslav integration. For example, the Belgrade party organization and, more particularly, the University of Belgrade, were the centers where the cadres from Serbia, Montenegro, Vojvodina, Bosnia-Herzegovina, Macedonia, and Kosovo were prepared for revolution.[49] Selection was based solely on personal merit, that is, dedication to the Communist cause, and there was little national friction—a unique thing among the interwar Yugoslav political parties.

From the mid-1930s onward the cadres became increasingly mobile, moving from one region of Yugoslavia to another. This circulation of Communist elites is particularly significant in comparison with the almost complete lack of circulation of other elites—political, cultural, or economic—among the nations of Yugoslavia (the only exceptions were the mostly Serbian military personnel, policemen, or civil servants who were transferred from one region to another). Moving all around the country, the young Communists were creating a Yugoslav consciousness in their party. For example, Aleksandar Ranković, a Serbian member of the Politburo, was in Croatia from January through March 1941, supervising the trade union activities of the Central Committee of the Communist Party of Croatia and helping solve its organizational problems.[50] Blagoje Nešković, the secretary of the party organization for Serbia during the war, was sent to Zagreb in July 1941 to investigate a crisis in the Central Committee of the Communist Party of Croatia. Back in Belgrade in August he proposed penalties to the Politburo, whereupon Tito, as the general secretary, made the final decision.[51] Such procedures, which totally disregarded the sovereignty of the Croatian and Slovenian parties, were very common and were not perceived as unusual by the party members. At the same time, Slovenian and Croatian Communists exerted strong influences in Serbia and other parts of Yugoslavia.

When the war began in Europe the CPY was at its peak—united, disciplined, well organized, experienced, and Yugoslavist. This fact was demonstrated clearly at the fifth conference of the CPY (actually a party congress, although it was not formally called that) in October 1940.[52] More than 100 leading Communists, well known to the party cadres all over Yugoslavia, assembled secretly in a rented villa in a suburb of Zagreb. Such boldness was a measure of the Communists' confidence, given the fact that they could all have been arrested.[53] The delegates to the conference had been elected at regional and district conferences attended by around 1,500 Communist delegates who had themselves been elected by the general membership. To be sure, both sets of delegates, as well as the members of the Central Committee, had in fact been selected from above, but it was nevertheless true that the leadership enjoyed the devoted support of the membership. The delegates were 53 workers, 14 peasants, 29 intellectuals, and 5 administrative personnel. All had been professional revolutionaries for many years. Their average age was thirty-three, their average length of party membership nine years, and their average time spent in prison two years. Around two-thirds had been tortured by the police at least once. Many of them were veterans, and some had held officer rank in the Spanish Civil War.[54]

The Popular Front

In its resolution of March 1935, the Central Committee of the CPY no longer described Yugoslavia as an imperialist creation.[55] It called for self-rule for certain regions, in particular for Croatia, without any mention of separation or full independence. The party was becoming increasingly aware that nationalism and chauvinism were dangerous, since they often played into the hands of profascist groups in Croatia and Slovenia. With a new level of political realism it recognized that inflamed nationalist passions could lead to open conflict among nations. It was no longer confident that such passions could be channeled toward Communist revolutionary struggle.[56] In June 1935 in Split, the plenum of the Central Committee decided to proceed immediately with the founding of the Communist parties of Croatia and Slovenia.[57] Yet the solution of the national question was no longer connected solely with the revolution. The party seemed ready to recognize that something could be achieved within the framework of the bourgeois state. Complete national liberation was, of course, still impossible without a Communist revolution, but the Communists were now ready to assist those political changes that could improve the lot of the oppressed nations. There were to be free parliamentary elections for all nations of Yugoslavia, the most important being the creation of a Croatian parliament; but parliaments for Bosnia-Herzegovina, Macedonia, Vojvodina, Slovenia, and Montenegro were also mentioned. This was a kind of federalism, although the word was not used. The plenum also demanded freedom of action for all cultural and educational institutions of the oppressed nations.[58]

In April 1936, first in Prague and then in Vienna, the plenum of the CPY Central Committee concluded that a single state of Slovenes, Croats, and other nations along with Serbs was possible as long as Serbian domination was abolished and full national equality established.[59] However, this plenum stipulated that while a current "monarcho-fascist dictatorship" lasted, Communists should not openly support the unity of the Yugoslav state, but should concentrate on demanding democratic reforms. The plenum also concluded that the party should struggle against the ideas and slogans that were contributing to the growth of Croatian fascism. The Communists thus indirectly admitted that their earlier unconditional support for the right of nations to self-determination and for the separation of Croatia had prevented them from being sufficiently critical of Croatian nationalism.

The Comintern did not support the decisions of this plenum. It accused the CPY of being too closely involved with the policies of "bourgeois" nationalist parties—especially the Croatian Peasant Party—and of interpreting the right of national self-determination too rigidly and thus unnecessarily associating itself with claims for separation. Greater emphasis should have been placed on autonomy for the oppressed nations as a solution to the national question.[60] The Comintern was thus conveniently forgetting that its own influence had played a considerable role in forming exactly the views that it was now criticizing. The Comintern now maintained that the CPY should openly oppose separatism. It should continue to support the right of self-determination, but it should advocate the transformation of Yugoslavia into a federal country with a democratically elected parliament.[61] Democracy should not, however, be based upon majority rule, which could lead to domination by the strongest nation. Neither the Comintern nor the plenum discussed the delicate question of the number of federal units and the borders between them.[62] Interestingly, the demand that Yugoslavia also be proclaimed a republic was dropped. This was tantamount to a temporary acceptance of the monarchy, which had hitherto been described as "great-Serbian" and even "fascist."

The Comintern's change of attitude toward Yugoslavia was noticeable at the founding congresses of the Communist parties of Slovenia and Croatia. The Communist Party of Slovenia (Komunistična partija Slovenije) was founded in April 1937 in Čebine near Trbovlje. Its manifesto stressed the threat posed by fascism to the very existence of the Slovenian nation because of German aspirations to Slovenian lands.[63] Yugoslavia as a "free union of fraternal nations" (with both a Slovenian national parliament and a Yugoslav federal parliament) was in the interests of the Slovenian people. The founding congress of the Communist Party of Croatia was held in August 1937 near Samobor. Tito spoke in the name of the Central Committee of the CPY.[64] The congress asserted that fascism was a threat to Croatia and that Croats could be free and progress only in fraternal cooperation with the other nations of Yugoslavia. The congress then called for free elections for a constituent assembly (parliament) in which mutual relations among the nations of Yugoslavia would be constitutionally established. The right wing's and fascists' demands for an independent Croatian state were severely attacked.[65]

The policy of the Popular Front became the official policy of the Comintern after its seventh congress, held in Moscow in July–August 1935.[66] In June 1935, under the Comintern's influence, the plenum of the CPY Central Committee had already accepted the idea of creating a mass movement against fascism. Blagoje Parović had stated:

> Not only the proletariat and the poor peasantry but the widest sections of the people will participate in the revolution. This is why for us one of the most essential tasks is to win over these sections of the people to the proletariat's struggle against the regime. We must search for ways, methods, and slogans that will move those masses toward us, avoiding everything that repels them or does not correspond to their level of readiness to fight.[67]

The Yugoslav Communists decided to adopt a strategy identical with that of Communists everywhere else in Europe: a unified political front of all "progressive" and "democratic" forces, under the influence or, if possible, leadership of Communists.[68] This required cooperation with the Communists' former enemies on the left, including the social democrats, whom the Communists had previously described as the "greatest enemies of the working class" and even as "social fascists." In Yugoslavia the Popular Front never became a coalition of political forces, since only a few minor political figures were willing to accept cooperation with the Communists.[69] The Popular Front was therefore primarily an effort by the CPY to capture the allegiance of the masses. The Communists were generally successful in presenting themselves as the most dedicated and best-organized champions of popular left-wing and progressive causes. This was in fact how many young Communists saw themselves. Their sectarianism and Marxist-Leninist dogmatism was modified or concealed. On the strength of such policies the CPY achieved considerable successes from 1935 until the beginning of the Second World War, and during the war largely continued with them. This policy of alliance with all progressive and antifascist forces during the Popular Front period enabled the Yugoslav Communists to acquire a reputation as a patriotic movement.[70] To be sure, they continued to attack "Serbian hegemony," but they were now also opposed to militant separatist movements and to the nationalist separatist ideologies of the non-Serbian nations of Yugoslavia.[71] The Ustasha movement, for example, was now considered to be a dangerous and "reactionary" enemy. The distinction previously made between the "reactionary" fascist character of the Ustasha leadership and the "progressive" national-revolutionary character of some of their followers from the poor peasantry was largely abandoned.

During the time of the Popular Front the CPY was transformed from an isolated Marxist-Leninist sect into the principal party of the left, radical in its enthusiasm and combativeness but moderate in its demands. The fact that political parties in the country lacked developed programs for social and economic change made it easier for the Communists to gain influence. During the Second World War, which in Yugoslavia lasted from April 1941 until May 1945, Communists created the Jedinstveni narodno-oslobodilački front (JNOF; United Front of People's Liberation) as a continuation of the policies of the Popular Front.[72] Its program demanded the liberation of Yugoslavia from Germany, Italy, and other occupying powers; national equality and fraternity ("brotherhood and unity") within a strong Yugoslavia; and democratic rights and social justice (social and economic reforms). The JNOF avoided revolutionary and Communist demands and made efforts to appear moderate in attributing primary importance to the mobilization for the struggle against fascism. The Popular Front of Yugoslavia (Narodni front Jugoslavije) was founded in August 1945 partly as a continuation of the JNOF. It included individuals, mass organizations, and political groups and parties that accepted its program and statute. No political group was allowed to preserve an independent political organization or structure. All were nominally represented through the participation of some of their leading members (seldom the best-known ones) in the Popular Front. Almost the whole spectrum of prewar parties was there, but under Communist hegemony they were shadows of their former selves.[73] The fourth congress of the Popular Front of Yugoslavia, held in February 1953, transformed it into the Socialist Alliance of the Working People of Yugoslavia (Socijalistički savez radnog naroda Jugoslavije), a mass organization controlled by the party whose membership included almost all employed Yugoslavs.

Because of their Popular Front policies, Communists appeared to many in the 1930s as the radical champions of the ideas of the Enlightenment. Since liberal-democratic forces had been weakened by the long rule of antiparliamentary regimes and by nationalism, Communism increasingly seemed to be the only force capable of making progressive reforms. The Communists thus succeeded in attracting leftist-inclined followers of other political parties. (Most of the parties were primarily "national," that is, primarily pursuing national interests, and therefore contained members of very different social and political views, including progressive and even socialist ones.) During the Popular Front period the party's influence among the young spread rapidly, often at the expense of other political parties.

In the late 1930s the idea of dividing Yugoslavia into independent states finally gave way to the idea of preserving the unity of the state while creating autonomous national units.[74] From now on the Communists would always argue in favor of federalism. They would not describe precisely the method of its achievement, but their preference would be for a referendum and plebiscite, rather than supporting the policies of "bourgeois" parties. Like Marković, they considered that sovereignty lay with the nation.[75] But Communists both in the Soviet Union and in Yugoslavia considered a federal system in a Communist country to be only a stage on the road to the final unification of the proletariat of all countries. It was thus not meant to be a permanent arrangement, let alone a stage toward a confederal system. (This view was part of the Communist creed beginning at least with the second congress of the Comintern, held in July 1920 in Moscow, which passed a resolution on the national question, the draft of which had been written by Lenin himself.)

The change from radical opposition to the state of Yugoslavia to patriotic support for its continuation and defense did not damage the party, since CPY members and supporters did not feel this reversal to be a betrayal of an element that had a central place in their Communist ideology. The Yugoslavism-in-fact of the anti-Yugoslav Communist Party (as it had professedly been in the late 1920s and early 1930s) was now built not only into the party's structure and organization but also into its program.

The Communist Party of Croatia and the Communist Party of Slovenia

In 1937 the CPY formed the Communist Party of Croatia and the Communist Party of Slovenia. Both remained completely integrated into the CPY, their primary task being to facilitate Communist activities among the masses of Croatia and Slovenia. (Although nationalism was very strong in both Slovenia and Croatia, in Croatia it was much more militant. Slovenian politicians often cooperated with the Belgrade regime and were represented in the government.)[76] The creation of the new parties was an integral part of the new policy of the Popular Front: the struggle for parliamentary democracy and federalism, and firm opposition to separatism. Communists in Yugoslavia still believed that ultimate national emancipation (which was never precisely defined) would not be possible without a Communist revolution. But whereas in the late 1920s and early 1930s revolution had been considered the only means of solving the national question, now there was much more room for reform within Yugoslavia. Croatian emancipation, for example, was for Communists no longer connected with world revolution. It was considered to be to a considerable extent achievable in a peaceful way and within the borders of the Yugoslav state.

The Comintern did not initiate the creation of the Croatian party in the early 1930s because there were simply too few active members in Croatia. The CPY had been weakened by mass arrests during Aleksandar's dictatorship and the escape into exile of many leading Communists. By 1940, however, membership in the CPY had grown to 6,455, of whom 3,164 were in Croatia.[77] (Many of these, however, were workers still primarily active as trade unionists rather than purely revolutionary cadres.) The creation of the Communist Party of Croatia in August 1937 was a symbolic gesture; the CPY remained united in its organization, leadership, and policies.[78] The real national emancipation of the Croatian people was to take place in conjunction with the other nations in a democratic Yugoslavia, and a demand was made for free elections in which Communists could participate. The Communist Party of Slovenia had already been founded in April 1937, and its manifesto proclaimed: "The Slovenian people demand such economic policies as will make them economically independent and guarantee to the Slovenian people a life worthy of a man . . . Taxation should be lowered and Slovenia given financial means proportionate to the taxes she is paying."[79]

Such national demands were typical of the Slovenian "bourgeois" parties, and Communists had accepted them in the late 1920s and early 1930s. But now the party was also in favor of Yugoslavia: "The future of the Slovenian people and its national existence will be guaranteed only in a free alliance of the fraternal peoples of Yugoslavia in the form of a federal state." Typifying the Communists' political style during the Popular Front, the new Slovenian party demanded moderate—that is, liberal-democratic—reforms: "The Slovenian people cannot develop without democratic reforms, that is, without freedom of association, assembly, a free press, and free speech . . . The will of the masses cannot be expressed except through the freedom of a general, direct, equal, and secret ballot."[80]

However, the creation of the Slovenian and Croatian parties did not signify an evolution of the CPY toward a federation, let alone a confederation of parties. Not only did the party keep its Yugoslav name (while emphasizing that this should not be interpreted to mean that it was propagating the creation of some nonexistent Yugoslav nation), but the principles of centralism were applied more than ever. The two new Croatian and Slovenian central committees did not acquire any more independent power for Croatian and Slovenian Communists than they had previously wielded.

The Central Committee of the CPY gave the Communist cadres a clear explanation of the reasons for the creation of the Croatian and Slovenian parties. In summarized form these were: to satisfy the demand of the Slovenian and Croatian masses that their parties bear the name of their nation; to increase the interest of the Croatian and Slovenian masses in the Communist cause; to underline the party's commitment to the struggle for the freedom of the Croats and Slovenes; to introduce a new element into the struggle for the "internationalist education of the masses"; to prove that Serbian workers and peasants did not oppose the Slovenian or Croatian struggle for national affirmation; to provide better conditions for the creation of Slovenian and Croatian party cadres; to strengthen the internationalism of the CPY; and to mobilize the Croatian and Slovenian peasants for the struggle for "national liberation."[81] At the same time the party reaffirmed its total opposition to any form of "bourgeois nationalism" and chauvinism. Before the creation of the Slovenian and Croatian parties the Central Committee had been firm in asserting that the organizational structure of the CPY would continue unchanged:

We are a party of revolution, an army of class war. We need a united and centrally led organization with a united headquarters that will lead, direct, and coordinate the fight in all sectors of the class struggle. We need Serbian workers and Serbian peasants to lead a struggle for the demands and for the freedom of Croatian and Slovenian workers and peasants, but for this we need a united party, one Central Committee that will lead the struggle of all organizations, and not three or five central committees that will each work for themselves. Both the Croatian and Slovenian organizations have and must have their members inside the Central Committee, but this Central

Committee is not and should not be some kind of a post box, a consultative organ, or a voiceless assembly of federal delegates tied to their mandates, but a plenipotentiary fighting headquarters of a revolutionary organization to which, from one congress to the next, all sectors and all units of struggle are subjected.[82]

The Communist Party of Serbia

The Communist Party of Serbia was not founded until May 1945. Although Tito was present and spoke at the founding congress, the event was not publicized and was seldom mentioned later.[83] The foundation was not considered an event of particular importance; it was largely a formality accompanying the administrative reorganization of Yugoslavia into republics: every republic had to have its party. (However, Montenegro got its party only in October 1948, and Bosnia and Herzegovina only in November 1948—after the Yugoslav-Soviet conflict came into the open.) The Macedonian party had already been founded in 1943, primarily in the hope that this kind of national recognition would rally the Macedonians around the CPY and attract them to the Partisan movement. Before the war Macedonians were officially considered to be Serbs and Macedonia to be Southern Serbia; after the occupation and dismemberment of Yugoslavia in April 1941, Macedonia became part of Bulgaria and the Macedonians were proclaimed Bulgarians.

The Serbian party had not been founded before the war because the leadership of the CPY did not think that there was sufficient demand from Serbian Communists and Communist sympathizers. And since the Serbian nation was not "oppressed," the "class struggle" did not have to be combined with the struggle for "national liberation." The CPY claimed that there was no Serbian national question, since the Serbs had solved it through the creation of Yugoslavia.[84] The party was basically right when it stated that the Serbian national question did not exist in prewar Yugoslavia. It inevitably came into existence in the late 1960s, when Yugoslav federalism began to develop into confederalism, and the Serbian people suddenly felt themselves dispersed in different units. But in the late 1930s the party could not have predicted such a development; it believed, in accordance with Marxist-Leninist teaching, that federal units would merge after the revolution. The idea that there could be a problem about the status of Serbs outside the borders of the Serbian federal unit did not occur to the CPY.

Though maintaining that there was no Serbian national question, from 1935 onward the party insisted that there was an enormous difference between the Serbian people and its ruling class (that is, between Serbian workers and peasants and the "great-Serbian bourgeoisie") and pointed out that democratic freedoms had been taken away from the Serbs as much as from any other nation. The party continued to speak of the "hegemony" in Yugoslavia of the Serbian military, politicians, and civil servants, united around the Serbian monarchy. Yet it was now considered wrong to speak of Serbs as the "oppressor nation," as the Communists often had in the late 1920s and early 1930s.

In 1943 and 1944 German military control of Serbia (as well as control by the Chetnik military units) was still too strong for a founding congress to take place.[85] Also, during most of the interwar period, the main enemy, as far as the national question was concerned, was "great-Serbian hegemony" (and, therefore, Serbian nationalism). This was why Serbian Communists were under particularly severe pressure not to voice any sentiments that might even indirectly be understood to be nationalist, and were never formally asked if they wanted a separate Communist party for Serbia.[86] Moreover, the example of the Soviet Union delayed the creation of the Communist Party of Serbia. The Russian Communist organization within the Soviet party (All-Union Communist Party—Bolsheviks) was also not organized on the national principle although it had the largest membership and by far the most influential organization.

At the founding congress of the Communist Party of Serbia, Edvard Kardelj, a Slovenian member of the Politburo, spoke in the name of the Central Committee of the CPY. Echoing the Communist line of 1935, he tried to explain why in 1937 the Communist Party of Yugoslavia had created only the Slovenian and Croatian parties and had begun preparations for the creation of the Macedonian party. He stated that "at that time it had been essential for our party in Croatia, Slovenia, and Macedonia to make a gesture to the oppressed peoples of Yugoslavia, to mobilize and activate the national-liberation movement." Since Yugoslavia was now built on federal principles, Kardelj continued, if the Serbian party did not exist, the "great-Serbian reactionaries" could say that the Serbian nation was not being treated equally.[87] Of course, one could ask if this same argument could not have been used by the "great-Serbian reactionaries" before the war. Indeed, there is some evidence that it had been. Yet such Serbian anti-Communist propaganda had only limited success, not only before the war but also during and after it, when it tried to prove that the CPY was anti-Serbian. The numerical strength of the Serbs in the CPY and in the Partisan army during the war was too strong a counterargument.

Unchanged Views on the National Question

Certain crucial characteristics of the CPY's policies toward the national question, and especially the Croatian question, remained unchanged from the very foundation of the party until the beginning of the Second World War.[88]

First, from the very beginning, Communists from the several nations of Yugoslavia found it easy to work together; from the national point of view, they did not experience their membership in the party, which was Yugoslav, or the party itself as artificial.

Second, Communists were aware most of the time that the CPY's all-Yugoslav organizational structure gave it a decisive advantage over all other political parties, which operated primarily within one nation.

Third, the party always opposed national hatred and chauvinism. Even when working with members of separatist parties, it made efforts to persuade them to abandon extreme forms of their nationalism. It never abandoned certain basic enlightened principles with regard to the national question. Although in the mid-1930s nationalism probably penetrated the Communist organization in Croatia more than any other in Yugoslavia, the majority of Croatian cadres were never nationalist.[89]

Fourth, the party always insisted that relations among the "toiling masses" of all nations be based on mutual understanding and solidarity.[90]

Fifth, the party persevered in its belief that the national question was of secondary importance for the Communist revolution; it constituted only one form, and not necessarily the worst one, of oppression in a class society. The importance of the national question depended on its usefulness to the party's revolutionary tactics at any particular time.

Sixth, the CPY refused to place overall blame on the Serbian nation for national oppression or to consider it fundamentally reactionary and imperialist in character.

Finally, a large majority of party members did not genuinely oppose the existence of Yugoslavia. Anti-Yugoslavism was never a dominant sentiment or a passionately felt cause of great importance to the party, not even when the dissolution of Yugoslavia was the party's official policy. The anti-Yugoslav line of the late 1920s and early 1930s was attractive to many Communists from Serbia and Montenegro primarily because of its radicalism, but they did not believe that a secession of non-Serbian nations was necessary once the revolution had triumphed. It was important for them, however, to be absolutely clear of any accusations of reactionary nationalism. In the name of Communist purity, they believed that it was their duty to give unreserved support to the oppressed nations.

four

National State and Genocide: The Ustasha Movement, 1929–1945

The Origins of the Ustasha Ideology

Viennese centralism was on the increase in the 1850s. In Croatia the opposition press was censored and otherwise restricted; the Croatian flag was banned. German was being introduced into the state administration and into the schools as an obligatory second language. Many educated Croats began to doubt that Croatian national emancipation could be achieved as long as there was union with Vienna and Budapest. During the second half of the nineteenth century a growing number of educated Croats felt a primary political loyalty to Croatia and focused their interests and activities on the Croatian people and their destiny. In this sense, the Croats were on their way to becoming a modern nation, a nation with a fully formed political consciousness.

Ante Starčević, the founder of the Party of Croatian Rights, was the most prominent voice of the new Croatian nationalism. He based his demands for Croatian independence on historical documents that proved the formal legal continuity of the Croatian state. For him Croatian statehood had never been extinguished. It had been confirmed rather than lost by the 1102 Pacta Conventa with the crown of Hungary. He would devote his life to attempts to transform Croatia (which had survived in legal documents and in the continuity of the Sabor) into a real sovereign state. Like many extreme Croatian nationalists, Starčević came from one of the mountainous regions of Croatia, which had a mixed Croatian-Serbian-Muslim population. As a young man he wrote poetry and later obtained a doctorate at the University of Budapest. The combination of his primarily theological and philosophical education and his lack of practical political experience made his nationalism dogmatic and unrealistic.

Starčević awoke to his specifically Croatian identity (as opposed to his original Illyrian/Yugoslav one) partly in reaction to the existence of an already largely formed Serbian identity both in Serbia itself and elsewhere where Serbs lived. The Serbian national consciousness was oriented to Belgrade. It was rooted in memories of medieval Serbia and the Serbian struggle against the Turks. Starčević's early commitment to Illyrianism changed to disillusion with the Serbian rejection of Illyrianist ideas, sharpening his conflicts about language and culture with Serbian literary and political figures from Serbia and Vojvodina. (Novi Sad, the largest city in Vojvodina, was the cultural capital of the Serbs under the Habsburg monarchy.) The internal logic of Starčević's ideological development was simple. He first developed a South Slav national consciousness, a sense of ethnic and linguistic identity that was "Illyrian," that is, both Croatian and Serbian. (In the second half of the nineteenth century all Croatian politics consisted of different versions of Illyrianism; it had become its basis and framework, since almost everyone accepted the language of the people and claimed to be interested in the culture, traditions, and welfare of the people.) But he could not develop a common Croatian-Serbian political identity. Separate Croatian and Serbian traditions and state ideas were too strong. As a result, Starčević was eventually "transformed" into a Croat.

With their insistence on the legal continuity of the Croatian state (whose sovereignty had never been formally annulled), Starčević and the Party of Croatian Rights irreversibly imbued the Croatian consciousness with ideas of state and sovereignty. This national consciousness rejected any political bonds, loyalties, or obligations outside the Croatian nation, either with Budapest or Vienna, or with Rome by way of Catholicism. It demanded that alliances be forged solely on the basis of national and, once independence had been achieved, state interests. Starčević's nationalism was the first purely Croatian nationalism, and he was the first major Croatian figure to be anti-Habsburg, although at times he seemed to accept the Habsburg rule. He broke with traditional Croatian political responses, which involved moving closer to Vienna in order to avoid domination by Budapest, or closer to Budapest in order to avoid domination by Vienna, and advocated equidistance from both. He preached the subordination of all other loyalties and bonds to the goal of Croatian sovereignty. Imperious and stubborn, unselfish and scrupulous, this "Cato of Croatia" would captivate the Croatian nationalist intelligentsia. (Even today, Starčević's grave in Šestine, near Zagreb, is a place of pilgrimage for Croatian nationalists.)

The similarity between Croats and Serbs allowed Starčević to be as expansionist in his territorial demands as the Illyrianists had been. In Starčević's view, almost all the people living between the German-speaking population in the north (Austria) and the Greeks in the south were Croatian in origin, and therefore to be included in any future independent Croatian state. He proclaimed with majestic arbitrariness that many Serbian historical figures (including the medieval Nemanjić dynasty) had been Croats of the "purest blood." The borders of his Croatia were almost the same as those of modern-day Yugoslavia. At the same time his Croatian nationalism made him utterly intolerant of any non-Croatian expression of national consciousness.[1]

Starčević's extreme nationalism was founded on the belief that medieval history conferred rights and legitimacy, and on his arbitrary and unscholarly interpretations of medieval documents, especially those relating to the boundaries of the medieval Croatian state. (He worshiped medieval times in a romantic, mystical way: old glory, noble blood, a great and powerful state that had been almost forgotten.) Another ingredient of his philosophy was the belief that the intrusion of any other national consciousness (especially Serbian) on the territory of his imagined Croatia was the result of treason, corruption, racial inferiority, or a mixture of the three.[2]

He believed in the unity of Croatia, a centralized and unified state encompassing, at a minimum, inner Croatia, Slavonia, the Military Frontier, Dalmatia, and Bosnia-Herzegovina. Over these territories the Croatian Sabor should rule with almost complete sovereignty. Starčević never doubted that only Croatia had legitimate rights to Bosnia-Herzegovina. He considered the Bosnian Muslims to be Croatian "blood brothers." He opposed any struggle against Ottoman feudalism in Bosnia-Herzegovina in the second half of the nineteenth century, because it was mainly the Orthodox Serbs there who fought against it. (He was, for instance, delighted at the defeat of Serbia in the war with Bulgaria in 1885.) As a purely Croatian nationalist, Starčević opposed the proponents of Austro-Slavism in the Sabor—those who favored a "trialistic" organization of the Habsburg monarchy in which South Slavs would be the third partner, with the same rights as the Hungarians acquired in 1867. He supported Croatian independence from Vienna; but he also opposed any idea of South Slav unity. He would not even agree to the official recognition of the appellation "Serb" and refused to accept the use of the Cyrillic alphabet (together with the Latin) in Croatia, something Vienna and the People's Party favored.

In Austria-Hungary the Serbs were sometimes called "Slavoserbi" (Slav Serbs). Without any scholarly evidence at all, Starčević proclaimed that the "Slavoserbi" were doubly "slaves," since they supposedly derived this name from the Latin words *sclavus* and *servus,* both meaning a slave. In the struggle against everything that did not fall within his own concept of Croatia, Starčević used intellectual strategies that strongly resembled some forms of later German National Socialist ideology and propaganda.

The anti-Semitism of National Socialists, for example, was based primarily on the belief that Jews were to be persecuted and, ultimately, exterminated because they were an inferior race, evil and dangerous to the "Aryan" race. But the National Socialist uses of anti-Semitism were more extensive than this simple credo. Sometimes not only Jews were considered Jews. Anyone of German origin who opposed National Socialism or who fell into any of a number of "subversive" categories such as that of pacifist or avant-garde ("decadent") artist, was considered by National Socialists to be "contaminated" by the Jewish "spirit"; such people were sometimes called "white Jews."

For Starčević the "Slavoserbi" were primarily a people who had a Serbian national consciousness, that is, the overwhelming majority of the Orthodox population of inner Croatia, Slavonia, Dalmatia, Bosnia-Herzegovina, and the Military Frontier. Starčević was neither particularly opposed to nor in favor of any religion. It was not the "deviations" of Orthodox theological dogmas and religious rites from Catholicism that upset him, but the link between the Serbian national consciousness and the Orthodox church. Only the Croatian national consciousness was legitimate in the territories he proclaimed to be Croatian. But for Starčević the "Slavoserbi" also included all people who seemed to him morally inferior, or of "impure" blood and origin, or who had migrated to Croatia and whom he considered to be slaves by their character and nature. Last but not least, they included all Starčević's political opponents, especially those from the People's Party.

Paradoxically, Starčević both included all Serbs in the Croatian nation and proclaimed them to be an inferior and evil race. His idea of Greater Croatia encompassed all Serbs as long as they were ready to abandon their own national consciousness and became Croats. But the moment they showed their own consciousness, they became "Slavoserbi." Starčević even developed his own version of the Croatian language and orthography (*korijenski pravopis;* "etymological orthography"), which in fact was not accepted in Croatia. The only attempt to introduce it was made during the Second World War in the NDH (Nezavisna Država Hrvatska; Independent State of Croatia). Its principal attraction lay in its differences from the Serbian orthography, which thus increased the difference between Croats and Serbs.

Starčević transformed the Croatian national consciousness, which was at the time primarily ethnic, cultural, and linguistic (the achievements of Illyrianism), into a modern political national consciousness, which envisaged the nation as a sovereign political community with common and unique political goals and a historical destiny. A man of great personal integrity, he became the father of modern Croatian nationalism. But he was also the progenitor of extreme Croatian nationalism, which sought to suppress and perhaps even to exterminate all those who had a different national consciousness. With him there entered permanently into Croatian politics the idea that all those who have a different national consciousness, or those whose political ideas are a hindrance to the realization of complete Croatian sovereignty, expansion, and homogeneity, are racially inferior and fundamentally evil beings. Mystical and fanatical, intolerant and violent, territorially expansionist and nationally homogenizing, Starčević's ideology contained all the important elements of the ideology of extreme Croatian nationalism in the twentieth century.[3]

Eugen Kvaternik, a follower and friend of Starčević, was the first Croat to break completely with the traditionally cautious style of Croatian politics and reject both Vienna and Budapest.[4] If Starčević was the first Croat with a "purely" Croatian national ideology, Kvaternik was the first revolutionary Croatian nationalist. Like Starčević a former student of philosophy and theology, he had largely abandoned Catholic teachings and church dogmas. Yet his political ideas remained mystical and dogmatic.

Initially Kvaternik saw Magyarization as a greater danger for the Croats than Habsburg centralism, and he supported the idea of a federal organization of the Habsburg monarchy. But soon he came to regard Vienna as the center of German political and cultural, as well as economic and military, expansion against the Slavs and began to struggle for the complete independence of Croatia. A prolific writer and journalist, he wrote proclamations appealing to the Croatian people to rebel against the monarchy. Later, as an exile in France, he tried unsuccessfully to obtain some help there for his activities.

Kvaternik's pseudo-romantic and mystical world view caused him to underestimate the strength of the monarchy after its defeat in the war with Prussia in 1866, and he decided to start an uprising with some members of the Party of Croatian Rights to establish an independent Croatian state in which only Croats would have political rights, and which would include Bosnia-Herzegovina, still under Ottoman rule. The insurrection took place in 1871 in Rakovica, a small town in the Military Frontier. Given the strength of the monarchy, the lack of popular support for revolutionary action, and the group's dilettante organization, the attempt was doomed from its inception. Kvaternik persuaded a few hundred people to join the uprising, but the regular army quickly dispersed them. A few days after Kvaternik had proclaimed himself the "regent" of Croatia and set up a provisional government, he and most of the leaders of the insurrection were killed.

Josip Frank, another follower and friend of Starčević, was a successful lawyer who attained popularity when in 1880 he wrote a dissertation on the disadvantages of the 1868 Nagodba (Agreement) between Hungary and Croatia, which increased Croatian dependence on the Hungarians and deprived Croatia of even its limited financial autonomy.[5] In 1895 he felt confident enough to leave the Party of Croatian Rights (with the approval of the aged Starčević) and found the Pure Party of Rights (Čista stranka prava) out of his own faction. Abandoning Starčević's bold defiance of Vienna, he soon developed into an Austrophile and a Habsburg loyalist. From the beginning of his political career until his death in 1911, Frank was a fanatical opponent of any cooperation between Croats and Serbs. Skillful in using nationalist slogans and radicalizing the people, he became in the first decade of this century a leading anti-Serbian demagogue and the instigator of the persecution of Serbs in Croatia. Usually described by Croatian historians as cynical and without scruples, this direct predecessor of extreme nationalism of the interwar period even attempted to create Croatian paramilitary "legions."

An Encounter of Two Ideologies: Communists and Croatian Nationalists in the 1930s

Immediately after the creation of the Kingdom of the Serbs, Croats, and Slovenes in 1918, Croatian separatists in exile (especially in Austria and Hungary) instituted activities against it. Most were former followers of Josip Frank ("Frankovci") who had been proponents of "hereditary Croat loyalty to the House of Habsburg" during the war and had opposed any form of Croatian-Serbian cooperation in Croatia, as well as the unification of Croatia with Serbia. Among these émigrés were also former Croatian officers from the Austro-Hungarian army and various adventurers, fortune hunters, and professional spies.[6]

After King Aleksandar established his dictatorship in January 1929, Ante Pavelić and Gustav Perčec founded the Ustasha—Croatian Revolutionary Organization (Ustaša—Hrvatska revolucionarna organizacija), a secret group formed abroad with the goal of achieving Croatian independence through terrorism and armed struggle.[7] The organization had a small number of adherents inside the country, and sympathy for it varied. In the 1930s the Ustasha movement became increasingly dependent on the states that were the Versailles treaty "revisionists": Hungary and Austria, Fascist Italy, and, in the realm of ideology, Nazi Germany.[8] These four countries were interested in changing the borders of "Versailles" Europe, and Germany and Italy were increasingly capable militarily of succeeding in such a task. The Comintern had hoped—under Stalin as under Lenin—that through its policy of support for struggles of "national liberation" it would become the leader of all those who considered themselves defeated and betrayed by the peace treaties after the First World War. Yet instead it was often fascist and National Socialist ideology and regimes that proved attractive to many dissatisfied nationalists in Germany, Italy, Hungary, Slovakia, Bulgaria, and Croatia.

It was not only the radical revisionism of Hungary, Italy, and Germany with regard to borders that attracted the Ustashas. These countries gave financial help, provided military training in their territory, and supplied the Ustashas with weapons and explosives for their terrorist activities. Italy also incited them to certain terrorist actions, and may even have been behind the Ustashas' assassination of King Aleksandar in October 1934; in any case it provided sanctuary to the organizers. Opportunism and dependence, as well as a fascination with the power of the fascist countries, helped to transform the Ustashas into a replica of a fascist movement. The Ustashas went into partial hibernation after the assassination of King Aleksandar in 1934: European public outrage at their involvement forced Mussolini to restrict Ustasha activities. These restrictions were continued, particularly after 1937, when relations between Yugoslavia and Italy became amicable.[9] It was during this later period that Ante Pavelić, a former lawyer who had represented Zagreb in the Belgrade parliament in the 1920s, became the undisputed leader of the movement.

In the 1930s Croatian separatist groups, called "Frankovci" even when they were not direct followers of Josip Frank, also increased their activities. The Frankovci were the largest student group at the University of Zagreb in 1940, closely followed by the Communists, but had neither a permanent organization nor an established leadership. There were, however, clubs and journals influenced by the Frankovci.[10] In the late 1930s many of them joined the Ustasha organization or tacitly accepted Pavelić's leadership. It is even possible to say that the Frankovci were a part of the Ustasha movement, as long as one remembers that most were not "sworn" Ustashas, that is, formally admitted members. After the creation of the NDH by the Axis powers in April 1941, the Frankovci enthusiastically supported the Ustasha regime and joined its military formations.

In the early 1930s the Ustasha movement was spreading in some of the poorest regions of Croatia and Bosnia-Herzegovina: Lika, Kordun, Dalmatinska Zagora, Banija, and western Herzegovina; armed attacks on the police and army were followed by mass arrests of those who sympathized with the Ustashas or supported them in any way.[11] The Communists cited economic reasons for the rebellions: "hunger, poverty, and terror of the regime." But the party also recognized that national oppression was a contributing cause. The *Proleter* announced in December 1932:

> The Communist Party salutes the Ustasha movement of the peasants of Lika and Dalmatia and fully backs them. It is the duty of all Communist organi-

zations and of every Communist to help this movement, to organize it and to lead it. At the same time the Communist party points out this movement's present shortcomings and mistakes, which can be explained by the fact that a considerable role is played by Croatian fascist elements (Pavelić-Perčec), who have no interest in developing a broad mass movement against Serbian dictatorship; they fear that such a movement might turn out to be not only against the Yugoslav dictatorship, but also against their own Italian masters. This is why they limit themselves to the actions of small units and individual terror.[12]

The CPY repeatedly instructed its cadres to struggle to turn the Ustashas into a mass movement and to resist individual acts of terrorism by Croatian fascists. The party maintained that the "great-Serbian dictatorship" could be overthrown only by mass action in both Croatian and Serbian regions. The party also argued for incorporating demands for social and economic justice into the struggle for national liberation, and accused Pavelić of desiring, in alliance with the Croatian bourgeoisie, a dictatorship similar to Italian Fascism.

In the 1930s Croatian separatists (Ustashas and Frankovci) along with the Communists made up the majority of political prisoners in Yugoslavia.[13] Some had been arrested for violence or terrorist acts, but most, especially among the Communists, had been imprisoned simply for their views, for their membership in the party, or for organizing peaceful demonstrations, protests, or clandestine publications. The majority of imprisoned Ustashas were peasants from the poorer mountain regions of Croatia and Bosnia-Herzegovina.[14] Their rebellions and protests were prompted as much by high taxes, a corrupt administration, and difficult conditions of military service (mostly under Serbian officers) as they were by the goal of Croatian national independence. The political consciousness of these Croatian peasants was based on mistrust and hatred of the Serbian political and military elite, a hatred of Serbs in general, and a hope that in some future independent Croatian state the peasantry would be better treated.

Their nationalist ideology was rudimentary. Many of these peasants hated Serbs in an irrational, intuitive way that had much of its basis in folk memory. It was a kind of proto-fascist sentiment and would prove a fertile ground for fascist ideology.[15] Most of them came from regions of mixed Croatian and Serbian populations, where national and religious conflicts and hatreds had a long history and had often become interwoven with personal animosities. (These mixed regions, however, also bred the opposite: a remarkable degree of religious tolerance and cooperation among Croats and Serbs, and Yugoslavism.)

Many regarded Pavelić as their leader because of his radicalism and persistence. Yet in the early 1930s he was not treated as a *Führer* or a

Duce in the Nazi or Fascist sense, nor was loyalty to him unconditional. Many peasants refused to identify him as a politician—a term that to them meant a readiness to compromise and a "soft," "antinational" style of politics that they associated with city dwellers. They preferred to think of him as a modern-day counterpart to the guerrilla leaders during the Ottoman Empire.[16] "Sworn" Ustashas, however, had to pledge absolute allegiance to Pavelić, and they were creating around him the cult of the leader. Imprisoned Ustashas liked to describe themselves as nationalists, a term that under the Habsburg monarchy had been associated with patriotism and republicanism, a populist concern for the social problems of peasants, and an interest in their culture and way of life.[17]

Imprisoned Communists showed an immediate interest in their fellow prisoners.[18] They called the Ustashas "national revolutionaries," hoping that the sacred word *revolutionary* would somehow help purge the movement of its dark chauvinistic sentiments and help move its members toward acceptance of Communist ideals.[19] That label was also expected to make cooperation with the Ustasha movement seem less strange to Communist followers. Communists further tried to persuade their fellow prisoners that "Serbian hegemony" in Yugoslavia was perpetrated by the "Serbian bourgeoisie" and served only its interests, while the Serbian "toiling masses" were being exploited as much as the Croatian. But the Ustashas' passionate and aggressive nationalism had long before generalized into animosity toward the whole Serbian nation. Marxist-Leninist concepts simply did not fit their perception of social reality; the Ustashas refused to make a distinction between Serbian national consciousness and "Serbian hegemony."[20]

In their conversations with Ustasha prisoners the Communists censured the collaboration of Ustasha leaders with Fascist Italy and Hungary, both of which had traditional expansionist demands on Croatian lands. Most Ustashas defended their leaders: these were the only outside powers that had been ready to support their struggle. The Communists blamed only the leadership for collaboration with the fascists and hoped that persistent political and ideological propaganda would influence the "healthy" elements among the Ustashas. The Communists thought that their attempt to influence the Ustashas would be more successful if they were to stress that the Communists also supported the dissolution of Yugoslavia and the creation of an independent Soviet Croatia forming part of a wider Yugoslav or Balkan federation, and of the Soviet Union as a future world-encompassing proletarian state. The Ustasha nationalists appeared not to doubt the sincerity of the Communists, even though many of the latter were Serbs. They did accept that these Serbs had, by becoming Communists, distanced themselves from traditional Serbian nationalism. Still, they could not identify with the idea of a Soviet

Croatia. Most of them were peasants, and thus were attached to the idea of private ownership of land. But it was not primarily fear of collectivization that turned them against the Communists (who in fact had tended to conceal their ideas and plans concerning land ownership). What the Ustashas truly wanted was a nationalist Greater Croatia that would encompass the territories of inner Croatia, Slavonia, Dalmatia, Bosnia-Herzegovina, and perhaps even some others, a state that would not form any alliance with other Yugoslav states. The Ustasha nationalists preferred an ethnically pure Greater Croatia, one cleansed (if necessary by force) of all Serbs. They also wanted their Croatian state to be a strictly centralized one. There was never any mention of regional autonomy or federalism for Slavonia, Dalmatia, or Bosnia-Herzegovina. This viewpoint was something the Ustashas had in common with Croatian nationalists in general, who seldom spoke of a federal constitutional arrangement for Croatia.

The abstract and vague nature of Marxism-Leninism in relation to the national question made these "full-blooded" Croatian nationalists suspicious. Moreover, in the CPY, members of the various nations worked together and had a common goal. Therefore, the Communists obviously regarded nationality as a peripheral matter. In a way, the Ustashas had correctly perceived that as far as the national question was concerned, the structure of the CPY was more significant than its proclaimed policy. The very fact that Croats and Serbs were working together in one political party—and a centralized and monolithic one at that—obviously suggested that Croats and Serbs would never be separated in the way the Croatian nationalists so fervently desired.[21]

Altogether, the Communists' attempts to transform the Ustasha nationalists into a left-wing movement and to win over their younger members to the Communist cause met with poor results—especially if one takes into account that the Communists were better organized, better disciplined, and better educated than the Ustashas and that some of their intellectuals were veritable masters of propaganda and persuasion. It was also significant that although the Communists did not find it difficult to persuade the Ustashas that the Croatian "bourgeoisie" was no better than the Serbian, or that many of the higher Catholic clergy of Croatia were not sincerely devoted to the cause of Croatian emancipation, they still could not change the Ustashas' general perception of Serbs. The Ustashas' passionate nationalist hatred was directed at the whole Serbian nation.

Before large numbers of nationalists had been organized into the Ustasha movement, it was easier for them to accept the support of the Communists and to cooperate occasionally with them. Moreover, during the dictatorship of King Aleksandar, from 1929 to 1934, the Communists themselves were far from being well organized and disciplined enough to compete effectively for the leadership of the masses. Small dispersed groups of Communist and Ustasha radicals and rebels, persecuted and often imprisoned, could and did make use of the fact that they had a common enemy—the Yugoslav state. From this there developed a certain degree of solidarity. But after the Ustashas had become an ideologically developed movement, common concern for the poor peasants and common opposition to the centralized Belgrade regime were not enough for continued cooperation. The Communists' pro-Yugoslav stand in the late 1930s further increased the animosity between Ustashas and Communists. It seemed to confirm the Ustashas' old suspicions that the Communists had never really been committed to Croatian independence.

By the late 1930s the Communists and the Ustashas had ended their cooperation, and relations between them rapidly deteriorated. An armed conflict could not take place, since the existing Yugoslav state was sufficiently strong to prevent it. But the intensity of the confrontation between adherents of these two movements all over Croatia, and especially at the University of Zagreb, left no doubt about how uncompromising and violent the struggle would be if it did come. Anti-Communism now assumed an extremely important place in Ustasha ideology. This development was partly in imitation of the ideology of the countries whose protégés the Ustashas had become, but it was also a result of the fact that from their initial separatism, anti-Serbianism, and the cult of the state, the Ustashas had developed an ideology of extreme nationalism that was simply incompatible with Marxism-Leninism.

As an ideology, the Ustashas' anti-Communism borrowed heavily from the European fascist movements.[22] The Ustashas considered Communism to be a product of the Asiatic and Jewish "spirit" and a sublimation of its wish to destroy and conquer European nations. They saw the contemporary European political situation as a struggle for survival, in a social-Darwinist sense, among nations and among ideologies. Considering themselves the only true representatives of the Croatian people, they proclaimed it their sacred duty to take part in this struggle. In that way they sought both to prove and to save the strength of the Croatian people. Since the nation was seen as an individual organism, the fight against Communism became a test of strength of the nation as a whole rather than of the individual. The Ustashas interpreted the aggressive, ruthless character of their own movement as the expression of the nation's strength and will. Political violence and terrorism were defined as the only way of protecting the very survival of their nation.[23]

To the Ustashas, Bolshevism was the enemy of the natural social order. The social order in Croatia, they thought, should be based on respect for the small peasant landowner, the preservation of patriarchal family values, and opposition to forced industrialization and urbanization;

religion and tradition were a part of the peasant way of life and contributed to the Croatian national identity. The Ustashas were equally opposed to "corrupt" parliamentary democracy and to Bolshevik interference in family life and the organization of the economy and believed that national government should be strong, authoritarian, and, naturally, in the hands of the Ustashas. In many respects the Ustashas were confused epigones of the European fascist and National Socialist ideologies, unable to create a coherent doctrine of their own and to unify different influences into one whole. They were at once a modern totalitarian and terrorist organization, conservative traditionalists, Roman Catholic clericalists (struggling against Orthodox Christianity, Jews, and Communist atheists), and primitive, peasant-populist rebels. Their ideology mixed pseudo-romantic populism with social-Darwinist ideas, racism with traditional nationalism, respect for the church with the glorification of armed struggle, revenge, and terrorism.[24] They romanticized family life and small propertyholders while glorifying the unity and corporatism of the modern fascist state. They set spiritual values, traditional morality, and religion against Marxist materialism. Yet their aggressive, militant language was permeated by biological (and, therefore, materialistic) concepts, such as blood, race, and instinct. Despite its later advancement toward fascism, the Ustasha movement never became truly fascist. It was primarily a pseudo-romantic, populist, terrorist nationalism. In southeastern Europe it was perhaps most similar to Corneliu Codreanu's Legion of the Archangel Michael in Romania. The Legion was also extremely nationalist, mystically attached to certain events in distant national history, oriented to the peasantry, which it romanticized, and influential in poor peasant regions with mixed population. However, for the Ustashas genocide was a central element in their program.[25]

Because of its contact with nature, peasant labor was considered to be an enduring source of morality and patriotism. For the Ustashas, nature and land "spoke" the language of extreme nationalism; therefore, the nationalists were the only natural political movement. This peculiar spiritualization and politicization of nature and matter were thought to be the very opposite of Marxist materialism, which was described as unethical, mechanistic, and nihilistic. Although they did not consider individuals to have any political rights, the Ustashas did believe that certain natural rights existed: the rights to private property and to ownership of small-scale means of production free of state control. The Ustashas were not completely hypocritical when they attacked Soviet totalitarianism for its total subjugation of individuals by the state. For although they were profoundly antiliberal, with no respect for the freedom of individuals and their rights, the dictatorship that they sought to achieve, though even more violent than Soviet totalitarianism, remained rather less than total, since it left a certain private domain to the individual.

The Ustashas' Rousseau-like romanticization of the peasant way of life and a natural society based on it had two important consequences. First, many political institutions (especially political parties and parliament) were considered to be not only superfluous or harmful, but unnatural. Second, since peasants were naturally just and their "instincts" and reactions always moral, there developed a peculiar cult of aggressive impulses, anger, revenge, and uninhibited hatred. The Ustashas were opposing Communist dogmatism with "instincts" and irrationalism.

Fascism and Nazism were largely a reaction to conflicts within nationally homogeneous societies, a form of solving class conflict and the crises of political institutions through violence and dictatorship. The Ustashas, however, had no developed program for internal affairs and only a rudimentary concept of what Croatian society should be like. They shared the cult of the state with the fascist and Nazi movements. But for the Ustashas the nation and the national state were the supreme goals, while for the fascists and the Nazis these were but instruments of the will for power. Fascism and Nazism were what might be called permanently dynamic movements that believed in a certain kind of life: militaristic, based on struggle and domination, ruthless. In contrast, the Ustashas were ultimately a static movement, since they aimed for a stable state of affairs: the creation of a homogeneous nation state.[26] The Ustashas envisioned a concrete political goal, their Croatian state. In that sense, their movement did not see further justification for its existence, once its goal had been reached. They believed that they were fighting against a foreign enemy (Serbs) and that once this struggle ended with victory, the triumphant soldiers would return to their normal way of life.[27] (This does not, of course, mean that the Ustashas would have abandoned political power had they succeeded in establishing the NDH as a stable state during the Second World War.)

Typically European nineteenth- and twentieth-century nationalists believed that a nation was an ethnic community with a common language, history, and territory struggling to increase its national cohesion and to strengthen its international position. This was not essentially different from what the Ustashas wanted. It was primarily in their methods of struggle and rule that they resembled the Nazis. For all their imitation of Nazism and fascism, the simple and, perhaps, terrible truth is that the essentials of the Ustashas' ideology were not much outside the mainstream of Croatian nationalism, and very close to the special tradition of Starčević, Kvaternik, and Frank. It was their methods that made them distinctive.[28]

Protecting the State

After the proclamation of the NDH on 10 April 1941, the Ustasha regime began to enact new laws.[29] Contrary to European and American traditions, by which the foundation of a state was accompanied by legislation that conferred certain rights and liberties on citizens, the first legal initiatives of the Ustasha state were directed at eliminating political opponents (real, potential, or imaginary) and taking away from the members of certain minority groups their national and citizens' rights. The Ustasha leadership had prepared such legislation while in exile. On 17 April a law was enacted whose declared purpose was "to defend the people and the state." It made capital punishment mandatory for all those who in any way offended "the honor and vital interests of the Croatian people" or who even "by attempt" threatened the Croatian state.[30] The deliberate imprecision of the crucial terms of this law was intended to provide the

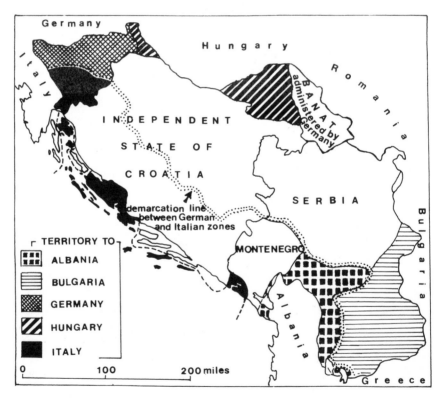

Occupied Yugoslavia, 1941

Ustashas with a legal framework large enough to allow the murder of political opponents or members of certain minority groups. The law was turned into an even more potent weapon by the shortening of trial procedures, the abolition of the right of appeal (the sentence had to be carried out not later than two hours after its pronouncement), and the preponderance of Ustashas among the judges.

The law was further supplemented with retroactive powers, the main purpose of which was revenge against prewar adversaries.[31] It was also an expression of the Ustashas' ideological belief that the Croatian state had always been a legal reality, even when its incorporation in another state deprived it of international recognition. For the Ustashas, the Kingdom of Yugoslavia was illegal not only in the sense that it had never been accepted by a majority of Croatian people through democratic processes (either elections or referenda) but also in the sense that it was actually violating the laws of a Croatian state that in the Ustashas' mind really existed.[32] By claiming that the Croatian state had always existed and that they had only liberated it by defeating the foreigners who had occupied it, the Ustashas were continuing, in an extreme fashion, the traditions of nineteenth-century Croatian nationalism, especially the ideology of Starčević and the Party of Croatian Rights, which had insisted on the legal reality and existence of the kingdom of Croatia inside Hungary and under the Habsburg monarchy.[33] Such a "real" state had to have laws, and to the Ustashas it seemed self-evident that some of the laws would be directed against the enemies of the state. Such laws were considered a natural element of the national state and a necessary precondition of its existence. According to this view, the retroactivity of their legislation was not retroactivity at all. Nor was the Ustasha struggle consequently ever aimed at establishing a new body politic, but only at liberating an ancient one. Revolution was restoration, a return to the "golden age," and the NDH was simply Croatia Restituta.

Thousands of people became victims of this "protection of the state" in the first few weeks of Ustasha rule. A large majority of them were Serbs (who had now become a minority group inside the NDH). The Serbs were considered to be an enemy nation and became the direct responsibility of the Ustasha police and Ustasha military and paramilitary units. The government soon introduced specifically anti-Serbian measures. Schools of the Serbian Orthodox church, for example, were closed. The Serbian Orthodox church itself was forced to discard the word *Serbian* in a general campaign to weaken its political influence and separate it from the Serbian national identity. However, the Ustashas were not primarily a Catholic movement.[34] Catholicism had meaning for them mostly as a part of the Croatian national tradition and a *differentia specifica* from Orthodox Christianity. They were not very interested in religious dogma.

Orthodoxy was not bad in itself, but because it was Serbian. Many Ustashas even envied the Serbian Orthodox church because since medieval times it had been less dependent on foreign centers and in that way had become proto-national. Their fanatical persecution of Serbian Orthodox priests was inspired by the fact that the Serbian Orthodox religion was part of the Serbian national identity, and the Serbian Orthodox church a defender of Serbian national interests.[35] In a similar vein, villages whose names contained words or expressions that were associated with the Serbian nationality or religion or were considered to be more typical of the Serbian vocabulary than of the Croatian, were given new names.[36] Use of the Cyrillic alphabet was banned. In addition, Serbs' movements were limited, they were no longer allowed to live in certain residential areas, and they had to wear a blue band with the letter *P* (for *Pravoslavac,* Orthodox) on their right arm.

The Ustasha Anti-Serbian Propaganda

After coming to power the Ustashas quickly established control over the Croatian press and radio stations and developed massive political propaganda against all opponents of the regime and against the Serbian nation. In numerous speeches and articles Ustasha functionaries portrayed Serbs in negative stereotypes, emphasizing that there was no place for them in the Croatian state: they were an alien people who had entered Croatian territory uninvited and had become an enemy of Croatia.[37]

Ustashas refused to tolerate any form of Serbian national consciousness within the territory of their state. To destroy that "evil" at its root, they waged a war against the Serbian nation as a whole. Initially Serbs were portrayed as a different "race"; then, suddenly, they were described as traitors who had betrayed their country, Croatia, to foreign interests. The Ustashas refused to acknowledge that having a Serbian national consciousness was not a political act or a deliberate choice. Such an admission would have made their anti-Serbian policies look like a campaign against innocent people. They therefore insisted that being a Serb was itself a political act and that those "who wanted to be Serbs" and "insisted on being Serbs" could justly be punished for that. They refined this form of rhetoric by associating Croatian national identity with extreme Croatian nationalist ideology, declaring all "true Croats" to be Ustashas or their supporters. Consequently, for the Ustashas one ceased to be a member of the Croatian nation by opposing their regime. The liquidation of all those in the NDH who were not loyal to the new regime was then justified as a purification of the Croatian nation itself.

Ustasha propaganda against the Serbs was often purely racist. This was primarily a result of the acceptance of Nazi terminology, but it also reflected the intensity of the Ustashas' commitment to the struggle against the Serbs. However, they never developed a coherent racist theory. The Ustashas spoke of a "pure Croatian race" but never defined the Croatian racial type. They made no attempt to establish which radical characteristics distinguished Serbs from Croats, although the Croats were officially defined as "Aryans." For the Ustashas the Serbs were definitely not Aryans; but they were not non-Aryans either, in the sense in which the Jews and Gypsies were defined. For the Ustashas the Serbs were a political enemy whom they described in racial terms and treated in the same way in which the Nazis treated people they considered both racially inferior and racially dangerous. It was a racist and genocidal hatred of a people who merely had a different national consciousness.

Jews or Serbs who could prove that they had been active prewar supporters of the Ustashas or of Croatian separatism could save themselves and acquire Croatian citizenship. In these cases some Jews also acquired the title "honorary Aryan." Such political loyalty was difficult to prove, and in any case very few non-Croats were, or ever could have been, sympathetic to the prewar extreme Croatian nationalism. Most exceptions were made for Serbs and Jews who were related to members of the Ustasha movement. (Some leading Ustashas were married to Serbian or Jewish women.) Racist anti-Semitism was, then, something the Ustashas accepted from the ideology of National Socialism, but it never became a central element in their ideology. Racist legislation against the Jewish population imitated the German model;[38] but no such systematic legislation (with an insistence on family origin and physical appearance) was enacted against the Serbs. The persecution of Serbs would, however, quickly become a system itself, since the Ustashas in fact considered them the greatest enemies of the NDH and made them the main target of their propaganda.

The structure and organization of the NDH were such that systematic persecution could begin without any previous comprehensive legislation or detailed written governmental instructions. All power was in the Ustashas' hands, and the laws and the legal system could be interpreted and applied in whatever way they desired. It was enough for leaders to give verbal instructions to the authorities in different regions of Croatia. And so in the general atmosphere of a violent anti-Serbian campaign, mass terror and genocide immediately began. Ustasha power outside the larger towns was in the hands of Ustasha district officials, who had full control of all military and police functions and partial control of the administrative and economic apparatus. As far as the enemies of the state were concerned (including the Serbian population), the power of these officials was supreme. A typical instruction was given on 2 May 1941 in Velika Gorica by one of Pavelić's closest collaborators, Milovan Žanić, minister of the Legislative Council: "This country can only be a Croatian country, and there is no method that we would hesitate to use in order to make it truly Croatian and cleanse it of Serbs, who have for centuries endangered us and who will endanger us again if they are given the opportunity."[39]

The Summer of 1941 and the "Serbian Discovery"

The collapse of the Yugoslav army and the disintegration of the Yugoslav state apparatus during the short war of April 1941 left many parts of the country in a state of lawlessness. In regions with mixed populations, especially those with a tradition of animosity between Croats and Serbs, some violent conflicts occurred. But after the NDH had been proclaimed on 10 April, the Serbian population showed considerable readiness to accept the new regime. Many fatalistically accepted that a "time of German rule" had arrived again and that the Croats and the Catholic religion would now have priority, perhaps more than in the Austro-Hungarian period but not in an essentially different way.[40] The Serbian population of Croatia consisted mostly of peasants who did not consider the violent establishment of the NDH with the help of foreign powers to be a sufficient reason for an armed rebellion against it;[41] the history of central and southeastern Europe is, after all, a tragic chronicle of the military conquest or violent overthrow of regimes. Yet Serbian hostility toward the new regime increased rapidly with the escalation of Ustasha terror against members of prewar Serbian political parties and organizations; former Yugoslav army personnel, police, government, and administrative officials; Serbian Orthodox clergy; and schoolteachers, small merchants, and tradespeople. Long before coming to power in April 1941 the Ustashas had prepared to liquidate all these elements of the Serbian population in Croatia.

The Serbs quickly learned that the NDH was an incomparably more violent state than either the Kingdom of Yugoslavia or the Habsburg monarchy. It showed a profound contempt for legal procedures and for human life. But the hope persisted that things would soon return to normal, once the Ustashas had firmly established themselves in power. It seemed contrary to all previous historical experience to assume that violence would increase, once power was firmly in the hands of the new rulers and all their political opponents exterminated. It was unthinkable and unbelievable to ordinary Serbs that the state would use its police and military to exterminate part of its own population.

Mass terror against the Serbs started after the bulk of German troops departed to the eastern front with the launching of the German invasion of the Soviet Union on 22 June 1941. As early as July and August there were large-scale massacres. Villages were destroyed one after another.

Sometimes all adult males were shot; more often the entire village population was slaughtered. The Ustashas would usually come to the village and command the peasants to assemble in the town hall, marketplace, or local Serbian Orthodox church on the pretext of reading a proclamation to them. Then they would tie the Serbs together, load them onto lorries or march them to the forest or a mountain crater, and murder them. Sometimes they killed them on the spot or locked them inside the church and then set it on fire.[42]

News of the massacres spread very quickly but often met with incredulity. The Serbs seem to have forced themselves to believe that the scope of terror was exaggerated, or that these were untypical incidents that would stop once higher state authorities learned of them. Also, many Serbs seemed confident that nothing would happen to them, since they were on friendly terms with local Croats and had never participated in the activities of the prewar Serbian nationalist organizations. There were even cases of people who, after surviving a massacre in some miraculous way, went to the Ustasha authorities. They simply could not believe that all that had happened had not been the result of a terrible misunderstanding that would be corrected after some explaining.[43] Finally, however, the Serbs began to realize that Ustasha actions were a systematic realization of a general plan. Thereafter the Ustashas had to rely on surprise attacks at dawn or late at night, when the peasants were at home and unprepared for escape or resistance.[44] Most Ustashas who had joined the organization after the creation of the NDH were extreme and militant Croatian nationalists. They were soon transformed into fanatical terrorists. Those who were reluctant to take part in mass terrorism were coerced through indoctrination, military discipline, incitement by direct example, or sometimes simply by threats and alcohol.

The Ustashas' war against prominent Serbs was creating a political vacuum and opening the way for the Communist revolution. The CPY was the best-organized force to lead the Serbs. By the beginning of 1942, it was apparent that the final struggle would be between the Communists and the Ustashas. But even this could not prevent some Communist intellectuals from cynically observing that the Ustashas, however cruel and unacceptable their methods were, had "done the job" for the Communists by liquidating the Serbian "establishment."[45] By its brutality the "black" revolution was destroying the old order and helping the "red" revolution.

The Nature of Ustasha Terrorism

One conspicuous trait of the Ustashas' genocide against the Serbs was their policy of involving as many of their members and sympathizers as possible in terrorist acts. In contrast, the German Nazis, with similar objectives of extermination, relied on relatively small, select, and semi-secret units that were kept separate from the rest of their movement. Moreover, Ustasha terrorism was to a considerable extent not concealed. Individual attacks on villages were planned and carried out in secrecy only in order to achieve surprise. The event was afterward made known publicly in the regions where it had taken place (though not directly in the Zagreb press), and the Ustashas boasted about their exploits.

There were many reasons for the participatory and open character of Ustasha terrorism. First, the Ustashas' state apparatus and administrative machinery were not large enough for an organized liquidation of Serbs solely in concentration camps (in 1941 there were around 1,900,000 Serbs in the NDH). Also, the economic system and the means of communication were largely under German control, and the Germans would not have allowed massive allocation of resources for this purpose, since they opposed large-scale terrorism against the Serbs. (The Ustashas initially tried to hide their terrorist acts from the Germans, but the Serbian uprising soon revealed to the Germans the enormity of the massacres.) The Ustasha policy toward the Serbs, which clearly stated that there was no place for them inside the NDH, planned to kill about half the Serbian population and to expel the rest to Serbia or force them to convert to Catholicism, which, the Ustashas believed, would eventually transform them into Croats.[46] The last two outcomes could be achieved only by inspiring a high level of fear in Serbs, and this was one of the reasons why the terrorism was well publicized.

Second, the Ustashas were a relatively small movement before the war, mostly isolated from Croatian society. Terrorism seemed to them to be the best method by which they could enter the mainstream of national politics. For even when they doubted that they would be successful in exterminating, expelling, or converting to Catholicism all the Serbs (and such doubts were common among Ustashas from the beginning of 1942), they still firmly believed that they had begun an irreversible Croatian-Serbian war and had made the very idea of a Yugoslav state unthinkable. By provoking Serbs into rebellion and sometimes even into reprisals against Croats, the Ustashas wanted to compel the Croatian nation to choose between subjugation by the Serbs or support for the Ustashas as masters of Croatia. The success of the Partisans prevented the Ustashas from achieving these goals. Moreover, in some places Ustasha terrorism had the opposite effect, alienating the Croatian masses from the Ustasha movement, which had become identified with violence and savagery.

Individual Ustasha military units also had a policy of involvement in terrorism against Serbs. The commanding cadres of the units—which consisted mostly of former émigré Ustashas—used all methods available to them to instruct recruits or volunteers in terrorism. There were several reasons for this strategy: a soldier who had committed a crime against Serbian civilians would not surrender easily to the enemy, for fear of revenge at the hands of the insurgents and, in the later stages of the war, trial as a war criminal; it directly involved his family, since they could become targets of revenge; such an act of violence would make him into a tougher, more ruthless fighter; and finally, terrorism was a kind of purification and purging of all vestiges of sentimentality, hesitation, and ordinary morality.

The marked similarities between the NDH and the Third Reich included the conviction that terrorism and genocide were necessary for the preservation of the state. In fact terrorism and genocide were extremely damaging to both states, to the point of endangering their very existence. The organization of concentration camps and the transportation of prisoners, for example, engaged enormous material and human resources that the Third Reich needed for war. The Ustashas' terrorism provoked massive Serbian rebellions as early as the summer of 1941, which would have caused an early collapse of the NDH had it not been supported by the German and Italian armies. In both Nazi Germany and the NDH, the main victims of terrorism were not enemies and opponents of the regime, but people who were for the most part ready to accept these regimes peacefully. The terrorism actually helped the real enemies of the NDH and the Third Reich. This readiness to risk their own survival proved that the Ustasha and Nazi leaders considered genocide a fundamental duty. Such commitment to genocide distinguishes these two states from most other despotic and violent regimes in history.

Nevertheless, there were very important differences behind these fundamental similarities. First, Nazi terrorism and genocide were in their style characteristic of a developed industrial state. Modern industrial equipment was used, and the terrorism was organized and supervised by a complex administrative network. Ustasha terrorism was primitive and traditional. No modern technology was used, and Ustasha administrative organization was poor.

Second, the Nazi terrorism was perpetrated by members of a literate, urbanized, clean, pedantic, organized, and disciplined central European nation. Ustasha terrorism, though by its scope and brutality outside even the worst Balkan traditions, still carried with it numerous distinctively Balkan traits.

Third, Nazi terrorism included plans, orders, reports, lists of victims, statistics. Most Ustasha orders were given orally, and the apparatus of terrorism functioned without precise plans. The Ustasha terrorist groups resembled gangs more than an organized army or organs of a state. Local Ustasha commanders pursued an arbitrary policy of terrorism, often choosing their targets and methods of extermination at random.

Fourth, since the Nazis were generally systematic and orderly, their terrorism was often depersonalized and bureaucratic. The perpetrators rarely knew the victims or had any direct, personal feelings toward them. Nazi hatred was abstract, "objective," and cold. So was their terrorism, although there were many examples of sadism. The Ustashas were direct, "personal," and warm: the first wave of terrorism was directed at people they knew, often at their own neighbors.

Fifth, from a certain literary-psychological point of view, Nazi terror, with its somberness, military discipline, bureaucratic pedantry, and ideological rigidity, was puritanical. In contrast, Ustasha crimes often became real orgies of violence.

Sixth, its ideology, technology, and totalitarian apparatus made Nazi terrorism essentially "modern," a part of the twentieth century. Even though the Nazis often spoke of "culture" and "decency," their ideology was a deliberate, conscious, and therefore modern negation of some of the most important traditions of European civilization. The Ustashas combined modern totalitarianism with primitive traditions of rebellion and revenge. They were terrorists first. Fascism came only later, and it was never fully absorbed, let alone developed.

The Myths of the State

The Ustashas' search for foreign support in the 1930s was not only a result of despair. It had its roots in the peculiar understanding of sovereignty, among many extreme Croatian nationalists, as meaning primarily ethnic homogeneity. They also felt that the right to political participation and citizenship in Croatia should be reserved exclusively for their Croatian conationals. Once these two were accepted as the most important elements of sovereignty, partial or even full submission to some external power did not seem so significant. Yugoslav and other scholars who claim that the NDH was not an independent or even a proper state at all usually give the following arguments: the NDH was created by the Germans and Italians after their victory over Yugoslavia; the Ustashas who ruled it never had the support of the majority of the Croatian people; their method of ruling was terroristic and genocidal, and therefore incompatible with any concept of legality and constitutionality; the NDH was obliged to pay for the upkeep of foreign armies on its territory and to make trade agreements with Germany and Italy;[47] it had no independent foreign policy; it gave a large part of its territory (Dalmatia) to a foreign power (Italy);[48] an enormous number of its inhabitants were totally opposed to it—not only all persecuted "minorities" (Serbs, Jews, and Gypsies) but also many Croats and Muslims; it could not, even with the entire mobilization of its own forces, control large parts of its own territory.

While all these arguments prove decisively that the NDH was not an independent and just state, only the last one suggests that it was not a state at all. A territory cannot be defined as being part of a state if armed units that are not only independent of this state, but opposed to it, control the territory. Beginning in the summer of 1941 the NDH encountered determined resistance from Partisan and Chetnik units. In the winter of 1941–42 the Ustashas lost control of large parts of Bosnia-Herzegovina.[49] These territories were partly controlled by Chetniks, who frequently fought not only against the Ustashas but also against Croats and Muslims. They were also fighting against the Partisans and in most cases were helped by the Italians, who increasingly wanted to weaken the NDH. The Partisans gained strength even more rapidly and soon controlled vast territories, where they organized political and other institutions. Further proof that the NDH was not really a state is the fact that although major operations against the Partisan forces in 1943 (the so-called fourth and fifth German offensives) took place mostly in Bosnia-Herzegovina, which was part of the NDH, the Ustasha troops played only a minor part in them, since their forces were insufficient against the Partisans.[50] Most of the troops in the fifth offensive, for example, were German. In May and June 1943 more than 80,000 German troops encircled the Partisan forces. Neither the Italian nor the German high commands believed that their Croatian ally was capable of surviving on its own.[51]

The Scope of the Ustasha Terror

Perhaps the most vexing question about the NDH is the actual number of Serbs killed by the Ustasha movement from 1941 to 1945, either in camps such as Jasenovac or, more usually, in *Einsatz*-style mass killings by Ustasha units. Estimates vary widely. The Yugoslav *Military Encyclopedia* states that there was a mass destruction of Serbs, Jews, and antifascists in Ustasha concentration camps and gives the following approximate figures: Jasenovac, 600,000; Jadovno, 72,000; Stara Gradiška, 75,000; Sremska Mitrovica, 10,000; and many more thousands in smaller camps.[52] Hermann Neubacher, a high-ranking Nazi official, estimates the total number of Serbian civilian victims in the NDH at 750,000.[53] The German general Lothar Rendulic claimed that there were 500,000 victims in the first months of the NDH's existence.[54] Many Serbian intellectuals in Belgrade cite one million murdered Serbs; some claim the same number for the Jasenovac concentration camp alone. The Croatian researcher Bruno Bušić asserted that the number of victims for the whole of Croatia (but without today's Bosnia and Herzegovina, which should have been added, since it was a part of the NDH during the war), including all nationalities and all camps, terrorism, and battles, was 185,327.[55] A Croatian historian, Franjo Tudjman, claims that the official number of 1,700,000 war victims for the whole of Yugoslavia is far too high. Since there simply are no exact statistical data about the war victims, he recommends calculating losses by scientific methods based on demographic statistics:

> According to two of the three most world famous methods for doing this, the overall demographic losses in Yugoslavia could amount at the most to about 2,100,000 (and according to the third half this). From this figure around 450,000 are accounted for by the lower birth rate, 500,000 by the German minority which left, about 200,000 by the Italian, Hungarian and Turkish minorities which left, about 200,000 by [Yugoslav] emigration, which leaves about 700,000–800,000 [Yugoslavs] to have perished.[56]

Tudjman then rightly points out that this is still an enormous figure and that few countries in the world have had a higher percentage of war victims. Still, if his estimate is correct it would mean that the whole of Yugoslavia lost less than the number of victims sometimes attributed to a single camp (Jasenovac). According to Tudjman the total number killed in all camps in Croatia was around 60,000, and they were of all nationalities: anti-Ustasha Croats, Gypsies, Jews, and Serbs. Given the number of Ustashas who worked in camps, as well as their level of organization and technology, including the transport apparatus at their disposal, it is indeed unlikely that numbers as high as those cited in the *Military Encyclopedia* could have been killed.

Tudjman, however, does not mention the number of Serbs inside the NDH who were murdered by the direct action of Ustasha units. And there seems little doubt that the greatest number of casualties were inflicted in precisely this way. It is unlikely that the exact number of those killed will ever be known. It was not determined after the war, and it will be extremely difficult to establish it after such a long time. Also, if the attempt is made, there will inevitably be disputes along nationalist lines, with nationalist Croatian historians trying to increase the percentage of those who were killed in battle or were victims of starvation, illness, or German or Italian terrorism. It is indeed often unclear whether a particular person was a victim of genocide or of Croatian counterterrorism (since in some regions Serbs retaliated, and these acts caused previously uncommitted Croats or Muslims to join the ranks of the Ustashas), or simply a victim of war (as a result of combat, starvation, or illness).[57]

In the most systematic and objective study so far of war victims in Yugoslavia, a Serbian scholar, Bogoljub Kočović, calculates the Serbs' losses in Croatia to have been 125,000, or 17.4 percent of their population there, and in Bosnia-Herzegovina 209,000, or 16.7 percent.[58] This means that in the NDH approximately one of every six Serbs lost his or her life during the war. After the Jews and Gypsies, this is the highest percentage of losses during the Second World War in the whole of Europe. The large majority were no doubt the victims of the Ustashas, although Kočović does not try to establish how many.

But regardless of the actual number of victims, the repression and terrorism of the Ustasha regime are without parallel in the history of southeastern Europe, and the genocide committed against the Serbs was the earliest total genocide to be attempted during the Second World War.[59] Neither Germany nor Italy forced the Ustashas to exterminate the Serbian population.[60] The Italians supported the Ustashas in the prewar period, but they never encouraged the Ustashas to commit genocide. In some regions Serbs regarded the Italian army as their protector against the Ustashas.[61]

Finally, Croats themselves, whether involved in political parties or not, were not exempt from Ustasha terrorism. Although many CPP members collaborated with the Ustashas, many others were killed or died in camps because of their leftist sympathies, their prewar opposition to the Ustashas, or their willingness to seek compromise with Serbs.[62]

five

Croatian and Serbian Political Parties, 1939–1945

Toward Croatian-Serbian Agreement

In the 1930s Serbian intellectual and political elites had become increasingly aware that Croatian national identity could not be transformed into a Yugoslav national identity, and that Croats should have some form of political autonomy. (Needless to say, there was considerable disagreement about the degree of autonomy Croats should have and about the borders of their territory.) They considered the solution of the Croatian question to be of crucial importance for the survival of Yugoslavia, as well as a prerequisite for the establishment of an efficient pluralistic political system and parliamentary government.

By and large the Serbian politicians of liberal-democratic and socialist views were relatively tolerant of and open to Croatian demands and the problems of other national groups. Their critical attitude toward Serbian predominance over other nations was often the basis of a critical attitude toward the political and social order in general. Serbs who totally opposed Croatian national demands were also unlikely to favor any reforms for more civil and political liberties (whether for trade unions or for political parties), among other reasons because these would inevitably give more scope to Croatian nationalism. Most intransigent Serbian nationalists, who promoted a centralist and unitarist Yugoslavia and a continued Serbian predominance in the government, civil service, and army, held authoritarian and conservative political views, rejecting parliamentarism and political parties and opposing reforms in the social and economic spheres. There was also often a correlation between Serbian politicians' attitude toward Croatian nationalism and their attitude toward Communism. Most extreme Serbian anti-Communists advocated harsh measures against Croatian nationalism, and those with a deep aversion to Croatian national demands frequently acquired militant anti-Communist attitudes.

At various times in the interwar period the Croatian Peasant Party sought support for its struggle for Croatian independence from Italy, Great Britain, France, Germany, and the Soviet Union.[1] In the 1920s France and Great Britain backed a strong Yugoslavia as an ally against Italy, the Soviet Union, and Germany. But in the 1930s these First World War allies of Serbia and supporters of the creation of Yugoslavia came to favor some kind of compromise with the Croats.[2] In the late 1930s Germany's annexation of Austria and occupation of Czechoslovakia and Italy's occupation of Albania prompted efforts by the ruling circle around Prince Pavle to appease Croatian nationalists.[3] Many leading Serbian politicians who opposed the autocratic regime of King Aleksandar and Prince Pavle also had concluded that there was a need for a new policy toward Croatia. Such views could have been found as early as the 1920s, especially among the leaders of the Democratic Party. But now they found support even among the Radicals, who since the creation of Yugoslavia in 1918 had most often formed the government and were the staunchest defenders and promoters of Serbian interests.

Prince Pavle combined a reactionary attitude toward parliamentary pluralism and social and economic reforms with a realization that one should look for a compromise with Croatian demands.[4] In February 1939 he dismissed Prime Minister Milan Stojadinović, among other reasons because of his refusal to take a new approach to the Croatian question.[5] The new prime minister, Dragiša Cvetković, owed his rise to power primarily to the patronage of Prince Pavle. He was not a popular figure in his native Serbia and had no standing among Serbian opposition parties. His cabinet included no one who commanded authority among Serbs.

Vladko Maček, the leader of the CPP, was the most influential politician in Croatia; most Croats accepted him as the defender of their national interests. Maček led the United Opposition, a coalition of Croatian and Serbian parties opposed to the dictatorship, in the elections of May 1935.[6] Even without a united program, the opposition won 1,076,346 votes, against the government party's 1,746,982.[7] While visiting Belgrade in 1938 Maček received a tremendous welcome from Serbs,[8] who viewed him as the leader of an all-Yugoslav democratic opposition to Prince Pavle's regime. His cautious approach, however, soon showed that Maček was unwilling to seek support from the Serbian masses. Even so, in the elections of December 1938 the United Opposition increased its base, winning 1,364,524 votes, while the government party under Stojadinović won 1,643,783.[9]

Though united with major Serbian parties against the authoritarian regime, Maček was showing readiness to make a deal with Prince Pavle whereby his acceptance of the undemocratic 1931 constitution would gain concessions for Croatian autonomy.[10] Negotiations between Prime Minister Cvetković and Maček from April to August 1939 produced the Sporazum Cvetković-Maček (Cvetković-Maček Agreement).[11] The CPP had in this way abandoned the program of the democratic opposition, whose main goal was fundamental change of the 1931 constitution. The Sporazum established the Banovina (province) of Croatia, under an extraordinary provision of that constitution. The Banovina consisted of the Savska and Primorska *banovine* and some districts in Bosnia-Herzegovina.[12] In shape and size it closely resembled the postwar republic of Croatia. Its boundaries were not considered as finally determined, but were to be settled by plebiscites in parts of Bosnia-Herzegovina. (However, no procedure for these plebiscites was laid down.)

Croatia was now the only *banovina* in Yugoslavia constituted at least implicitly on the principle of nationality.[13] Since it was named for the people who composed a majority within it, and since only a minority of Croats were left outside its borders, the Banovina came close to resem-

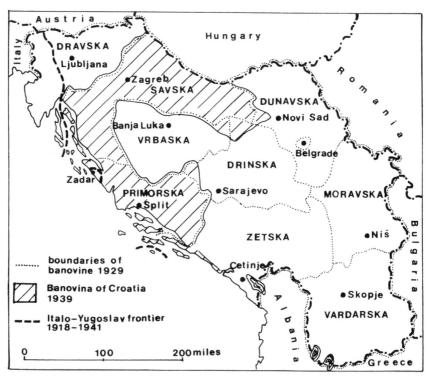

The banovine *of Yugoslavia, 1929, and the Banovina of Croatia, 1939*

bling a nation state.[14] It became a self-governing province with a special status inside the kingdom. Equally important was the fact that the Banovina was governed by politicians whom the populace regarded as protectors of the national interest. All other *banovine* were administered by civil servants chosen primarily for their loyalty to the crown and the central government. For Croatian politicians the main task now was to achieve even more independence from external influences on the Banovina, especially those from Belgrade.[15]

Like other *banovine*, the Banovina of Croatia was headed by a *ban*, the head of the local executive who was also a formal representative of the king. In Croatia, however, he was meant to be responsible not only to the crown but also to an autonomous Croatian parliament, the Sabor. Croatia was autonomous in many aspects of social, political, cultural, and economic life: agriculture, trade, industry, forestry, mining, construction, social and health policy, physical education, justice, education, and internal administration.[16] Among the sectors reserved for the central government, the most important were foreign affairs and national defense. Croatian autonomy was further strengthened by the appointment of Maček as vice-premier of the Yugoslav government and the inclusion in it of five members of the CPP. Juraj Šutej, a distinguished member of the CPP, became the minister of finance, and Ivan Šubašić became *ban* of Croatia.

The Cvetković-Maček cabinet consisted of five members of the Yugoslav Radical Union (the government party founded by Stojadinović); five representatives of the CPP; one representative each of the Independent Democratic Party (Samostalna demokratska stranka), the Agrarian Party (Zemljoradnička stranka; the name generally used for the Union of Agrarians), the Slovenian People's Party, and the Yugoslav Muslim Organization; and one member without party affiliation. Maček understood his vice-premiership primarily as a position from which to fight for Croatian interests and only secondarily as one from which to participate in governing Yugoslavia. In Croatian internal politics he retained full control of the CPP, which had all but monopolized political power in Croatia.

The CPP was not in principle opposed to parliamentarism and a multi-party political system inside Croatia. Yet for Maček all issues concerning the political system were matters to be accepted or rejected on an ad hoc basis, and both his political instincts and his rule over the CPP were authoritarian.[17] Since the death of Stjepan Radić there had been no elections of party leaders, and the CPP's General Committee, formally the ruling body of the party, held no regular meetings. Appointments depended primarily on Maček, who tolerated no internal dissent or opposition. Under Maček the CPP never developed a program to establish liberal-democratic political institutions for Croatia or to recognize minority rights for Serbs there. The Banovina of Croatia was to be organized as a centralist and unitarist state, with no local autonomy (let alone federal units); nor was it to have a legally constituted system for the protection of civil and political liberties.[18]

On the one hand, many influential members of the CPP and many administrators of the Banovina of Croatia sympathized with the Frankovci and the Ustasha movement, and sometimes even secretly cooperated with them. On the other hand, a strong left wing in the CPP, which was moderate in its national demands, sought close cooperation with Serbs both inside and outside Croatia, and, mostly because of its antifascist orientation, was sympathetic to Communism and the CPY.[19] The CPP could accommodate people with completely opposed ideologies, as long as they favored more political autonomy for Croatia. Yet such a political party, with no clear political ideas or firm organizational structure, would be unable to adapt to the difficult circumstances of war and civil war. The overwhelming majority of CPP members would remain passive during the war. Its right wing, in particular the paramilitary formations Peasants' Defense (Seljačka zaštita) and Citizens' Defense (Gradjanska zaštita), both modeled on the Austrian Heimwehr and Hungarian Honwed and sometimes even led by former Austro-Hungarian officers, later joined either the Ustasha movement or the regular army of the NDH, while the left joined the Partisans.[20] In both right- and left-wing alliances, the CPP remained an inferior partner, preserving only a token independence.[21]

The Sporazum found little support among Serbian political parties, and the Serbian Orthodox church and the armed forces opposed it. Although anti-Croatian sentiment was not particularly entrenched, these conservative Serbian institutions believed that any concessions to Croats would weaken the unity of the Yugoslav state and endanger Serbian interests.[22] Opposition to the Sporazum, however, was not limited to conservative Serbian nationalists, who were in any case unlikely to support any restrictions on centralism and unitarism. A number of respected Serbian political and intellectual figures who on the whole favored a new approach to the Croatian question (as well as rejecting the constitution of 1931) were critical of the Sporazum. They considered Maček's deal with Prince Pavle a betrayal of democratic principles, rendered more serious by the fact that it had been committed by the leading Croatian political party and their former ally in the United Opposition.[23] Relations between Croatian and Serbian politicians, and between Croats and Serbs in general, which had improved considerably during the United Opposition, were now strained; many Serbs felt that Croats were supporting Prince Pavle's autocratic regime in exchange for concessions to their national demands.[24]

The undemocratic nature of the Sporazum, some Serbian political figures pointed out, was demonstrated not only by the fact that Maček, though the leader of the United Opposition, had abandoned its main goal of changing the constitution of 1931. Equally important was the fact that the CPP had come to power in Croatia not through elections, but through an agreement with the crown.[25] The CPP had succeeded in uniting the majority of Croats, and there was no doubt that it would have easily won elections in Croatia; yet it was also obvious that the CPP was only a halfhearted supporter of liberal democracy and not deeply committed to the creation of parliamentary political institutions.

Adapting his policies to the successes of fascism and Nazism in western Europe, Maček favored extremely harsh measures against Communists and other left-wing groups, and showed considerable tolerance toward the right-wing separatist intelligentsia. In the Banovina the activities and publications of German and Italian sympathizers were encouraged, although organized Ustasha groups were not allowed, because the CPP considered them a dangerous opponent and contender for the leadership of Croatia. Some CPP journals and publications praised Germany for its economic efficiency and "orderliness." As a healthy nation with a strong leadership and respect for the national principle, it was a natural defender of small nations and of their right to national independence. That a peasant party of a Slav nation could entertain such colossal illusions is understandable only in light of the CPP's complete lack of clear ideological principles and intellectual perceptions, its provincialism, and its total concentration on Croatian-Serbian relations.[26]

The Sporazum: An Unsolved Yugoslav Question

The Sporazum did not establish federalism in Yugoslavia; it only created an autonomous Croatian unit.[27] It attempted to solve the Croatian problem while ignoring all other national issues in Yugoslavia. These were, however, inseparably linked. By giving in to Croatian demands for autonomy, the Sporazum inevitably raised both the Serbian question and the problem of the organization of Yugoslavia as a whole. Slovenes, for example, resented the fact that they remained part of the centralized state while Croats were gaining autonomy. In previous years Belgrade had made concessions to the Slovenes in order to gain their support against Croatian demands. The Sporazum made deals of this kind impossible.

Croats, Slovenes, and Serbs were the only three recognized nations in Yugoslavia. But Macedonians and Montenegrins also sought some form of autonomy. In addition, there were non-Slav national minorities—Albanians, Hungarians, and Germans—with similar demands. Finally, the South Slav Muslims of Bosnia-Herzegovina were clearly more than merely Yugoslavs of Muslim faith, and they desired some form of self-rule. The Sporazum addressed none of these problems.

As a Croatian nationalist party, the CPP was concerned solely with Croatia and Croatian problems. It accepted Yugoslavia only as an unavoidable political reality that would be difficult, perhaps even impossible, to change. For CPP members, Yugoslavia was not their country, although they did not consider it a foreign, enemy state as did the Ustashas. Many members of the CPP hoped one day to achieve complete Croatian independence. For all these reasons, the CPP had no policies for Yugoslavia, nor was it interested in creating them. It was because of such attitudes that Maček found it so easy to abandon the United Opposition and make a deal with Prince Pavle. Although he was not a wholehearted separatist, he was definitely a halfhearted supporter of Yugoslav unity. He had no Yugoslav political consciousness; he journeyed from Zagreb to Belgrade to defend Croatian interests, not to make policies for the whole of Yugoslavia. For Maček, Yugoslavia was an arena for Croatian foreign policy.

This lack of interest in Yugoslavia as a whole, combined with powerful Croatian nationalist sentiments, disqualified the CPP from participating in the government of Yugoslavia. Ironically, however, through the Sporazum the CPP had become the leading political force in Yugoslavia. The Yugoslav Radical Union, the government party that supported Prime Minister Cvetković and from which most Serbian government members were drawn, was less a party than an organization of people working for, and dependent on, the government. It had no popular support among Serbs (or any other nation of Yugoslavia) and was intensely disliked by Serbian political parties as an instrument of the autocratic regime.

The 1931 constitution remained in force after the Sporazum was adopted. So while the rest of Yugoslavia was legally, politically, administratively, and militarily one centralized, unitary state, Croatia was an autonomous part within it with extensive political rights. It was a *corpus separatum* within a country where so much was interconnected and interdependent. In some respects the problem resembled the one posed for Great Britain by Ireland in the second half of the nineteenth century. William Gladstone's recommendation for Irish home rule precipitated an intensive debate both inside and outside the British Parliament. One of the central questions raised was whether Irish members of Parliament should have seats both in Westminster and in the Dublin Parliament. If this system had been introduced, they would have been making independent decisions for Ireland while preserving the right to legislate on British matters. In a similar way, Croatian politicians, after gaining autonomy for Croatia, still participated with Serbs (who, moreover, were not even authentic Serbian representatives, since they owed their election to the bogus parliamentary system of the 1931 constitution) and others in the government of Yugoslavia. Thus the Croats participated in making decisions both about Yugoslav and purely Serbian matters while having great independence in governing Croatia.[28]

Serbian politicians exaggerated the threat that the Sporazum represented to Serbian interests. The Serbs' numerical superiority in the country as a whole, and their preponderance in the crucial institutions of the state, were a sufficient guarantee that their interests would not be seriously endangered, at least for the time being. Yet it was true that a political system with such a confused distribution of powers and responsibilities could not function effectively. It was an ambiguous mixture of federalism and confederalism. Croats were both more independent in Croatia and more influential in the Yugoslav government than simple federalism would normally allow. In Belgrade, for example, they had, among other things, the right of *liberum veto*.[29]

Some historians have taken a more charitable view of the Sporazum, interpreting it as a merely temporary solution that, for all its imperfections, contributed to the resolution of the Croatian national question and marked a step toward the creation of a federal Yugoslavia. Yet in many ways the Sporazum was an obstacle to solving the national problem in Yugoslavia. After achieving autonomy for Croatia, Croatian politicians had become a conservative force, opposing any change in the 1931 constitution. They did not want the Sporazum to be a first step in the transformation of Yugoslavia into a federal state. Lacking political vision, limited by pragmatism and short-term goals, they refused to seek some way to regulate relations among Yugoslav nations. In addition, the Sporazum laid the foundation for an ineffective government. Not only did it not take into account the international situation and the fascist and Nazi threats to Yugoslavia; it also prevented Croatian politicians, who shared power in Belgrade, from acting in the interests of the Yugoslav state. Because they feared losing their power base in Croatia, they never accepted responsibility for the destiny of the entire country. Instead, they used their newly acquired power primarily to protect and promote Croatian national interests.

The Coup d'Etat of 27 March 1941

Prince Pavle's reputation among Serbs was dangerously low. Less of an autocrat than King Aleksandar, he was just as opposed to political parties, but lacked Aleksandar's popular advantage as a successful military commander from the Balkan Wars and the First World War, and as the recognized protector both of Serbian interests and of the unity of Yugoslavia. Prince Pavle's contempt for Balkan politics and his aloof, aristocratic manner deepened the mistrust of the Serbian people, who took great pride in the peasant origin of the Karadjordjević dynasty and in its members' unsophisticated life style.

During 1940 the international situation became increasingly dangerous for Yugoslavia. Europe was falling under German domination, and in October 1940 Italy, which already had Albania under its control, attacked Greece. Romania and Hungary joined the Tripartite Pact in November 1940. Bulgaria would follow suit in March 1941.[30] At the beginning of 1941 Yugoslavia was nearly surrounded by Italy, Germany, and their allies; only Greece was still resisting the Italians. Germany exerted constant pressure on Yugoslavia to join the Tripartite Pact, and on 25 March 1941 the country's leaders relented; Cvetković signed the pact with Hitler.[31] The negotiations had been secret, and their outcome was a shock for most Yugoslavs. Under the conditions imposed by Germany, however, Yugoslavia was not obliged to participate in the German and Italian war operations, nor would German troops be stationed in its territory.[32]

On 27 March a group of Serbian officers overthrew the government of Prime Minister Dragiša Cvetković, forced Prince Pavle to resign, and declared King Petar II, eldest son of the late King Aleksandar, to be of age, six months before his eighteenth birthday.[33] The Serbs' accumulated dissatisfaction with Prince Pavle's policies and autocratic style was one of the causes of this almost bloodless coup. The crucial cause, however, was his decision to join the Tripartite Pact. The coup prompted enthusiastic popular demonstrations in many Serbian towns, especially in Belgrade. There were also demonstrations in Ljubljana, the capital of Slovenia, but without the participation of the largest political party there, the Slovenian People's Party. The CPY had not expected the coup but expressed its support, urging the new regime to ally itself closely with the Soviet Union. Communists participated in the demonstrations and became a dominant political force in the streets and squares of Belgrade.[34] Only in Croatia was there little popular support for the coup, and the CPP was unwilling to compromise itself by supporting what seemed to many Croats to be a purely Serbian affair.

The conditions of adherence to the pact did not put immediate great demands on Yugoslavia. Yet potentially and in the longer run they did, since they had placed Yugoslavia in the "new order" in Europe and accepted the leadership of Nazi Germany and Fascist Italy. Serbs feared that the pact was only a first step toward making Yugoslavia part of Germany's and Italy's war effort and a fascist state. They doubted both Hitler's sincerity and Prince Pavle's ability to preserve sufficient distance from Germany.[35] Popular mistrust of Prince Pavle and the secretiveness that surrounded the joining of the pact and its exact wording only increased their suspicions. The coup was an emotional reaction, an outburst of anger against an alliance that went against Serbs' feelings, historical memories, and traditions. Those who took over the government, however, were frightened of provoking Germany and soon made attempts to mollify it.[36]

The Sporazum contributed to the general Serbian animosity toward Prince Pavle, but abolition of the Sporazum was not a motive for the coup.[37] Slogans shouted during the Belgrade demonstrations were anti-German and favored political democratization.[38] Croats, however, were suspicious that the officers who had organized the coup would try to restore a centralist and unitarist Yugoslavia. They were also worried by the sudden reactivation of Serbian political parties, who were mostly not sympathetic to the Sporazum. Fear of war with Germany and Italy, in some cases combined with admiration for the powerful and "orderly" Third Reich, contributed to the CPP's negative attitude toward the coup. In any case, Maček was in the government with Cvetković and, therefore, at least partly responsible for the signing of the pact. Indeed, Maček regarded adhesion to the pact as the only course to prevent war.

General Dušan Simović, the most prominent military figure involved in the coup, tried to create a coalition government representing all parties "that had roots in the people." This included all major political parties except the CPY. Simović hoped to get the CPP to participate in the coalition government, but Maček laid down conditions. He required that the Sporazum be confirmed, that the police force in Croatia be put under the direct control of the *ban* of Croatia, and that the implementation there of all new legislation, both Croatian and Yugoslav, be the executive responsibility of the *ban*.[39] Simović accepted these demands. It was natural that a Croatian leader should be suspicious of a coup by Serbian officers and that he would consider it his duty to protect the Sporazum. Yet Maček was preoccupied solely with achieving additional gains for Croatia. Neither he nor anyone else in the CPP possessed the moral and spiritual strength or political vision that the situation demanded. At the time of the coup, when Churchill praised Yugoslavia "for finding its soul," Maček chose cautious neutrality and kept the Croats outside that event.[40] Maček agreed to join the Simović government only on condition that it try to placate the Germans, and offered to travel to Berlin to appease them. He was the most prominent and vocal among those in the government who insisted that the new government confirm Yugoslavia's acceptance of the pact and make concessions.[41]

On 6 April 1941, Germany led the Axis attack on Yugoslavia.[42] Belgrade was bombed, with severe losses among the civilian population.[43] Zagreb was spared because the Germans recognized the anti-Axis coup as primarily a Serbian affair and counted on the Croats as potential allies.[44] In less than a fortnight Yugoslavia was defeated.[45] The enemy had the advantages of modern equipment and of surprise.[46] All political maneuvering came to a sudden though only temporary end, and the government went into exile.

Velimir Terzić, a retired general of the Yugoslav People's Army, argues that the lack of solidarity between Croats and Serbs, and Croatian unwillingness to fight for Yugoslavia, decisively contributed to Germany's quick defeat of the Royal Yugoslav Army.[47] He reports numerous incidents of troops fighting against each other rather than against the enemy. Despite the considerable evidence he supplies in support of his thesis, he seems to exaggerate the importance for the defeat of Yugoslavia of Croatian unwillingness to fight. Some Croatian units did desert the Royal Yugoslav Army, but many demonstrated their readiness to resist the Germans.[48] The majority of Croatian officers in the armed forces remained loyal until 10 April, when the NDH was proclaimed. After that they judged that Yugoslavia had ceased to exist as a state and no longer commanded their loyalty.

Enthusiasm for defending the country was greater among Serbs, but defeatism spread quickly through the higher ranks of the Serbian-dominated officer corps. The chief reasons for the defeat were lack of energetic political and military leadership, the army's comparatively poor equipment, and its old-fashioned approach to strategy and tactics. The army reflected the weakness of the entire political system.

The Government in Exile

The government in exile was the continuation of the one formed after the coup of 27 March.[49] It was a coalition, designed to bring together all important political parties and create the national unity needed to face war and occupation. Despite its impressive collection of distinguished political personalities, it was weak, because it was deeply divided. Prime Minister General Simović had no political experience and distrusted politicians and political parties.[50] The legality of the government in exile rested on the 1931 constitution, which made government ministers responsible solely to the king. King Petar II was therefore both the sovereign of Yugoslavia and the final political arbiter.[51] It was only a matter of time before external influences would cause this unstable young man to use his enormous powers against the government ministers.

The government was created on the supposition that internal politics should be laid aside until the end of the war, so as not to interfere with efforts for the liberation of the country. This approach seemed to be simply one of common sense for an exiled government faced with a long war and foreign occupation. Yet it was impossible to sidestep the national question. Croats and Serbs within the government were in constant conflict with each other. Formally speaking, the government was constituted according to political parties rather than national representation. Juraj Krnjević, Ivan Šubašić, Juraj Šutej, Ilija Jukić, and Rudolf Bićanić, for example, were the CPP's representatives in the government. Yet they saw themselves primarily as representing the Croatian nation. They considered it their most important task to speak to the Allies on its behalf, rather than to participate in government policies of Yugoslavia.

There were several Serbian political parties in the government in exile. But this was just one of the reasons why Serbian ministers never formed a bloc unitedly representing the Serbian nation. They were divided in other ways too—individual against individual, "Yugoslavs" against "Serbs," those who were losing faith in Yugoslavia against those whose faith remained.[52] Yet, on major issues relating to Croatian-Serbian relations and the future organization of Yugoslavia, they had much more in common with one another than they had with Croats. Croats, therefore, often perceived them as a bloc and consciously sought to destroy their actually nonexistent unity, often causing a government crisis in the process. In all changes of prime ministers in the government in exile, the Croatian-Serbian conflict would play a decisive role.[53] Indeed, it contributed decisively to the failure of the government in exile.

Under the Sporazum, Croats in the Cvetković-Maček government had parity with, and even superiority over, Serbian politicians, since the latter had little popular support. But after 27 March and in the government in London they confronted ministers who represented at least the vestiges of genuine Serbian political parties, and which were certainly more representative than Cvetković's Yugoslav Radical Union: the People's Radical Party, the Democratic Party, the Agrarian Party, the Yugoslav National Party (Jugoslovenska nacionalna stranka), and the Independent Democratic Party.[54] The Independent Democrats had some Croatian members and before the war had allied themselves with the CPP. They were not, however, a party with major influence.[55]

Divisions between Croatian and Serbian ministers were very deep: at times they seemed to consider each other members of foreign, and in some cases even enemy, nations. The CPP members of the government could not accept relations between Croats and Serbs as a matter merely of internal affairs to be settled after the war. But they obviously did not consider them to be a matter of external affairs either, since their participation in the government implied an acceptance of Yugoslavia. They were aware that if they attempted to conduct relations with their Serbian colleagues as if between two sovereign and independent nations, their relations with the British and, later, the Americans would be endangered. Such a policy would have been seen as indirect acceptance of the NDH, which was an Axis creation.

Although Simović's government had confirmed the Sporazum, Serbian ministers avoided publicizing this fact. Anti-Croatian feeling among Serbs in Yugoslavia after the establishment of the NDH, and especially after the Ustashas' massacres of Serbs in the summer of 1941, was a serious issue for the London government. Also, the government in exile included several Serbs who were outspoken critics of the Sporazum, a fact that increased Croats' feeling of unease. Yet, except for a few extreme Serbian nationalists, Serbs believed that there could be no return to centralism and unitarism and also rejected the idea of an independent Greater Serbia. Few Serbs in the government were secretly planning the restoration of Serbian hegemony. Yet they showed little sensitivity to Croatian fears about the position of Croatia in some future Yugoslavia. The CPP ministers were for their part intolerant, and their approach to the national problem was often dogmatic. The conflict between Croats and Serbs came down, in essence, to the almost confederal status of the Banovina of Croatia, which most Serbs claimed to accept—but not, from the Croatian point of view, with sufficient determination and trustworthiness—and to the Croats' refusal to commit themselves to restoring Yugoslavia or engaging in all-Yugoslav politics.[56]

Croats in the government in exile wanted to be the representatives of a sovereign Croatian nation (and they were to a certain extent accepted as such), but in fact the CPP was just one of several parties in a coalition government. The structure of that government was undefined: was it a coalition of political parties, a federation, or a confederation of nations? Croatian ministers insisted that they were under no obligation to accept majority decisions.[57] In this way they effectively gave themselves the right to block any decision of the government. The use of this *liberum veto* gave them the status of a sovereign nation.[58]

The Anti-Yugoslavism of the Croatian Peasant Party

Vladko Maček remained in Yugoslavia after the Axis invasion in April 1941.[59] Although he refused an offer from the Germans to form a Croatian government, he issued a proclamation exhorting Croats not to oppose the occupying forces and to cooperate with the new regime. He did not urge people to join the Ustasha movement or to support the German and Italian war effort.[60] His proclamation reflected a spirit of nonresistance and "waiting for better times" (a typical response of the CPP when confronted with an aggressor). The Ustashas considered Maček an enemy, since he was opposed to their terrorist methods and had made a compromise with the Belgrade regime. Yet Maček's proclamation, whose effect was considerable, helped the Ustasha regime to consolidate power.

Maček was soon arrested and placed in a concentration camp. Later he was interned on his farm in his native village and until the end of the war took no part in politics. His representative in the government in exile was CPP secretary-general Juraj Krnjević, who had been in exile during most of the interwar period and was little known in Yugoslavia. He had a reputation as an intransigent Croatian nationalist and a hater of Serbs.[61] Krnjević became a deputy prime minister in Simović's government.[62] As early as August 1941 Krnjević, describing himself as "chief representative of the Croatian people," and without any consultation with the Yugoslav government, tried unsuccessfully to enter into negotiations with British foreign secretary Anthony Eden about the postwar borders between Italy and Croatia.[63]

Krnjević exemplified in an extreme form the thinking of most Croatian nationalists, both in the CPP and in the Ustasha movement. Starting from the correct but immensely exaggerated perception that Serbian political parties lacked sufficient understanding of Croatian problems, he developed an elaborate interpretation of Serbian politics to the effect that differences among Serbian political parties, or even differences between them and the royal dictatorship that had abolished them, were superficial and in many cases a ruse designed to confuse and divide Croats in their struggle for their national rights.[64]

In all his political activities Krnjević supported the idea of an independent Croatian state.[65] He decided not to support the NDH primarily because he believed that Germany and Italy would be defeated.[66] (In general, the CPP's attitude during the war—an attitude that would ultimately prove fatal to it as an effective political force—was one of keeping open as many options as possible.) In contacts with representatives of Croatian communities in the United States, for example, Krnjević made his separatist nationalism quite obvious, and inside the government he felt under no obligation to give an account of his actions.[67]

Konstantin Fotić, the Yugoslav diplomatic representative (and later ambassador) in Washington, began to consider Croats an enemy nation soon after the first massacres of Serbs in the NDH, and eventually came to argue that the concept of a Yugoslav state should be abandoned and that Serbs should concentrate their energies on creating an independent Serbian state.[68] Fotić, unlike Krnjević, had not been anti-Yugoslav before the war. Also, as an experienced diplomat, Fotić was more subdued and discreet in his anti-Croatian pronouncements than was Krnjević in his anti-Serbian ones. Yet even Krnjević, for tactical reasons, never openly declared himself against Yugoslavia.

Both Krnjević and his Serbian counterpart Fotić were separatists. They worked for the Yugoslav government solely because they thought it temporarily advantageous to do so. Both also had expansionist ideas; each claimed territories of the other nation for his own nation.[69]

Krnjević and Fotić were probably the most intransigent nationalists among the exiled politicians, but their antagonism gives a not unrealistic picture of the deep divisions that existed in London.[70] The government tolerated Fotić and was reluctant to check Krnjević, who was its senior minister and deputy prime minister. So they could proceed with their activities.[71]

The Impact of the Ustasha Genocide

The worst conflict between Croats and Serbs in the government in exile occurred in the late summer and autumn of 1941, when the first news of massacres of Serbs by the Ustashas reached London.[72] The Croatian ministers' reluctance to discuss and publicly condemn these atrocities outraged the Serbs. Even the Serbian politicians who had previously been close to the CPP (for example, some representatives of the Agrarian Party) found their relations with Croats strained. Croatian members of the government tried to minimize the Ustasha massacres, explaining them away as reactions to prewar Serbian oppression.[73] With complete disregard for the nature and magnitude of these events they compared them with the persecution of Croats in prewar Yugoslavia, citing as one example the expulsions of Croatian schoolteachers accused of nationalism during the dictatorship of King Aleksandar.[74]

Serbian politicians were united in their insistence that Croatian ministers make a strong public statement about the massacres, expressing their revulsion against and rejection of Ustasha policies. The Serbian ministers were themselves under pressure, since Serbian public opinion at home was turning against both the Croats and the idea of Yugoslavia as a common state for Serbs and Croats. They considered it essential to show that the government in exile, including its Croatian members, was firmly opposed to the Ustasha regime. Croatian members of the government, however, suspected Serbian politicians of exaggerating the number of victims of the massacres in order to undermine the position of Croatian ministers in the government and their relations with the British. Considering the reputation some of the Serbian politicians had as intriguers and haters of Croats, such suspicions were not unfounded. It is also true that the number of victims was exaggerated. Nonetheless, the actual number of victims was enormous. And yet, in the face of planned and systematically executed genocide, Croatian politicians remained completely dominated by sentiments of national prestige.[75]

Because the Croatian ministers never firmly and openly rejected the anti-Serbian policies of the Ustasha regime, the Yugoslav government remained in existence in name only.[76] As individuals, many Croatian and Serbian ministers lacked neither intellectual ability nor integrity nor political experience. Yet in retrospect their behavior seems grotesquely inadequate. During the greatest tragedy of the Yugoslav peoples they could not overcome the paralysis of national exclusivism. They remained until the end of the war the prisoners of their national ideologies.

One of the goals of Ustasha terrorism was to undermine the idea of a unified Yugoslavia by making cooperation between Croats and Serbs impossible. In a sense the Ustashas achieved this goal, since the conflict between Croats and Serbs in the government in exile was considerably worsened by the Ustasha massacres. But what the Ustashas actually destroyed was the interwar Yugoslavia of national political parties. The Partisan movement, on the other hand, was strengthened by the Ustasha policies. In the fratricidal civil war that followed the Ustasha massacres, Communist national policies increasingly attracted people from different nations of Yugoslavia.

The Chetniks as a Serbian Movement

In January 1942, King Petar II, under pressure from most political parties, dismissed Prime Minister General Simović.[77] Simović's distrust of politicians whom he considered to be destroyers of Yugoslav national unity had brought him into conflict with other members of the government.[78] The Croats had been particularly opposed to Simović. Although his Yugoslavism seemed sincere, it was no recommendation in their eyes. They saw it as masked Serbian hegemonism and a threat to their national aspirations. Furthermore, if Croats had to choose between dealing with an autocrat such as Prince Pavle or with Serbian political parties, they preferred the autocrat, as being less directly identified with Serbian interests. At the same time, given a choice between Serbian political parties and Serbian officers, Croats favored political parties. The royal dictatorship of January 1929 had not directly relied on the military. But the army, though passive until the coup of 27 March, hovered in the background and was regarded as one of the pillars of the centralist and unitarist Yugoslavia. It was more predominantly Serbian than any other institution in the country.[79] The Croats' deepest political instincts, therefore, warned them that a Serb in uniform was the least ready to give in to Croatian demands.[80] He would always consider the centralized and unitarist Yugoslav state a prerequisite for the defense of the country, and interpret quests for autonomy as threats to the survival of the country. Simović appeared to Croats not only as a Serbian general, but also as a leader and unifying figure for all Serbian parties in the government. Without him, they believed, this Serbian bloc would disintegrate.[81]

The new prime minister was Slobodan Jovanović, a legal scholar, the most distinguished Serbian historian between the wars, and the president of the Serbian Royal Academy of Sciences. His brilliant analyses and sharp wit destroyed many myths of Serbian nationalism. Yet he was also the president of the Serbian Cultural Club, founded in 1937, which tried to promote the cultural and political unity of all Serbs of Yugoslavia (and, after the Sporazum, to establish a kind of Serbian *banovina* in Yugoslavia), and a critic of the Sporazum from a constitutional point of view. Furthermore, he was a supporter of the Chetnik movement of Draža Mihailović. Before the war, Jovanović had neither the ability nor the ambition to involve himself in politics.[82] Yet circumstances placed him in a position of leadership at the most difficult time of the war.[83]

Jovanović's support for Mihailović, however, can be only partly explained by lack of reliable information about the activities of the Chetnik movement.[84] Jovanović was an anti-Communist, and he approved of what he understood as the Chetniks' primary concern with Serbian national interests. The latter further alienated Croats from Serbs in the government in exile.[85] As in the case of the Ustasha genocide, the government was unable to take a united attitude toward the Chetnik movement, particularly toward the Serbian chauvinism of the majority of its leaders. Serbian members of the government tended to glorify Mihailović and the Chetniks as heroes of the resistance to the occupiers, while Krnjević and Šutej feared the Chetnik anti-Croatian policies.[86] The latter tried systematically to undermine the prestige of the Chetniks among the Allies. In many ways their criticism of the Chetniks' anti-Croatian policies was justified. Yet the complaint of the Serbian ministers about Krnjević's and Šutej's lack of loyalty to the government was not completely unjustified either. As members of the government in which Mihailović was minister of war (and, therefore, their colleague) they were engaging in anti-Chetnik propaganda behind the backs of the Serbian ministers. This propaganda on the part of Croatian members of the government and Croatian exile groups undoubtedly influenced the Allies' abandonment of the Chetniks and recognition of the Partisan movement, which ultimately facilitated the Communist victory.[87]

During 1942 the Yugoslav government in exile made a mistake that enormously helped the Partisan movement. It instructed Mihailović to avoid open confrontation with the Germans until the Allies landed in Yugoslavia, and to send as many troops as possible to the territory of the NDH to protect Serbs there from the Ustasha massacres. Mihailović had at that time generally ceased fighting the Germans, and Chetniks in Montenegro, Herzegovina, and Dalmatia had already collaborated with the Italians in their operations against the Partisans. Moreover, Mihailović did not have large, mobile units that he could send to the NDH. (His guerrillas, unlike the Partisans, were traditional and, therefore, local). Yet once these orders from London became known, they reinforced the perception promoted by efficient Communist propaganda in Yugoslavia and Great Britain, that the Chetnik movement and government in exile were inclined toward passivity and collaboration with the occupiers of Yugoslavia and concerned primarily with the struggle against Communism and the preservation of Serbian predominance in Yugoslavia.[88] In particular the order to fight the Ustasha movement, which was not accompanied by any instructions about how to treat Croats and Muslims and Chetnik commanders who had committed atrocities against them, seemed like an attempt to continue and even escalate the Croatian-Serbian war.

In June 1943 Jovanović resigned as prime minister, primarily as a result of a crisis in Croatian-Serbian relations.[89] Jovanović had prepared a draft of a "Declaration of War Aims and the General Aims of the State Policy of the Yugoslav Government," arguing for a federal system and pluralistic parliamentary political institutions. It was meant to be a basis for Croatian-Serbian cooperation both in the government in exile and in the country, and to enable the government to concentrate on designing policies for the conduct of war.[90] Nevertheless, Croats led by Krnjević, though accepting the general line of the draft, considered Jovanović insufficiently Yugoslav or democratic to implement such a declaration. The Croats exercised their *liberum veto* and precipitated a government crisis.[91]

Miloš Trifunović, an old politician from the People's Radical Party and an opponent of the Sporazum, was appointed prime minister by the king. Trifunović's appointment was expected to elicit Krnjević's cooperation, since Jovanović had been removed and Krnjević had in principle accepted the declaration. But Krnjević then began to oppose the declaration, demanding new amendments that included a special reference to the Sporazum.[92] The Croatian-Serbian conflict was then exacerbated by other issues, and Croatian ministers declared that they would no longer collaborate with their Serbian colleagues; but they did not leave the government. On 10 August, after less than two months in office, Trifunović resigned.

The king's appointment of Prime Minister Božidar Purić, who had been Yugoslav minister to France before the war, was largely the result of intrigue. Partly because of British pressure, Petar II was exploiting his powerful constitutional position.[93] Purić's government was a nonpolitical, administrative one, consisting mostly of civil servants. Though partly a British creation, it resisted their demands to withdraw support from Mihailović, instead reappointing him minister of defense. Since it had no political authority, the government decided not even to attempt to bring about Croatian and Serbian cooperation.

In June 1944 Ivan Šubašić, a leading figure in the CPP and the prewar *ban* of Croatia, became prime minister at Churchill's suggestion. He was sworn in as a one-man government, combining his premiership with all ministerial positions. The British believed that as a Croat he was more likely to abandon Mihailović and come to terms with the Partisan movement, and this proved to be the case. He recognized the Partisans (formally called the People's Liberation Army of Yugoslavia; Narodnooslobodilačka vojska Jugoslavije) as the only Yugoslav force fighting the occupiers and accepted their provisional administration in territories they controlled. As a result of an agreement with Tito in June 1944, he did not reappoint Mihailović as minister of defense, and later dismissed him as chief of staff of the Supreme Command.[94] In the provisional Yugoslav government of March 1945, which was led by Tito, Šubašić and a few other London politicians who supported him represented only a small minority. This was the end of the Yugoslav government in exile.

Anti-Communism, Nationalism, and Liberalism

The Yugoslav government in exile found little support among Croatian communities in the United States or among Croats at home.[95] The main reason was its unconditional support for the Chetnik movement, which most Croats considered to be a great-Serbian movement committed to national domination, "revenge" against Croats and Muslims, and the creation of a Greater Serbia or Serbian-dominated Yugoslavia. Croats also knew that some members of the Chetnik movement thought that Croats and Muslims should be expelled from all "Serbian" lands (including the whole of Bosnia-Herzegovina and parts of Croatia).

The government in exile was aware to some extent of the extreme Serbian nationalism of many factions of Mihailović's movement. Yet it made little effort to combat or even moderate that nationalism. There were important reasons for this passivity. First, in 1941 and 1942 the British government desperately needed a heroic resistance movement for propaganda at home and in occupied Europe. Therefore, both the government in exile and the British considered it useful to idealize the Chetniks. Second, the horror of the Ustasha massacres caused Serbs in the government to excuse Chetnik atrocities against Croats and Muslims. The Serbian members of the government were afraid of losing the support of Serbs at home if they criticized Mihailović or his movement. Third, they believed that the best way to combat Communist propaganda against the Mihailović movement was to deny all its claims completely. Fourth, the government in exile had little direct contact with Mihailović, and its control over him and his movement was limited. The leading members of the Mihailović movement, as well as commanders of independent Chetnik units outside Serbia (in Bosnia-Herzegovina, Croatia, and Montenegro), respected neither politicians in general nor the government in exile in particular, nor, in many cases, even Mihailović. Mihailović's formal position was leader of what was pompously named the Yugoslav Army in the Fatherland (Jugoslovenska vojska u otadžbini). Despite his high rank, however, Mihailović was primarily a unifying figurehead for the Chetniks: he had little actual control over Chetnik commanders in Serbia, and none at all over those elsewhere.

Because the London government's support for the Chetnik movement was unacceptable to Croats, the Partisans (who were fighting the Chetniks and promised a solution to the national question in Yugoslavia based on national equality and federalism) emerged toward the end of the war as the Croats' only alternative.[96] The participation of Croats in the Partisan movement and in the CPY, with Croat Tito as the leader, persuaded many uncommitted Croats that after the war the Partisans would abolish Serbian hegemony. Participation in (or support of) the Partisan movement was a way for many Croats to defend their own nation against accusations (which were frequent after the Ustasha massacres, both in Yugoslavia and among the Allies) that it had allied itself with Italian Fascism and German Nazism.

So it was not only pro-Yugoslav and pro-Communist Croats who, as the war continued, began to support the Partisan army. At least for the time being, the idea of an independent Croatian state was so compromised by the Pavelić regime that no Allied country would support it.[97] Thus, a Communist-led Yugoslavia began to seem the best solution for Croats. (Tito and the Partisan leaders claimed that they were not aiming to introduce Communism after the war. But to most politically informed people it was obvious that the Communists would rule Yugoslavia. The only question was whether they would be content with hegemony or would seek a complete monopoly of power.) Even some prewar Croatian opponents of Communism came to support the Partisan army, believing that it offered the only chance for Croatian emancipation and even the survival of the Croatian nation. But it was not only national self-interest that moved those Croatian non-Communists who supported the Communist-led Partisan army. The Partisans' heroism, their success in uniting different nations, the presence among them of large numbers of young people, intellectuals, and talented artists and writers, and their hopes of creating a new society—all had a powerful emotional impact on the uncommitted.

The Serbs' situation was different. Serbs in the government in exile and Serbian anti-Communists in general had little to fear but Communism. Although the Ustashas continued killing Serbs, the threat to Serbs' very survival in the NDH ceased about midway through the war. They faced no danger of postwar domination by another people. Nor would the territories in which they lived be given to a foreign state. They knew that they would be treated well by the victorious Allies. In the eyes of the world the Serbs had two resistance movements, the Partisans and the Chetniks. It mattered little that these two groups fought against each other or that Chetnik commanders often collaborated with Germans and Italians in their struggle against the Communists. Mihailović had, after all, been organizing a movement against the triumphant Wehrmacht as early as 1941, and until the end of the war the Allied airmen who were parachuted over Serbia could count on the Chetniks to help them return to their bases.[98]

The attitude of Serbian members of the government in exile toward the Partisan movement generally followed the pattern established in prewar Yugoslavia: the more nationalist an individual's political views, the stronger his anti-Communist sentiments.[99] In connection with Serbian anti-Communism, however, the situation was often paradoxical. In general, Communism as an ideology and political practice is criticized chiefly because it severely limits individual freedom. Many of its opponents consider it the very opposite of liberal democracy, perhaps even its most total and "totalitarian" negation. Yet in the government in exile and in Yugoslavia itself, liberal-democratic Serbian politicians and intellectuals were the ones who showed much greater readiness to compromise with the Partisan movement than did the intransigent Serbian nationalists, to whom individual freedom and rights meant little in comparison with national interests.

For many of them, the Communists, though severely limiting individual freedom, seemed to offer the only hope of protection of individual rights, indeed of individual survival. Yugoslavia was being torn apart and devoured by civil war between nationalist extremists, who naturally magnified all differences between peoples. The nationalists focused on differences in religion, nationalist traditions, and ideologies. The Communists' rejection of traditional national ideologies and their successful struggle against "fratricidal war" converged with liberal democrats' belief in individual rights, for that belief led them to oppose nationalist extremism during the war, which in turn made them pro-Yugoslav (though neither centralists nor unitarists). Antinationalist and pro-Yugoslav attitudes led naturally to support for the only group that represented the whole of Yugoslavia and had fought successfully both against the powers that occupied it and those engaged in nationalist civil war.[100]

Counterrevolutionaries without Counterrevolution

Postwar Yugoslav historiography claims that the government in exile represented and defended the "old" Yugoslavia and its social, economic, and political order. This description is true in the sense that a large majority in the London government opposed the Communist revolution and its program, which demanded a radical transformation of Yugoslavia. The government in exile, however, was not fighting for a return to the *status quo ante bellum.* Though opposed to the Yugoslav Communist revolution (which was threatening to remove its members from the Yugoslav political scene forever), it never engaged in a real counterrevolution (that is, in a united effort against the CPY and the Partisan movement).

However, the failure of the Yugoslav government to create a program of counterrevolution was not due solely to the primacy of national feeling over fear of Communism or to Croatian-Serbian conflict. The ancien régime, which the counterrevolution should have defended, was itself rather amorphous. What, indeed, was the ancien régime? The dictatorship of King Aleksandar and the unitary, centralist state that it established? Or the "order" of the Banovina of Croatia? Or Serbian parliamentarism before the First World War, the memories of which were still strong in many Serbian politicians? Yugoslavia had existed for a very short time and had never properly constituted and stabilized itself. It did not have any generally accepted political institutions, nor did it have an established all-Yugoslav political elite. It was divided by different cultural, religious, political, and regional traditions. Above all, there was deep disagreement between the two largest nations over its structure and its most essential institutions.

So, although the government in exile knew that it was against Communism, it did not know, and perhaps could not know, what it was for. The Communists, on the other hand, had a clear program. Their ideological unity helped them to achieve organizational and political unity. They viewed their future, or believed they viewed it (and in this case it is not important if it was a reality or a phantasm), with more clarity than the politicians in the government in exile "saw" the past order in which they had participated.

six
———

Federalism and Yugoslavism, 1943–1953

The Communist Rise to Power

In applying to Yugoslavia Hugh Seton-Watson's three-stage model of the Communist seizure of power in eastern Europe, Dennison Russinow notes that "the CPY had entirely skipped the first [stage], a 'genuine coalition' with non-communist parties, and had paid only passing respect to the second, the 'bogus coalition,' in order to achieve international recognition and formal legitimacy."[1] This "one-and-a-half" stage theory shows in a succinct way that Yugoslav Communists were faster than any other Communist party in eastern Europe in taking power and in moving from hegemony over other parties (the "bogus coalition") to a complete monopoly of power (the "monolithic stage" in Seton-Watson's terminology).

Most of the time during the war the CPY tried to unite all "patriotic," "antifascist" forces in an all-Yugoslav "national-liberation struggle." This policy proved sufficiently broad to draw many members of different political parties into the Partisan movement. In its propaganda the CPY often claimed that it was just a leading member of a democratic coalition in which independent groups enjoyed equal rights. When it occasionally admitted its primacy (the term *hegemony* was never used), the CPY tried to present it as benign. It justified it as a prerequisite for the organization of the armed struggle and for the suppression of the "fratricidal war." In its wartime propaganda the CPY vehemently rejected any suggestion that it might be imposing a hegemony with a malevolent purpose, such as preparing a "dictatorship of the proletariat." The CPY's leaders frequently reiterated that the party's dominance was purely a measure of expediency dictated by the needs of the "national-liberation struggle." The party pretended that its preponderance was only temporary and promised freedom for all political parties (except those that had collaborated with the enemy) after the liberation of the country.

The CPY's hegemony over other parties during the war was not imposed primarily by force. It was largely a consequence of the sheer military and political "weight" of its Partisan movement. In 1945–46 the party quickly moved into the monolithic stage, encountering less resistance than did other eastern European Communist movements. The strength of the party and the considerable popular support it gathered under enemy occupation helped the CPY, but so also did the degree of nationalist strife, primarily between the Croats and Serbs, and the ensuing political vacuum. The parties of the different nations of Yugoslavia were not only unable to create a common front against the Communists; they also often failed to prevent the Communists from inciting them against each other. The parties were also palpably fragile. Their weakness stemmed from the long period of royal authoritarianism of King Aleksandar and Prince Pavle, when continual conflict between Croats and Serbs had prevented the parties from uniting to oppose the pseudo-representative regime effectively. When the war came, none of the parties was able to organize resistance to the occupying powers. They found themselves incapable of struggling successfully against either the occupiers or the Communists.

The prewar Serbian predominance alienated all non-Serbian national groups. The Croatian national ideology became more attractive and more radical, until the mass of Croats opposed the very idea of a Yugoslav government. The conflict between the Croats and Serbs was the most important single cause of the malfunctioning of the prewar Yugoslav political system. During the war, it paralyzed the Yugoslav government in exile. It also accounted for the largest number of victims on Yugoslav territory in the Second World War, in the Ustasha genocide and in the internecine massacres and countermassacres by extreme Croatian, Serbian, and Muslim nationalists.[2]

The main criterion in most definitions of power and state power is a monopoly of military power over a given territory. In this sense, the CPY can be said to have already seized power at the moment during the Second World War when it became militarily stronger than all other Yugoslav military formations. At the latest, the Partisans can be considered to have established such military superiority in September 1943, when, upon Italy's capitulation, there was an enormous increase of territory, new recruits, and weapons and ammunition. (Italian troops in Yugoslavia surrendered most of their equipment to the Partisans.) Anyone who could have known then not only that the Axis would lose the war, but also that the western Allies would not invade Yugoslavia in order to suppress the Communists, could have predicted that postwar Yugoslavia would be a Communist state.[3]

The Yugoslav Communists, then, had already seized power during the war. After September 1943 the Partisans simply enlarged the territory under their control and further reinforced the power and hegemony of the CPY. Toward the end of the war, when the remnants of the old political parties tried to reenter the political arena, the Communists controlled almost all of Yugoslavia. The preclusion of any real political activity by non-Communist parties, rather than the destruction of a liberal-democratic political system (which simply did not exist), allowed the Communists to enter the monolithic stage.

Elsewhere in eastern Europe, Communist-led resistance gained control over larger territories only after the arrival of the Red Army and after the war seized power with the decisive help of the Soviet Union. In Yugoslavia, however, the Soviet Union did not have a significant part in the Communists' rise to power. Although the Red Army fought the retreating Wehrmacht in parts of Yugoslav territory in the second half of 1944, the Yugoslav Communists had by that time already inflicted decisive defeats upon their opponents in the civil war.[4]

When the Second World War ended in Europe in May 1945 the CPY, at the head of the victorious Partisan army, proceeded to consolidate its political power. The CPY was committed to the abolition of all other political parties. It anathematized any system in which different parties coexisted and competed, in which any one party held power as a result of free elections and only for a limited period, and in which the opposition was regarded as a necessary counterbalance to the party in power, and freedom of speech, press, and assembly were universal rights.

There were two ideological motives for the CPY's rejection of political pluralism. First, Marxism regards political parties as a "superstructure" of the capitalist social and economic order, whose hidden purpose is the perpetuation of that order. Second, Leninism maintains that a monopoly of power by a Communist party is a prerequisite for the revolutionary transformation of society. Reinforcing these ideological considerations was the temptation to enjoy the spoils of victory. The CPY's members were united in their belief in the need for the "dictatorship of the proletariat," that is, their party's monopoly on power. But some felt that the party should not try to establish a permanent monopoly over political, social, and economic life and should soon cease to rely on coercion as a means of enforcing its policies.

All prewar politicians, especially those who had spent the war in exile and had backed the non-Communist forces, were prevented from organizing their parties after the war. The CPY also used every opportunity to compromise its political opponents by portraying them as collaborators with the fascist occupiers of Yugoslavia. It used its control of the armed forces, police, and judiciary, all of which it had created during the war, to achieve its political goals. The Department for the Protection of the People (Odeljenje zaštite naroda), for example, was founded in May 1944 to serve as the CPY's military intelligence and political police. It had at that time been a part of the Partisan army.

For many Yugoslavs in the immediate postwar period, the non-Communist political parties lacked credibility or legitimacy, for a number of reasons.[5] (This, of course, was also a view that the CPY actively promoted in its propaganda.)

1. Many Yugoslavs considered political plurality to be a potentially destructive internal force. They felt that it would tend to cause strife and prevent the healing of the civil war wounds, especially those resulting from Croatian-Serbian conflicts.

2. The suppression of political parties in Yugoslavia in the interwar period and the lack of a developed democratic tradition in large areas of the country prevented many Yugoslavs from identifying with any political party or group. Often they simply had no comprehension of a multiparty system or of free elections.

3. Even the most important political parties had only a few dedicated political activists. In this sense even parties with large followings were weak.

4. A number of prominent politicians from the prewar parties had been members of the government in exile during the war, and their reputations had been sullied by the constant nationalist conflicts inside the cabinet.

5. The prewar political system was considered to have been corrupt, since many politicians had abandoned their parties in order to curry favor with King Aleksandar or Prince Pavle.[6] More important, the parties' failure vigorously to defend liberal democracy undermined the very foundation of a pluralist political system, since it lent an aura of normality to nonrepresentative rule.[7]

6. Each of the major prewar political parties drew its constituency from only one nation whose interests it primarily defended, and had no program for the national question in Yugoslavia as a whole. In contrast, the CPY was not only an all-Yugoslav party; it had also led an all-Yugoslav resistance movement and a substantial Yugoslav army recruited during the war. The CPY found backing for its brand of Yugoslavism among broad segments of the population, especially among the young. By calling public attention to those members of prewar parties who had joined nationalist forces that fought against both the Partisans and other extremist national groups, the CPY had considerable success in discrediting entire parties.

7. For most prewar Serbian parties, preserving the integrity of the state was more important than the form of the constitution or the preservation

of the liberal-democratic system. For the Croats, liberal democracy likewise took second place. Although they rarely expressed a demand for an entirely independent state, the concept of full sovereignty always underlay their nationalism. This autonomous Croatian state unit, and not parliament and free elections, was their chief goal.

The CPY and the CPP

In August 1941 the CPY leaders instructed the Central Committee of the Communist Party of Croatia (CPC) to try to cooperate with the CPP in creating resistance groups. Some CPP leaders had seemed to favor active and even armed resistance. In fact, however, the CPP never issued a public call for active resistance. On the contrary, it prescribed passivity and nonresistance. As early as the autumn of 1941 the Communists had begun to regard the CPP as their main political rival in Croatia (the Ustashas lacked any lasting political support) and concentrated on influencing and winning over its rank and file. The CPC tried to provoke Croatian peasants to rebellion with such radical tactics as precipitating armed clashes between the Ustashas and the peasants, with the calculated risk of Ustasha retaliations. As the war dragged on and its burdens and horrors seemed to demand drastic solutions, the continued passivity of CPP leaders alienated Croatian peasants in some regions. Toward the end of 1942 and the beginning of 1943, some local CPP leaders did start to cooperate with the Partisans; inevitably they fell under the control of the well-organized Communists.[8]

During the war the CPP proved unable to create a single armed Croatian unit. All speculation about the party's ability to form clandestine groups from among the conscript soldiers in the NDH or to bring the latter into the Allied camp turned out to be vastly exaggerated. To be sure, the Croatian peasants favored the Allies rather than the Germans, and many had supported the CPP in the interwar period and might do so again in the future. But that was all. Their resistance to the Ustashas had been unorganized and lacked leadership. When organized armed groups with Croatian members appeared, they were without exception under Partisan command. In the first half of 1944 the British concluded:

> There is no indication that [the CPP] has, or has had, any armed resistance organisation functioning under its control . . . Since April 1941 the CPP has shown no sign of constructive activity, nor has it developed any effective resistance movement of its own. [There was not even] a nucleus for any resistance group which might receive Allied backing as an alternative to support for the Partisans. The Partisans, for their part, appear to be attracting to their ranks a growing number of [CPP] adherents.[9]

During the war the Communists insisted that the only true representatives of the CPP were those who had joined the United Front of People's Liberation (JNOF; Jedinstveni narodno-oslobodilački front), an organization controlled by the CPY through which it continued its prewar Popular Front policy and which, needless to say, supported the Partisan movement. The CPP members who did join the JNOF were soon under the complete control of the CPY. The Communists made a considerable effort to adapt the ideas of Antun and Stjepan Radić, the founders of the party, to their own purposes, exaggerating the importance of "progressive" elements in the party ideology. The Croatian Republican Peasant Party had renounced its republicanism and changed its name to the Croatian Peasant Party in 1925. In 1945 the pro-Partisan leaders of the CPP hailed the formal abolition of the monarchy as the fulfillment of the republican hopes and dreams of the Radić brothers. But republicanism had never been a central issue for the Radićs. Their primary concerns had been the economic and social position of the Croatian peasantry, and Croatian national interests.[10]

The Communists described their federal organization of the Yugoslav state as another fulfillment of the goals of the Radić brothers. Indeed, the Radićs had tended to favor peaceful coexistence between Croats and Serbs, so it was not impossible that some kind of federal solution to the Croatian-Serbian conflict would have been acceptable to them. Yet they would never have accepted it under Communist domination. The CRPP's brief membership in the Comintern-controlled "Green International" was nothing more than an attempt by the desperate Stjepan Radić to find support wherever possible after his party had been banned. But the propaganda of the CPY and of the pro-Partisan leaders of the CPC interpreted the "Green International" episode as a sign of Radić's deep sympathy for the Soviet Union.

In general, the Communists tried to present to the Croatian peasant masses a mixture of their own and the CPP's ideology. Using the vocabulary and symbols of the CPP, and frequently imitating the CPP's demagogic rhetoric, they attacked the rich, advocated peasant socialism, proposed social reforms, and promised prosperity. They stressed the CPP's collectivist sentiments, often with stories and proverbs from village life. At first sight the peasant-populist ideology of the CPP appeared to be the very opposite of Marxism-Leninism: it emphasized the sacredness of family life and the importance of religion and tradition; it idealized nature and the peasant way of life. But the CPP ideology was not at all liberal democratic. It merged collectivism with openly authoritarian attitudes. The idea that a plurality of interests, political concepts, and parties could enrich and strengthen the nation was alien to the CPP. Politics was seen as one of the urban vices, and the corruption that was supposedly part of its nature was contrasted with the imputed sincerity and deep patriotism of peasants. The individual was seen principally as a member of social groups such as the family, village, and nation. Individualism was identified with selfishness, and the nation itself was not perceived as a complex, pluralistic entity, but as an enlarged patriarchal family. The Communists used the CPP's collectivist and authoritarian ideas to achieve their own goals. They helped pro-Communist CPP members to publish the journal *Slobodni dom* (Free Home), which supported Communist policies, in Croatia; in Bosnia-Herzegovina the pro-Communist faction of the CPP published a counterpart, *Hrvatski glas* (Croatian Voice).[11] *Slobodni dom* was full of stories, parables, and proverbs showing the need for unity and portraying the slightest opposition to the CPY as damaging to the unity and interests of the Croatian nation. It attacked the anti-Communists in the CPP and accused all Serbian opposition parties of favoring the restoration of prewar centralism and Serbian hegemony. These attacks by a Croatian political party upon Serbian political parties, and vice versa, made the CPY appear to be the sole alternative to Croatian-Serbian conflict. And they helped the CPY to achieve its goal: the abolition of all non-Communist parties, including the CPP. After the war *Slobodni dom*'s circulation quickly decreased. Even so, the Communist government of Croatia subsidized the journal until 1962, when it was finally allowed to die. Thus the CPY extinguished with relative ease the last remnants of the CPP, a party that had been one of the strongest in Yugoslavia throughout the interwar period.

On 13 June 1943 the Regional Anti-Fascist Council of the People's Liberation of Croatia (ZAVNOH; Zemaljsko antifašističko vijeće narodnog oslobodjenja Hrvatske) was created at the initiative of the CPY. Several influential members of the CPP belonged to ZAVNOH. But their faction of the CPP was prevented by the Communists from retaining its organizational structure, and all its efforts at independent political activity were frustrated. It was not allowed to hold meetings and recruit members, to reorganize its political cells and local units, or to give independent directives to those that still existed. With the approval of the Communists, the CPP members of ZAVNOH formed a new executive committee, which tried to deprive the old CPP leadership of its legitimacy. When CPP members in the Partisan movement demanded to be allowed to rebuild their own organizations, the CPY insisted that all activities be confined within "committees of people's liberation" (*narodno-oslobodilački odbori*). These committees were completely dominated by the CPY; they were, in fact, the civil and administrative sections of the Partisan army. The CPY justified the subjugation of the CPP as warranted by the struggle for national liberation: all forces had to be united under one leadership.[12] For tactical and propagandistic reasons the CPY allowed the pro-Partisan part of the CPP leadership to remain visible and vocal, but it retained complete control of its political "basis" through the committees of national liberation. This arrangement, established in wartime, made it relatively easy for the Communists to eliminate the CPP completely upon liberation.

In April 1944 the pro-Partisan CPP factions formed a new Croatian Republican Peasant Party in the village of Taborište in Kordun, at the center of a large territory under Partisan control. From the very beginning its leaders were aware that the independence of this new CRPP was illusory; the JNOF was not a democratic coalition. Yet most members seemed sincerely to believe that they were serving the best interests of the Croatian people. They were disappointed by the passivity of the old CPP leadership, admired the Partisan struggle, and believed that in wartime Croatia, divided as it was between the forces of the NDH and those of the Partisan movement, their choice must be for the latter. They expected the CPY to have a leading political role in postwar Yugoslavia. What they did not suspect was that the CPY would transform its wartime hegemony into a complete monopoly of power, extinguishing all forms of independent political activity.

The CRPP accepted the program of the JNOF and abandoned the prewar program of the CPP. In August 1945 the JNOF changed its name to the Popular Front. After the second congress of the Popular Front in September 1947, the CPY stopped sponsoring and supporting the CRPP. It had done its job for the Communists. In October 1950 the CRPP publicly acknowledged that it was no longer an organized political movement.

The Popular Front proclaimed, among other things, the abolition of the monarchy and the establishment of a republic with a federal system, the separation of church and state, and the nationalization of crucial branches of heavy industry. All prewar political parties that had joined the Popular Front were pressured into accepting its entire program. Those who in any way resisted were accused of never having sincerely accepted the program of the Popular Front and of having joined it for tactical reasons only. Serbian groups usually also heard that they were opposed to federalism, were seeking a return to centralism and great-Serbian hegemony, and were secret supporters of the Chetnik movement. Croatian groups were accused of harboring separatist tendencies, of scheming to establish a new NDH, and of sympathizing with the Ustashas. In fact, the CPY interpreted any opposition to its postwar rule as a prolongation of the country's internal wartime conflicts. This practice became institutionalized: as recently as the early 1980s the party-controlled press still accused democratic critics of the regime of sympathies for the Chetniks or Ustashas.

The Constitutional Development of Yugoslavia and Croatia

During the war the CPY organized a congress of its People's Liberation Movement. At its first meeting, on 26 and 27 November 1942, this "Partisan parliament," the Anti-Fascist Council of the People's Liberation of Yugoslavia (AVNOJ; Antifasištičko veće narodnog oslobodjenja Jugoslavije), proclaimed itself the only legitimate representative of the peoples of Yugoslavia. At its second meeting, on 29 and 30 November 1943, in the town of Jajce in one of the largest Partisan-controlled territories of Bosnia-Herzegovina, AVNOJ announced that after the war Yugoslavia would be organized on a federal basis.[13] Communist leaders considered it important to reassure Yugoslavia's national groups that there would be constitutionally guaranteed national equality after the liberation of the country. They also stated, however, that final decisions about the organization of the country would be made by popular vote after the war.[14]

The constitutional development of Croatia closely followed that of Yugoslavia, since both were directed by the CPY, of which the CPC was an integral part. ZAVNOH, the first Croatian "Partisan parliament" founded in June 1943, was a Croatian replica of AVNOJ. Similar councils were created in other territories that would become republics after the war. These were big steps toward the creation of the Yugoslav federation.

Postwar Communist historians emphasize the democratic character of the second meeting of AVNOJ and of the first meeting of ZAVNOH, supporting this claim by the fact that they were attended by delegates from different parts of Yugoslavia and Croatia. However, the delegates were either Communists or carefully selected fellow travelers and sympathizers. Both AVNOJ and ZAVNOH represented a continuation of the Popular Front tactics of the late 1930s: an alliance of all "progressive forces" against fascism. The crucial difference was that the Communists now completely dominated all other political groups.

Parts of the territory that ZAVNOH controlled were reconquered by Axis forces before passing again into Partisan hands. The local committees of people's liberation—the political-administrative cells that formed the basis of ZAVNOH—then resumed their efforts to achieve stability. ZAVNOH's main efforts were directed to increasing the territory under its control and consolidating it by establishing political, judiciary, and administrative structures. But it also denied the Yugoslav royal government in London the right to represent Croatia—a decision very popular with Croats, since the royal government and the Kardjordjević dynasty were considered instruments of Serbian interests. Further, it nullified the November 1920 Treaty of Rapallo, which had acknowledged Italian sovereignty over the Istrian peninsula, the city of Zadar, and some Adriatic islands, and announced the incorporation of these territories into Croatia and Yugoslavia.[15] Finally, it pronounced illegitimate all international treaties, agreements, acts, deeds, debts, and alliances made by the government of the NDH.

Many Croats accepted the solution to the national question proposed by AVNOJ and ZAVNOH. Great-Croatian solutions had been completely compromised by the Ustasha movement, and those attempted by the Chetniks and the Yugoslav government in London inspired mistrust and fear among Croats, since both were seen as representing great-Serbian ideology. ZAVNOH demonstrated to the Croats that the Communists were responding to their demands for national autonomy. Its activities and proclamations gave the Partisan movement in Croatia an aura of Croatian patriotism, and the Partisans were increasingly perceived as a mass movement at the same time Yugoslav and Croatian. In April 1945 ZAVNOH proclaimed itself the only Sabor (parliament) of Croatia, the supreme organ of the sovereign state power and the highest legislative body; it then proceeded to form the government of Croatia.

The Yugoslav Constitution of 1946

Toward the end of 1945 elections were held in Yugoslavia for the Constituent Assembly. The only list of candidates was that of the Popular Front, but it was possible to vote against it. The Popular Front probably would have won this first postwar election even if opposition had been allowed;[16] but Yugoslavia's Communist leaders wanted an overwhelming majority. For if the opposition had received a large enough share of votes, it would have been legalized and become a permanent factor of political life. Through the monopolistic use of mass communication and the intimidation of opponents and critics, the Communists garnered about 90 percent of the vote.[17]

On 29 November 1945 the newly elected Constituent Assembly abolished the monarchy and proclaimed Yugoslavia a republic based on the federal principle.[18] The constitution was adopted in January 1946, and the country was named the Federal People's Republic of Yugoslavia (FNRJ; Federativna Narodna Republika Jugoslavija). The Federal Assembly of the Federal People's Republic of Yugoslavia, consisting of the Federal Council and the Council of Nations, was established as the supreme legislative body.[19] This rubber-stamp parliament enacted laws valid for Yugoslavia as a whole, and (following the pattern of Soviet federalism) in the case of any discrepancy between them, federal laws superseded those of individual republics.

Six federal ministries were created: foreign affairs, defense, transportation, a merchant navy, post, and foreign trade. The ministries of the republics were either republican or federal-republican. The independence of republican ministries was partly nominal, since they were supervised by federal economic, planning, and political bodies. The "mixed," federal-republican, ministries—finance, interior, judiciary, industry, mines, trade and supplies, agriculture and forestry, labor, and construction— were to manage particular branches of the state administration indirectly through the ministries in individual-republics and directly in certain enterprises that were of importance to the state as a whole.[20]

The Four National Equalities of New Yugoslavia

The Yugoslav federation, as laid out in the proclamation of the second meeting of AVNOJ and the constitution of 1946, was founded on what could be termed "four equalities." These would survive numerous constitutional changes until the late 1960s and early 1970s, when relations among the Yugoslav nations were radically altered.

First, all Yugoslav citizens had equal rights and duties, regardless of nationality, race, or religion. Article 21 of the 1946 constitution stated: "Every legal act, which would give privileges to citizens or limit their rights on the basis of their belonging to a different nationality, race, or religion, as well as any preaching of national, racial, or religious hatred and disunity, is unconstitutional and punishable by law."

This article was a formal expression of national equality through "nation blindness," analogous to the "color blindness" sought in the United States. Such nation blindness had already existed in the CPY before the war and, during the war, in the Partisan army and Partisan-controlled territories. Most Partisans and Partisan sympathizers had considered nation blindness in the economy, educational system, army, and other realms to be not only the essential element in the solution of the national question, but more or less its complete solution. This was also how they had understood the wartime slogan "Brotherhood and unity": members of different nations of Yugoslavia would fight, work, and live together, with equal rights and duties.[21] As Communist power was extended to all areas of social and economic life, the principle came to be generally applied. This was indeed an important achievement of the Yugoslav revolution.

Second, the six republics of the new Yugoslavia—Bosnia and Herzegovina, Croatia, Macedonia, Montenegro, Serbia, and Slovenia—were proclaimed to be equal in all aspects of their rights and duties. This proved true in practice: no republic dominated any other. In official state and party documents, however, the equality of the republics was said to be based on their sovereignty. Yet in fact the republics were not sovereign. Not only were they ruled by the CPY, but the constitution itself severely limited the sovereignty of the republics. Article 9 stipulated that certain rights delineated by the federal constitution belonged only to the FNRJ; and article 11 demanded that the republics' constitutions conform to the constitution of the FNRJ.[22]

The republics' borders were created on partly national and partly historical principles. Because of the mixed population, it would have been impossible to create purely national republics even if that had been the primary concern of the CPY. Yet the republics were defined as sovereign homelands of sovereign nations: Croatia of Croats, Serbia of Serbs, and

Yugoslavia after 1945

so on. Minorities in the republics, however, had the same rights and duties as the majority. They therefore had the right to take part in all decisions affecting the sovereignty of the predominant national group and its republic. At the same time minorities were defined as part of their own nation; thus, the Serbian minority in Croatia was a part of the sovereign Serbian nation.[23] This meant that Serbs were entitled to sovereign rights within three sovereign republics—Serbia, Bosnia and Herzegovina, and Croatia—two of which were the sovereign homelands of other sovereign nations.[24] The same was valid for Croats, who lived not only in Croatia but also in Bosnia and Herzegovina and in Serbia. Finally, since all citizens of Yugoslavia had the same rights everywhere in its territory and could move freely from one republic to another, a citizen of any republic had the right to political participation in any other, if he decided to settle in it.[25]

Third, all nations of Yugoslavia were defined as equal. Article 1 of the 1946 constitution stated: "The Federal People's Republic of Yugoslavia is . . . a community of peoples with equal rights." There were five of these peoples: Croats, Macedonians, Montenegrins, Serbs, and Slovenes. South Slav Muslims in Bosnia and Herzegovina and other parts of Yugoslavia were not recognized as a nation, although they were often mentioned as a separate group. The mixed population of Bosnia and Herzegovina, for example, was always described as consisting of Serbs, Croats, and Muslims.[26] Equality of nations was a reality to the extent that there was no "leading nation" (whether in the CPY, the government or the state apparatus) to parallel the role and position of the Russian in the Soviet Union.

The fourth, and final, "equality" was established when the CPY considered it necessary toward the end of the war to speak of the equal contribution of all nations of Yugoslavia to the struggle for national liberation, and especially of the equality of Croats and Serbs in this respect. Characteristic of the mood of Yugoslav patriotism that prevailed in the Partisan movement and among broad segments of the population, this equality applied only to the South Slav nations of Yugoslavia. Non–South Slav minorities (especially Germans and Italians, but also Hungarians and Albanians) were excluded.

The CPY was reluctant to acknowledge that different nations of Yugoslavia had varied widely in their participation in the Partisan struggle. The party considered such blindness to differences essential in healing the wounds incurred during the bitter civil war. Also, to proclaim one nation superior to another in the national-liberation struggle seemed to the CPY to be very close to proclaiming it more revolutionary. Since the hierarchy of power in Yugoslavia was based on adherence to revolutionary ideals (the CPY as the revolutionary elite was the leading force in the country), a nation that was "more revolutionary" than its counterparts might also demand more power and a privileged position. In order to justify equality of rights, the CPY had to present the nations of Yugoslavia as having contributed equally to the revolution. Nor could the nations appear to have varied in the extent of their crimes and collaboration with the enemy.

The party's views on the contribution of different nations to the "national-liberation struggle" underwent great changes during the war. The CPY and Tito publicly lamented the lack of mass Croatian participation in the Partisan army in 1941 (blaming it primarily on the opportunistic policies of the CPP),[27] and in 1941 and 1942 often praised the Serbs for their mass participation in the Partisan army.[28] In 1941 and 1942 party propaganda described the extermination of Serbs in the NDH as an especially monstrous crime. Toward the end of the war the party spoke only of crimes against the peoples of Yugoslavia in general. The CPY never identified the whole Croatian nation with the Ustashas, and the Croatian people were never blamed for the Ustasha crimes. However, the CPY could not help admitting in 1941 and 1942 that a part of the Croatian population, especially in regions mixed with Serbs, supported the Ustasha movement. As the war drew to a close, the party's tone changed. Guilt for the crimes rested more and more on the ruling class— unpatriotic and antinational capitalist exploiters in Croatia. National conflict was reinterpreted as class conflict. Thus Ustasha genocide became a kind of "white terror": "oppressors" and "counter-revolutionaries" terrorized the "working people." Toward the end of the war and immediately after it national hatred was in general blamed on the ruling class and not at all on the "working people," despite the glaring counterevidence provided during the war. The war experience, in which simple peasants often fought each other, was conveniently forgotten. The purpose of the Communists' postwar reinterpretation of history was not only the consolidation of their own power, but also the strengthening of national equality.

Postwar Yugoslavism

Proceeding from the assumption that, once capitalism was abolished, there would be no national and colonial oppression,[29] Yugoslav Communists did not consider it necessary to draw up complicated federal arrangements or institutions. National freedom and equality would inevitably follow from a successful revolution. The party's confidence in the certainty of national justice for the oppressed nations was strengthened by the lack of national discrimination in the Partisan army during the war and the general success of Yugoslavism immediately after the war. The

Yugoslav constitution and other legal documents that guaranteed national rights were seen as primarily a formal institutionalization of something that already existed, a kind of legal advertisement of the Communists' success in solving the national question.

The Communists' wartime slogan "Brotherhood and unity" was not only intended to counter fratricidal war and disunity. It also symbolized their policy of pan-Yugoslav solidarity, cooperation among the nations of Yugoslavia, Yugoslav integration, and, ultimately, the creation of a Yugoslav national consciousness. The federal structure was not meant to erect barriers between the different nations of Yugoslavia. "Federalizing" the country and conferring national sovereignty on the republics occurred alongside the CPY's creation of organizations that, though divided into republican subbranches, were in their essence all-Yugoslav. Brigades of young volunteers were formed to work in different parts of Yugoslavia. The Alliance of the Communist Youth of Yugoslavia (Savez komunističke omladine Jugoslavije) had particular responsibility for propagating Yugoslavism among the young. The Yugoslav People's Army (Jugoslovenska narodna armija) continued the Yugoslavist traditions of the Partisan army, while units of soldiers made up of different national groups usually served outside the territory of their own republic. The Popular Front, the Anti-Fascist Front of Women (Antifašistički front žena), and numerous other organizations were Yugoslav in orientation. Professional, cultural, artistic, scientific, and sporting organizations were usually divided into republic subbranches, but all had influential headquarters in Belgrade.

The potential for creating a Yugoslav national consciousness seemed to be reinforced by the very existence of a united Yugoslav Communist party and by its successes in organizing and leading the Partisan army, which was also Yugoslav in spirit. If members of Yugoslavia's various national groups had worked and fought together in the party and the Partisan army in wartime, why should cooperation not be possible in peacetime? The Communists pointed out tirelessly that they had made decisive and irreversible progress toward the creation of a Yugoslav national consciousness and that Yugoslavism had, to a large extent, already become a reality. In addition, if one believed in a future Communist society, as Communists and their sympathizers did immediately after the war, then one believed not only in inevitable progress to a classless society of freedom, equality, fraternity, and abundance, but also in the establishment of a society in which Communist ideology was accepted by everyone and not just by the avant-garde. In other words, in the Communist future everyone would be a Communist. And since the party was Yugoslav, everyone in the not-too-distant Communist future would, therefore, be a Yugoslav.

The wartime and postwar Yugoslavism of the CPY was also in part the result of applying the ideology of Marxist-Leninist internationalism to internal Yugoslav national problems. Communists in general were opposed to "bourgeois" nationalism and believed in the creation of an international, or, more precisely, global, Communist society.[30] They also foresaw the complete disappearance of national consciousness, that is, of loyalty to a particular nation state. It followed that in countries and territories where they were active, Communists should try to prevent national conflicts, to minimize the importance of national differences, and to unite the working people of different nations. But if they did these three things in Yugoslavia—that is, if they fought against Serbian, Croatian, and other nationalism; if they attempted to reduce the differences between the nations of Yugoslavia and worked to unite all its working people (and that meant the majority of people)—then they were in practice working for Yugoslavia and Yugoslavism. The "internationalism" of the Yugoslav Communists was transformed into Yugoslavism.

For Yugoslav Communists after the war, Yugoslavism meant the eradication of political loyalties to particular nations in Yugoslavia and their transformation into a Yugoslav national consciousness. This process did not, however, presuppose the disappearance of ethnic and cultural differences or the abandonment of individual national languages. The ethnic, cultural, and linguistic characteristics of the nations of Yugoslavia ought to survive within the "new" Yugoslav national consciousness.

In brief, during and immediately after the war the CPY conceived of its Yugoslavism in three distinct ways: Yugoslavism was antinationalism—opposition to all the nationalisms of the nations that constitute Yugoslavia; Yugoslavism was patriotism—primarily the struggle for the liberation of Yugoslavia from the Germans, Italians, and others who had occupied it; and Yugoslavism was internationalism—the unity of the working people, who would disregard nationality in the struggle for a social revolution. The CPY incessantly pointed out the need for solidarity among the peoples of Yugoslavia and for their close cooperation in "our common struggle to build socialism," as well as stressing their common origin and ethnic and cultural similarities. Support for Yugoslavism was expressed in party documents, in books and articles dealing with Yugoslav politics, and in the writings and speeches of the leading party functionaries.

In the postwar years Josip Broz Tito, the leader of the party and the armed forces and the undisputed ruler of Yugoslavia, privately believed in the possibility of creating a Yugoslav nation. (The official CPY policy was one of strengthening Yugoslavism and developing Yugoslav national consciousness, but not of creating a Yugoslav nation.) Tito's vision of the future Yugoslav nation was not fundamentally different from that of the interwar supporters of the creation of a Yugoslav nation. Tito, of course, regarded the social and political system of prewar Yugoslavia as capitalist and backward, and thus as incapable of creating a Yugoslav nation.[31] He probably perceived backwardness as the main cause, since he could not have been unaware of the historical examples of nation-building by capitalist countries. But for Tito the power of socialism to create a new Yugoslav nation was not based solely on its supposed ability to overcome "backwardness" by promoting development and industrialization. In his mind, socialism was inseparable from the rule of the Communist party. This organized and powerful political force would utilize its all-encompassing "leading role" in society to educate new generations in the spirit of Yugoslavism.

In a speech in Zagreb in May 1945, immediately after its liberation, Tito promoted Yugoslavism and insisted that the borders of republics should not divide but unite the peoples of Yugoslavia.[32] This statement at first appeared contradictory; how could borders unite? At best they could be open, so that the divisions they caused might not be deep. Tito was actually reminding Croats that republics had been created primarily in order to dispel fears of Serbian hegemony over other nations and over Croats in particular. When understood in this way borders could indeed reduce the possibilities of national tension and conflicts, and Yugoslav federalism could indeed be a basis for the development of Yugoslavism.[33] The creation of federal units was a step backward in comparison with the Yugoslavism of the party and of the Partisan army during the war. For Tito, however, it was not an irreversible step backward but a preparation for the development of Yugoslavism.

At the founding congress of the Communist Party of Serbia in May 1945, Tito urged Communists to avoid arguing about republic borders.[34] Villages and towns within the borders of any republic belonged to the whole of Yugoslavia, he stated, and federal units were not to be considered independent states. On the contrary, there should be only one strong state for all Yugoslav nations: Yugoslavia.[35] Tito further argued that Communists should be the uniting bond among the peoples of Yugoslavia, and thus should fight against the "reactionary ideology" of nationalism. Yugoslav Communists should understand Yugoslavism as an indispensable part of Communist internationalism, he concluded, and regard all opposition to Yugoslavism as a form of "reactionary" nationalism.

The Right to Secede and the Fear of Separation

Drafted by Politburo member Edvard Kardelj with the help of legal scholars, the 1946 constitution of Yugoslavia almost replicated the Soviet constitution of 1936.[36] Critics of Yugoslav Communism often mention this as a proof of the "Stalinist" nature of the postwar Yugoslav political system.[37] But in fact this constitution of 1936 was not particularly Stalinist, since it guaranteed a multitude of rights to individuals and to nations. The fact that the Soviet leadership could nevertheless practice mass terror and national oppression was just a proof of the irrelevance of constitutions in Communist countries. The Soviet constitution guaranteed to its nationalities not only the right to self-determination and the right to secede, but also an independent foreign policy and independent armed forces.[38] The constitution of Yugoslavia did not grant republics the right to an independent foreign policy and armed forces. Tito was also initially opposed to granting them the right of self-determination (including the right of secession). Considering that such a right would have been a sheer formality (since all the power was in the hands of the CPY), it is significant that Tito was even concerned about it. His apprehension was primarily caused by the extremism and crimes of the separatist nationalist movements, especially of the Ustashas during the war. He finally consented when he was reminded that such a right was a part of the program of the CPY before the war, that the Comintern advocated it, and that it had roots in the traditions of most European socialist parties.[39]

The drafters of the constitution then worded article 1 to state that Yugoslavia was "a community of equal peoples that, on the basis of self-determination, including the right of secession, have expressed their will to live together in a federal state." This was principally an acknowledgment of the abstract existence of that right before the creation of "new Yugoslavia."[40] Moša Pijade, a member of the Central Committee, was probably the most persistent defender of what might be called a "once and for all" interpretation of the unification of Yugoslav nations. Fearful that the constitution might be interpreted as permitting separation, Pijade insisted that, according to article 1, Yugoslav nations had exercised that right once and for all at the moment when they decided to join in a Yugoslav federation. In other words, the creation of Yugoslavia was irreversible, the decision of Yugoslavia's peoples irrevocable, and the right to secede and to create a separate state neither permanent nor inalienable.[41] Since, however, there was no particular historical moment or event when the peoples of Yugoslavia actually expressed their desire to live in Yugoslavia (there never was, for example, a referendum), Yugoslav Communists sometimes argued that the Partisan national liberation struggle represented such an act of state building and state constituting.[42]

This line of reasoning was never incorporated into official party and state documents, but it was tacitly accepted. For example, Vladimir Nazor, the president of the Croatian Sabor, believed that the Partisan struggle was a kind of all-Yugoslav referendum in favor of Yugoslavia. He said that the people had voted for the creation of new Yugoslavia with "lead balls," and that this fact made voting with rubber balls (which were used in elections because a large percentage of the population was illiterate) superfluous.[43] Before the war, Nazor had been one of the best-known Croatian poets. Though a non-Communist, he joined the Partisans because he was dismayed by the persecution of Serbs in the NDH and saw the Partisans as the only force capable of stopping the escalation of civil war between Croats and Serbs. For Nazor and many others, the fear of renewed conflict between Croats and Serbs reinforced their Yugoslavism.

Soon after the constitution of Yugoslavia was proclaimed in January 1946, the six republics devised their own constitutions. These repeated the general principles of the Yugoslav constitution and added articles relating to the specific problems of their areas of jurisdiction. The constitution of Croatia, adopted on 18 January 1947, granted the right of secession to the Croatian nation but did not describe this right as either inherent or inalienable. The constitution of Croatia did not state precisely whether Croatian participation in the Yugoslav federation was based on an irreversible renunciation of some or all of Croatia's sovereignty, or if this sovereignty remained intact.

In any case the republics' right to secede was chimerical. There was no political organization other than the CPY, let alone a nationalist one, that could organize a movement for separation; and the party's policy was to strengthen Yugoslavia and Yugoslavism and to punish any form of nationalism and separatism. Article 21 of the constitution, which stated that "any preaching of national, racial, or religious hatred and disunity" was unconstitutional and punishable by law, was used as a legal basis for criminal proceedings. This article, together with certain paragraphs of the criminal code, was interpreted very loosely by the Communist police and courts to suppress all forms of nationalism and separatism.

Revolution and the New Nationalism

Seen in the context of the civil war and prewar Serbian predominance, federalism and Yugoslavism were great steps toward national tolerance and cooperation among the nations of Yugoslavia. There were, however, new forms of nationalism, nationalist prejudice and persecution, which arose in the euphoria that enveloped the CPY after its victory.[44]

The party regarded its ideology as corroborated by history and believed that its power could not be challenged by any internal force. It did not see any obstacles in economic affairs, national relations, or society in general that it could not overcome. The CPY's pride was further increased by the high standing it enjoyed in the world Communist movement, and by the praise it received from the Soviet leadership. This revolutionary zeal spread through the Yugoslav population, particularly among young people. As a result Yugoslav Communists felt free to interfere in the affairs of other Communist parties. At various times, in various combinations, and in various ways they gave advice, criticism, military help, economic help, protection from Soviet pressures, and offers of alliance, economic cooperation, and cultural exchange to the Albanian, Bulgarian, French, Greek, Hungarian, and Italian Communists. Many Communist as well as non-Communist movements and states inevitably perceived such an ambitious policy as a form of rather presumptuous nationalism.

The CPY almost always saw itself as a superior partner in its relations with all other Communist parties, except with the Soviet one. The Soviet party saw itself as a superior partner in its relations with all other Communist parties, including the Yugoslav. Soviet foreign policy, including relations with other Communist parties, was consciously and consistently imperialist. Managed by Stalin and Molotov, it aimed at the global expansion of the Soviet state through propaganda, diplomacy, support for "progressive movements," economic aid, and, when the opportunity presented itself, military intervention. Yugoslav Communists in these postwar years did not try to impose their rule upon the Communist movements and countries of southeastern Europe. Nor were they planning to exploit them economically or to force them to adopt Yugoslav culture. Yet they were possessed by a passionate desire to spread the revolution in southeastern Europe and were certain that Yugoslavia should be at its center. Such ambitions and aspirations in the world Communist movement and in international affairs in general were a form of nationalism. And many Yugoslavs, gripped by revolutionary enthusiasm, believed that Yugoslav peoples were superior to many other nations in their courage and love of liberty. This Yugoslav nationalism influenced attitudes toward non-Yugoslav minorities, especially the Hungarian minority in Vojvodina and the Albanian minority in Kosovo, which were treated with deep mistrust anyway because of their wartime support of the occupying forces.

The worst displays of Yugoslav nationalism were the expulsions of the German minority from Vojvodina into Germany and of the Italian minority from Dalmatia and Istria into Italy.[45] (It is unclear, however, how many Germans and Italians left from fear of retribution, even before they encountered the Partisans, and how many were forced to leave.) During the war the majority of Germans in Yugoslavia did welcome the occupation of Yugoslavia and supported the Third Reich, and a considerable number volunteered for the German army and the SS. Yet to hold an entire national group responsible for war crimes and to punish it collectively was incompatible with the proclaimed principles of the Yugoslav Communist revolution. The expulsion of the Germans was partly influenced by similar expulsions from other eastern European countries, but it also reflected simple hatred and desire for revenge. It was also a means of compensating the people from poor mountainous regions devastated by war (such as those in Bosnia and Herzegovina, Lika, Dalmatia, and Montenegro) with the rich and fertile land of Vojvodina.

The inventory of forms of nationalism in postwar Yugoslavia would be incomplete without mention of a peculiar version of supranational nationalism, whereby the Soviet Union tried to create an ideology of Slav unity and solidarity that would transcend individual nationalities. This neo-pan-Slavism was employed to increase Soviet influence in the Slav countries. Its roots lay in the Soviet war propaganda, which used Marxism-Leninism with restraint, but was full of Russian patriotism often expressed in the language of traditional Russian nationalism and populism.[46]

Toward the end of the war Soviet leaders revived traditional pan-Slavism. Nazi persecution of Slavs and Nazi anti-Slav racism were used to increase the Slav nations' sense of common identity.[47] Soviet pan-Slavist propaganda claimed that the Soviet Union and the "great Russian nation" were the protectors and leaders of all Slavs. All-Slav committees were formed on Soviet initiative with branches in capital cities of Slav countries. However, when the Soviet-Yugoslav conflict came into the open in 1948, Yugoslav contacts with eastern European Slav nations ceased. Soon afterward pan-Slavism was expunged from the official ideology.

The Establishment of the Borders of Croatia

Article 12 of the Yugoslav constitution of 1946 stated that the borders of republics could not be altered without their agreement.[48] However, all major decisions about the creation of republics, including their borders, made by the leaders of the centralized and monolithic CPY. ZAVNOH did not specify at first what it considered to be the territory of Croatia, but the NDH was generally regarded as an expansionist enlargement reflecting the demands of extreme Croatian nationalists. In November 1943 Bosnia and Herzegovina, which had been integrated into the NDH, formed its own antifascist council and was recognized as a separate unit. The party finally decided that Croatia should comprise most of the territory of the prewar Banovina of Croatia and all Croatian lands taken by Italy on the basis of the Treaty of Rapallo. Croatia thus increased its territory considerably in Dalmatia and with Istria but lost the part of Bosnia and Herzegovina that had been included in the Banovina of Croatia before the war. The incorporation of this territory into the new republic of Bosnia and Herzegovina respected the historical borders of that province, confirmed at the Congress of Berlin in 1878.

The establishment of the borders of the republics aroused only minor disagreements among the Communists and no great excitement among the general population, with the exception of Croatian and Serbian nationalists. But they did not dare to express dissatisfaction, since it would have been immediately identified with "Ustasha ideology" or "Chetnik ideology."

The Croatian Communist leader Andrija Hebrang voiced his reservations about the borders of Croatia to his colleagues in the CPC. However, he found no significant support for his views, since these closely resembled traditional Croatian nationalism. There was more interest in the CPC for Hebrang's view that Srem should be included in Croatia.[49] This region, between the Sava and Danube rivers, was historically a part of the province of Slavonia, and the Partisan movement in Srem had been closely connected with the Slavonian Partisans and the CPC during the war. But its contacts with the Communists in Serbia had also been strong. Moreover, the Serbs were a majority in Srem, and their wartime experience with the Ustashas was no different from that of Serbs in other parts of the NDH. Great numbers had participated in the Partisan movement and were committed to the new Communist Yugoslavia. When the Croatian proposals reached them, they protested.

The border in Srem between Serbia and Croatia was finally established solely on the basis of nationality: its meandering path between villages reflected whether a majority of Croats or of Serbs lived in each place.[50] Most of Srem went to Vojvodina, an autonomous province of Serbia; a few western districts went to Croatia. Although the Croats were a majority in several areas of Vojvodina, the CPY feared that to include those areas in Croatia would leave the Hungarian minority in Vojvodina too strong in relation to the Yugoslav population. Also, their inclusion, since they were not always directly bordering with Croatia, would have relegated parts of the Serbian population to Croatia.

Another small disagreement (never publicly expressed) in establishing Croatia's borders arose concerning the status of Boka Kotorska, the area surrounding a large bay in the south Adriatic, which became part of Montenegro. It was contiguous to Montenegro, and the majority of its population wanted to be a part of that republic. Yet until the end of the First World War it had been part of the Austro-Hungarian province of Dalmatia, and Croatian nationalists traditionally claimed that this fact entitled Croatia to it.[51] Minor changes of borders between republics continued into the 1950s, negotiated directly between the republics.[52]

Toward the very end of the war and immediately afterward Communists in Dalmatia demanded autonomy for that province, partly in order to increase their power and political status. They based their demands on Dalmatia's historical autonomy and the relative autonomy of the Partisan movement there. Some Dalmatian Communists claimed that Dalmatia had a long-standing political identity (along with Slavonia and inner Croatia, it was one of the three kingdoms into which Croatia had been divided since the late Middle Ages), and that during the war the Dalmatian Partisans had often fought under independent command.

This demand for autonomy also reflected the fact that Dalmatia was traditionally the most pro-Yugoslav Croatian province.[53] Moreover, after the NDH had recognized its incorporation into Italy in accordance with the Rome agreements of May 1941, the animosity of the population toward the Ustasha movement became enormous and support for the Partisan army very strong. Toward the end of the war and afterward, many Dalmatians saw Yugoslavia as the only guarantee of Dalmatia's independence from Italy and deeply resented even the mildest forms of Croatian separatism. However, the demands for Dalmatian autonomy met with energetic resistance from other Croatian Communists and were soon abandoned.

Another plan rejected by Croatian Communists and by Tito was one proposed during the war by Moša Pijade, a member of the Central Committee of the CPY, together with some Serbian Communists, for an autonomous region for Serbs in Croatia. Serbs lived dispersed in different parts of Croatia, mostly together with Croats. But in part of the territory of the former Habsburg Military Frontier (Lika, Kordun, and Banija), there were approximately a dozen semiconnected districts in which Serbs represented a majority. Yet since this territory was small, and since Serbs and Croats were already united in the Partisan units and within the CPC, there seemed to be no need for Serbian autonomy. Political considerations also played a part in the rejection of this plan. Toward the end of the war and immediately afterward the CPY was fighting to gain the support of the Croatian masses and considered that the creation of a Serbian autonomous region in the center of Croatia would have been unpopular with them.

Serbs were strongly represented in the CPC, especially in the lower and middle ranks. There was also a considerable number of Serbs from Croatia in the Yugoslav People's Army and police (their representation decreasing from lower to higher ranks). Both phenomena were the result of Serbs' mass participation in the armed struggle, which in turn was to a considerable extent a consequence of the Ustasha terror.[54] The rights of Serbs in Croatia were guaranteed by the constitution of Croatia. The Serbian cultural organization Prosvjeta, founded by the Communists and their sympathizers in the autumn of 1944 in the Partisan-controlled territory of Croatia, had a primarily political purpose: to show Serbs in Croatia that their national individuality and national rights would be respected in the new Croatia. The educational and other institutions of

Serbs in Croatia, some of which were formed during the last phase of the war, were created with the help of the government of Croatia. In the late 1940s and early 1950s these organizations withered away or merged with similar Croatian organizations.

The cultural autonomy of Serbs in Croatia was from the start meant to be primarily symbolic; in general, Serbs were expected to work together with Croats in all aspects of social, economic, and cultural life. The educational program, for example, was adopted for the whole of Croatia, and there were no separate Serbian newspapers or radio stations or even radio programs. Children in all schools in Yugoslavia were taught both the Latin and Cyrillic alphabet, but in Croatia Latin was dominant. The prevailing view after the war was that the people of Yugoslavia should build one common socialist Yugoslav culture, learn the history of all the Yugoslav peoples (and in so doing stress their common traditions), and read the literary works of writers from all parts of Yugoslavia. Neither Croatia nor any other republic was encouraged to develop a separate cultural life; rather, they were expected to integrate themselves into one Yugoslav culture. There were no attempts to develop cultural autonomy for Serbs in Croatia because Croatian culture was itself becoming a part of Yugoslav culture.

As long as Yugoslavism was strong and Croatia was participating in the creation of an all-Yugoslav culture, Serbs in Croatia seemed to accept inclusion of their organizations and institutions in the Croatian ones and did not insist on developing cultural autonomy. But in the late 1960s and early 1970s, when the Yugoslav federation began to transform itself into a confederation, and Croatia began to transform itself into a uninational state, Serbs in Croatia inevitably began to perceive themselves as a national minority. In "Yugoslav Croatia" Serbs could easily feel at home and a part of the community, but this was much more difficult in a "Croatian Croatia." Serbian intellectuals in Croatia and other parts of Yugoslavia began to make demands for Serbian cultural and educational autonomy.

Immediately after the war the position of Croats in Bosnia and Herzegovina was rather difficult. Large numbers of them had participated in the Ustasha movement, while many Serbs had joined the Partisans.[55] Croats in this province were underrepresented at all levels, especially in the army and the police, and the authorities regarded any insistence on Croatian national individuality with particular suspicion. (A similar response met any expression of Serbian national feeling in regions that had supported the Chetnik movement during the war.) In western Herzegovina, where the Ustashas were particularly strong, Croats were considered almost an enemy population. There was also a tendency (which was never allowed to develop) among the lesser Serbian party functionaries in Bosnia and Herzegovina to see Serbs in that republic as a nation that was progressive, revolutionary, patriotic, and pro-Yugoslav, and Croats as reactionaries, counterrevolutionaries, traitors, and chauvinists.

The All-Yugoslav Character of Political Power

The CPY's experiences through many years of clandestine struggle, as well as during the war, seemed to show that for the achievement of revolutionary goals, principles of unity and centralism were superior to any other organizational model. Also, both the Soviet party and the Soviet state were organized along those lines. Further, the Marxist-Leninist approach to economic affairs presupposed centralized planning: large enterprises, heavy industry, five-year plans, and so on.[56] Yugoslav Communists therefore considered a unitary and centralized state a prerequisite not only for "fighting the class enemy" but also for "building socialism."

Postwar Yugoslavia was both centralized and unitarist, but in a way that differed considerably from either the Soviet Union or prewar Yugoslavia.[57] The great majority of Serbian Communists were genuinely enthusiastic about Yugoslavia and totally rejected any traditional Serbian aspirations for predominance. Though dependent on the decisions of federal institutions, party leaders of republics were far from being simply officials appointed from above, whose sole function was to execute obediently orders and plans emanating from the center. They were people with their own revolutionary, wartime, and political biographies, with roots in the party of their region and nation, and with reputations and personal authority. They had a certain independent political weight and authority and could make themselves heard at the party center.

Many Croats played an extremely important role in party and state institutions outside the borders of Croatia. They were strongly represented in the highest positions in the diplomatic service, the army, and the state security service. Josip Broz Tito, a Croat, was the central political personality of Yugoslavia from 1945 until his death in 1980 and (for varying lengths of time) held the offices of secretary general of the CPY, prime minister, minister of defense, president of the republic, marshal of Yugoslavia, and supreme commander of the armed forces.[58]

The Conflict with the Soviet Union

The conflict between Yugoslavia and the Soviet Union that came to a head in the summer of 1948 considerably increased Yugoslav patriotism. Stalin's attempts to control and subjugate the CPY and to integrate

Yugoslavia into the Soviet empire met with resistance from Yugoslav Communists. These, however, did not subsequently eliminate internationalism from their ideology, nor did they ever define themselves as "national communists." (This label, like the label "Titoism," was invented by western commentators and political analysts, who remain to this day the sole users of such terms.) But no matter how passionately they claimed that it was Stalin who had betrayed Lenin's internationalism and that they had always remained faithful to it, Yugoslav Communists became completely isolated in the world Communist movement. Communist parties without exception followed Soviet instructions and joined the campaign of abuse directed against Yugoslav Communists. Previously admired and envied by other Communist parties as the world's "purest" and most successful revolutionary movement during and immediately after the Second World War, and as the only one that could be compared with Soviet Communists, the Communists of Yugoslavia now became "imperialist agents" and "fascists." The Yugoslavs countered with passionate attacks on Soviet imperialism and also began to emphasize the individuality and "originality" of the Yugoslav revolution, as well as the fact that they had received no Soviet assistance (military or otherwise) during the first few years of the war.[59]

Outside pressures brought to the fore the need for ideas and policies that would promote internal unity in Yugoslavia. The party began to underline especially the deep historical roots of Yugoslav identity and even more to affirm common Yugoslav historical traditions and cultural affinities. It particularly praised nineteenth-century political and cultural figures who had propagated the Yugoslav idea.[60] Some influential Croatian and Serbian Communist intellectuals even tried to promote a certain romantic revolutionary Yugoslavism and defined the spirit of independence and rebellion as the essential characteristic of South Slavs.[61] They based their views on the example of South Slav medieval Christian heretics who had opposed the power and dogma of both Rome and Constantinople, and the enormous power of resistance the South Slavs showed during their struggles for independence from the Ottoman and Habsburg empires. Both the struggle for national liberation during the Second World War and the challenge to Stalin's hegemony over the Communist world were presented as the greatest twentieth-century achievements of this Yugoslav fighting spirit. This romantic ideology never became official party doctrine, but it was encouraged all over, particularly in education.

During the critical years of the conflict with the Soviet Union, loyalty to Yugoslavia was firmly established as being superior to international Communist loyalty or loyalty to one of the nations that constitute Yugoslavia. However, good Communists and good Yugoslavs were not expected to abandon either internationalism or their nationality. Yugoslavism was nevertheless expected to be their first loyalty in the event of conflict between Yugoslavia's independence and interests on the one hand, and internationalism or any particular nationalism on the other. Official Yugoslav Communist doctrine asserted that there could be no conflict among these three loyalties, except through a distortion of one of them. If these loyalties were "healthy" and "socialist," they would coexist harmoniously. Stalinism was presented as a perversion of internationalism, and "bourgeois" nationalism as a perversion of loyalty and affinity to one's nation. Similarly, prewar centralism and unitarism were seen as abuses of Yugoslavism.

This strengthening of Yugoslavism did not result in a permanent expansion of the state apparatus or further limitations on individual freedom. Conflict with the Soviet Union did indeed initially increase the power of the state, especially of the army and the state security service. A stronger army was needed to defend against possible Soviet invasion, as was a more active state security to root out Soviet spies and supporters. But the resistance to Soviet pressures also encouraged demands for change. When the immediate threat of the Soviet invasion decreased, liberals in the party began to struggle for democratic reforms.[62] The liberal reformers saw the enormous power of the party's bureaucracy as the main obstacle to the free development of Yugoslav social and economic life in general.

At the party's sixth congress in Zagreb in November 1952, the CPY leadership concluded that the Leninist type of monolithic, disciplined, centralized, and hierarchical party was obsolete once the conditions of clandestine work and armed struggle had disappeared.[63] In a postrevolutionary society such a party inevitably thwarted the development of democratic socialism. At the congress the CPY changed its name to the League of Communists of Yugoslavia (LCY; Savez komunista Jugoslavije), and the Politburo was renamed the Executive Bureau. The LCY leadership decided that the party should be transformed into a movement of socialist forces, and should not command, but become primarily an ideological center. It should not demand unanimity from its members, especially not on theoretical questions. The power should devolve toward the "basis," toward factories and communes. Genuinely free discussions should take place there, and freely elected delegates should be sent to higher political bodies and assemblies. At no point, however, was this democratization meant to strengthen the independence of the republics at the expense of federal bodies, or to increase national loyalties at the cost of Yugoslav patriotism and Yugoslavism in general. On the contrary, introducing direct democracy into boroughs and factories and democratizing the party were expected to promote Yugoslavism.

Self-Management and Yugoslavism

During the 1950s the LCY developed the concept of self-management into the ideological foundation of the economic, social, and political order. Party theoreticians defined it as the only way of developing socialism and as something all countries should adopt. Yet although the concept was meant to be of universal validity, self-management was still considered a specific creation of the Yugoslav revolution and was supposed to prove the superiority of the Yugoslav model of socialism. Through workers' control of the economy and through citizens' direct democratic control over political bodies, self-management was meant to curb the power of the bureaucracy. In this way, it would democratize society and move it toward the withering away of the state and the establishment of a classless and stateless Communist society. Although self-management should cause Yugoslavia as a state to wither away, Yugoslavism was expected to continue developing. Direct democracy in economic and political life would unite the nations of Yugoslavia without coercion, and the bonds thus created would be strong and lasting.

In the 1960s Yugoslavia began to reform its federal structure. The Communist bureaucracies of the six component Yugoslav republics and two autonomous provinces (supported by Tito and by Kardelj, at that time seemingly Tito's heir) favored decentralization, strengthened the independence of their "mini"-states, and increased their own power. Self-management was now interpreted as a force contrary to Yugoslavism. The concept of Yugoslavism was increasingly associated with the federal levels of bureaucratic power in Belgrade, while self-management was regarded as favoring the autonomy and sovereignty of the republics and autonomous provinces. Every aspect of self-management that had previously been considered opposed to any kind of bureaucracy and to the state apparatus in general was now used as a criticism of the Yugoslav federal bureaucracy and the central administrative apparatus in Belgrade. Every gain in the power of political and economic bodies of the component republics and provinces as opposed to the center was now proclaimed to be a strengthening of direct democracy.

Like many other central concepts in the ideology of Yugoslav Communism, self-management could be interpreted in almost any way, if the relationship of power so allowed it. In the late 1960s power was being transferred into the hands of those who favored more independence for the constituent republics and provinces. The fact that their interpretation of self-management was contrary to the whole postwar Communist theory and practice about the relations among the Yugoslav nations did not seem to matter in the least. Yet the logic behind the initial idea that self-management would weaken the republics and provinces and strengthen

Yugoslavism was more convincing. For if one believed that socialism united nations, then it was natural to expect that self-management, as an important step in the development of socialism, should contribute to greater unity among the nations of Yugoslavia, and in this way to Yugoslavism. Moreover, since the six republics of Yugoslavia had certain characteristics of states, and self-management was meant to be an antistatist way of organizing the society and economy, and to contribute to the withering away of the state, it should inevitably lead toward the weakening of sovereignty and independence of the republics. It was expected that Yugoslavia as a state would also wither away once the system of self-management was sufficiently developed, but that Yugoslavism would remain. The first to wither away would be republics as states, since they expressed traditional national consciousness and were not indispensable to the development of socialism. For all of these reasons "conscious" socialist forces were expected to be Yugoslav, and in general Yugoslavism was a positive goal.

The Constitutional Law of 1953

The constitutional law of 1953 radically changed the 1946 constitution of Yugoslavia and was recognized by Yugoslav legal scholars as almost a new constitution.[64] By abandoning the previously sacred Soviet model and creating a new and "original" constitution, Yugoslav Communists were emphasizing their independence from the Soviet Union and trying to create a legal symbol for the individuality of the Yugoslav revolution.[65] The constitutional law was meant to be an instrument for achieving greater democracy, that is, to serve as a legal framework for the development of a socialist system that would be different from Soviet Stalinism. Since there was indeed a wave of liberalization in the early 1950s, the new law was greeted enthusiastically by many people both inside and outside the party. Of the many constitutional experiments and innovations in postwar Yugoslavia, including the last constitution of 1974, this was the only one that aroused genuine hopes for more freedom.

The constitutional law defined Yugoslavia primarily as a union of producers and a community of people whose "socialist consciousness," based on the practice of self-management, superseded their national consciousness. The sovereignty of the individual republics was founded on the working people (the producers) and not the people as a whole. The People's Republic of Croatia, for example, was proclaimed to be "a socialist state of the working people of Croatia, united by their free will with the working people of other republics in the Federal People's Republic of Yugoslavia."[66] With their superior socialist consciousness, the working people would create a united Yugoslav national consciousness. Party theoreticians insisted that there was one single Yugoslav working class, and since it was the main element of the working people, it seemed obvious that the working people would unite all the nations and republics of Yugoslavia.

The constitutional law of 1953 abolished the Council of Nations (one of the two chambers in the Yugoslav parliament), which represented the interests of republics and autonomous provinces. The Federal Council, which was the legislative assembly for the whole of Yugoslavia, remained, enlarged by the addition of some representatives from the Council of Nations. Although the parliament had only symbolic power, this change emphasized a tendency toward a "withering away" of republics. The ideology of the workers' control over economy and society through self-managing bodies was applied to the organization of the Yugoslav federation, and a new second chamber was created and named the Council of Producers. The constitutional law omitted the right of secession, mentioned in article 1 of the 1946 constitution. Although even that article implied that the creation of Yugoslavia was irreversible, its absence from the new constitution was a clear sign of further development toward Yugoslav unity.[67]

The Culmination of Yugoslavism

In the 1950s the party generally accepted the view that the national question in Yugoslavia had been completely solved.[68] It regarded Yugoslavism as a new "content" within the old "form," which would remain national, that is, Croatian, Macedonian, Serbian, and so on. These two Hegelian-Marxist concepts meant, in the context of the national question in Yugoslavia, that the individuality of nations (especially their linguistic and cultural identities) would be preserved, but that there would be a very high degree of communication and solidarity among the nations of Yugoslavia, combined with a primary loyalty to Yugoslavia and a sense of belonging to one community.

The party's belief that the future belonged to socialism and Yugoslavism seemed to be corroborated by young people's enthusiastic support for both. The new generation seemed to "breathe, think, and feel Yugoslav."[69] Although there was no coercion by the state apparatus forcing people to "breathe, think, and feel" in that particular way, any expression of nationalist and separatist ideas and demands, was punished by imprisonment, as was any opposition to Yugoslavism. The police and the courts interpreted these as "enemy propaganda" inspired by extreme nationalism. The Communists promoted Yugoslavism through the party-controlled mass media and educational system. But Yugoslavism among young people, which was at its peak in the 1950s, was not primarily a result of Communist indoctrination and coercion. Many felt genuinely attracted to the ideals of the revolution and socialism; the memories of fratricidal war were still fresh; and the legend of the Partisan struggle was still alive. Also, after the conflict with the Soviet Union, a strong and united Yugoslavia seemed to be the only way to preserve independence.

Communist theoreticians emphasized that the new Yugoslavism was not forced upon other nations by one hegemonistic nation, and that there was no similarity between it and the brand promoted by King Aleksandar. In its propaganda the party rejected political identification with any area smaller than the whole of Yugoslavia and stressed the idea that although the new Yugoslavism was not an attempt to create a new nation, the working people of Yugoslavia were of their own accord "merging into one whole."[70] Yugoslavism was to be something more and "higher" than the "old" national consciousness, which it would somehow include in itself in a changed form.[71]

The development of socialism was seen as both necessary and sufficient for the development of Yugoslavism, and Yugoslavism as something that promoted the development of socialism. This belief in the interdependence between socialism and Yugoslavism was, however, based not only on utopian hopes that a socialist and, ultimately, Communist society would unite people in fraternity and freedom, but also on certain rational and positivistic ideas. Mass literacy, education, and secularization would free the people from the "vestiges of the past" in their national consciousness, and industrialization would bring about general prosperity, large cities, and modern transportation. These developments would promote contact and communication among the peoples of Yugoslavia, and they would live more and more as a community. A redistribution in economic growth would reduce the discrepancies between the standards of living in different regions and republics. This process would also help to bring people socially and culturally closer. Similarity in people's conditions and ways of life would be not only a powerful unifying force but also a barrier to nationalist conflicts that had arisen in the past from economic inequalities.

In 1953 Edvard Kardelj gave the most complete and in some respects most radically pro-Yugoslav interpretation of the Yugoslav federation and of the future of Yugoslavia in general.[72] The "old type" of federation, that is, the one created immediately after the war, had been rendered obsolete by the development of socialism. On the basis of the common interest of the working people, and within the framework of an already developed and unified sociopolitical system, a "unified Yugoslav community" was coming into being. This new community was overcoming the national consciousness of individual nations without at the same time becoming a nation in the "old sense."

Conclusion

The Croats and the Serbs as separate nations have a history whose beginnings are lost in the depths of time. Their national identities are rooted in the memories and traditions of their medieval kingdoms. Despite the fact that they are old nations, neither their national identities nor the states they created were continuous. Hugh Seton-Watson calls such states as France, Britain, Sweden, Holland, and Russia "old, continuous," because they were formed over centuries by strong dynasties that consolidated their territorial expansion through homogenization.[1] The instability of the Croatian and Serbian medieval states, followed by the Ottoman conquests, interrupted the development of either two clearly separate identities or a homogeneous proto-Yugoslav one. In the nineteenth century the Croats and the Serbs found themselves lacking the strong state tradition that allowed the "old, continuous" nations to emerge as modern nation states.

The development of modern national consciousness in central and eastern Europe is usually described in terms similar to the following: "Here the ethnic community formed itself into a politically conscious nation, which then sought to secede from the large scale empire into which it had been incorporated and set up its own state, and then to unify within the expanded frontiers of that state all those who were felt to belong to the ethnic culture."[2] This statement is only partly true of Croats and Serbs. Ethnically and linguistically they were not separate, so differentiation rested primarily on historical memory, traditions, and religion. One could even say that Croats and Serbs are ethnically almost homogeneous, but are heterogeneous from the standpoint of national consciousness and loyalties. In fact the whole of Yugoslavia could be defined as a mono-ethnic state with three closely related languages (Macedonian, Slovenian, and Croato-Serbian or Serbo-Croatian) and many different national political consciousnesses.[3] When Yugoslavia was created in 1918, the South Slavs were not one nation. They had largely different political and state loyalties. Between the two world wars, national ideologies developed further and became widely disseminated.

In the interwar period the revolutionary loyalties of the Yugoslav Communists and their general attitude to the national question were cosmopolitan and internationalist. At the same time, Yugoslav Communists were also believers in Yugoslavism. Even when, in the late 1920s and early 1930s, the CPY became radically opposed to the continued existence of the Yugoslav state, Yugoslavism persisted among the party cadres. The CPY's call for the dissolution of Yugoslavia was primarily a revolutionary tactic designed to gain the support of dissatisfied nationalists within Yugoslavia. As good followers of Lenin, the Yugoslav Communists believed that by adopting this policy they were channeling the revolutionary energies of the "nationally oppressed masses." For Serbian Communists, opposition to a Yugoslav state in which Serbs were predominant in politics, the civil service, and the military served as final proof to their non-Serbian Communist comrades and their own revolutionary conscience that they had abandoned their nationalist prejudices and had committed themselves unconditionally to the defense of the "oppressed."

The Comintern considered the CPY too weak to be able to influence events in Yugoslavia. It therefore instructed the CPY to support anti-Yugoslav nationalists rather than try to moderate them and lead them directly toward Communist revolutionary actions. In this way the CPY was supposed to assist revolutionary upheavals in a country that the Soviet Union considered a potential enemy. It was only in the mid-1930s, in the period of the Popular Front, that Yugoslav Communists began to support the continuation of the Yugoslav state, although they continued to argue for national equality and the right of separation for non-Serbian nations. This was a more balanced approach to the national question than the previous one, and it meant blending Yugoslavism with demands for national emancipation. Toward the end of the Second World War this approach translated into the adoption of a federal system for Yugoslavia and a call for Yugoslav patriotism.

Both before and during the war there was little liberal-democratic opposition to Communism. Anti-Communism was mostly allied with authoritarian ideologies, and there was at the same time a direct correlation between the degree of anti-Communism and the degree of nationalism. During the war, both in the country and in the government in exile, nationalism was the dominant form of political consciousness. It brought Croats and Serbs into conflict with each other and prevented them from forming a united front against either the German and Italian occupiers or the Communists. In the context of a primarily nationalist civil war the Communists, with their federalist-Yugoslavist policies on the national question, appeared to be an enlightened movement. This perception of them played a decisive role in helping them achieve power.

In the immediate postwar period the CPY aimed to create a united Yugoslav political consciousness on a threefold basis: ethnic and linguistic similarities and common traditions, the wartime "national-liberation struggle," and the "building of socialism." Yet the Communists did not want to eradicate the individual characteristics of the nations of Yugoslavia. They believed that the new socialist society and the attraction of a glorious Communist future would cause people to think less of the past, overcome their inherited historical loyalties, and identify with the whole of Yugoslavia. The Communists were against assimilationism but favored one common state loyalty, blending the national cultures of Yugoslavia and adding new Yugoslav content to them.

During and immediately after the Second World War the Yugoslav Communists accomplished much toward solving the national question, and almost completely eliminated the conflict between Croats and Serbs. Toward the end of the war the CPY also showed its ability to build a state that would later prove sufficiently strong to survive the conflict with the Soviet Union. Clearly, Communist Yugoslavia was a viable political entity. But ultimately Communism, either as an ideology or as a one-party monopoly of power, could not permanently unite the nations of Yugoslavia and create a unified Yugoslav national consciousness.

Marxist-Leninist ideology concerning the national question was largely derived from the eighteenth-century Enlightenment: it wanted to overcome the past and reject it. When applied to Yugoslavia, exactly because of its similarity to the Enlightenment, it helped the Yugoslav Communists to perceive the common ethnic, linguistic, and other characteristics of Croats and Serbs behind their individual national traditions. In the nineteenth and twentieth centuries radical attitudes to social problems often strengthened such perceptions. Political leaders interested in peasants, workers, or both, perceived them as largely outside history or as victims of history. This increased the "thinking away" of historical traditions associated with the ruling classes. Marxism and the Enlightenment also shared a belief that humanity could create new human beings and a fundamentally different society. In 1919 a leading Croatian Communist intellectual and advocate of Yugoslavism, August Cesarec, wrote in *Plamen* (The Flame): "the task for us is to erect an insurmountable barrier, to dualize time and divide it into the black past and the white future."[4] For him, Croatian and Serbian nationalism were also things of the past. The future, of course, brought with it Communism but also included Yugoslavism.

From that time until the 1960s, Communist Yugoslavism was based on a belief that the differences between Croats and Serbs were negligible, since they were principally based on historical memories, tradition, and religion, all of which belonged to the past. For Communists these three elements could not be parts of the human consciousness of the future, let alone an important source of meaning or a foundation for deep loyalties. They would inevitably be erased by socialism, progress, and Communism. Although the Communists were correct in their perception of the differences between Croats and Serbs as primarily rooted in history, they were mistaken in thinking that because of this they were irrelevant. One could say with some irony that the major problem, both for Communist Yugoslavism and for eighteenth- and nineteenth-century Yugoslavism, which was based on "enlightened" and "progressive" ideas, was that they were not conservative enough. If either movement had contained a modicum of conservatism it would have recognized the importance for Croats and Serbs of tradition, religion, and, above all else, historical memory and would not have been surprised that peasants, workers, and "exploited" masses in general accept these values.

From the mid-1920s onward the CPY interpreted the crisis in Croatian-Serbian relations as caused primarily by "oppression," and expected that there would be no further conflict once Communist revolution abolished "Serbian hegemony." This again was an illusion. Serbian predominance exacerbated the crisis, but the main cause was the existence of national ideologies. As Ivo Banac correctly points out, "If anything, the national movements against centralism—particularly prominent among the Croats—merely completed the process whereby each group's national individuality was firmly set."[5]

The centralism of the interwar period (which was combined with unitarism during the dictatorship of King Aleksandar), with Serbian predominance in politics, administration, and the military—what the non-Serbian nationalist parties and the Communists exaggeratedly called "great-Serbian hegemony"—was undoubtedly damaging to the Yugoslav idea. But it is still doubtful if the just solution to the national question, with, for example, equal representation of Croats in all realms of public life, would have fundamentally changed the situation. The Croatian national ideology was fully formed. Yugoslavia was not the Croats' state; Belgrade was not their capital. Few of them admired Serbian writers, artists, and historical personalities. There were no common Croatian-Serbian cultural centers and universities. Interaction between the intellectual, political, and commercial elites was also rare.

The politics of interwar Yugoslavia can be partly interpreted as an alliance between the ideology of Yugoslavism and wholly or predominantly Serbian institutions: the monarchy, the military, the civil service, the Serbian Orthodox church, and the People's Radical Party. While the Serbian nation as a whole did not identify itself with the royal dictatorship of January 1929, did not economically benefit from it, and suffered the persecution of its political parties just as the Croats did, it is still true that King Aleksandar, as a protector of Serbian interests, enjoyed a certain support and sympathy among the Serbs that was conspicuously absent among the Croats. But there the dissimilarity between interwar Serbian and Croatian nationalism seems to end. Both Serbian and Croatian nationalism in their authoritarian forms (which, indeed, was the form in which they most frequently appeared) prophesied a myth of social harmony and blamed the "foreigners" for all present and past social conflicts, arguing that the nation itself was by its nature unified. This belief that the nation was a united organism, that is, the denial of its internal complexity and of conflicts within it, led to the assumption that political pluralism was not only unnecessary but also harmful: it might weaken the unity of the society. Connected with this was a tendency to deny the right to political participation to all but conationals.

Historians and sociologists have pointed out the mutually exclusive character of the Croatian and Serbian national ideologies.[6] Yet their exclusivity seems limited to their rivalry over certain territories (such as Bosnia-Herzegovina). In their ideological content, especially in their concept of the state, they were almost identical. Seton-Watson's claim that in interwar Yugoslavia the "really important issues that underlay Yugoslav politics [were] the conflicts between Serbian centralism and Croatian federalism" is only partly true.[7] The Croatian national movement never challenged the principle of centralism. It opposed centralism dominated by the Serbs and strong state power concentrated in Belgrade but did not seem to object to Croatian centralism and strong state power whose seat would be Zagreb. The Croatian nationalists never envisaged Croatia as a federal state, nor did they ever plan to give any kind of autonomy to Serbs or Italians or any other national group inside Croatia. Bosnia-Herzegovina was to be completely incorporated into Croatia; Muslims there were almost always simply proclaimed to be Croats of a different religion; and Serbs in Croatia were either considered Orthodox Croats or Vlachs to be assimilated, or sometimes—whether called Serbs, Vlachs, or Orthodox Croats—a lower, evil race to be expelled or exterminated. The Croatian political elite rarely recognized non-Croatian national groups as nations whose culture, traditions, historical memories, and loyalties, though different from Croatian ones, were nevertheless legitimate, and which gave them the right to participate in the political life of Croatia.

Despite instances of Croatian-Serbian political collaboration (such as the Coalition of 1905 and the United Opposition in the late 1930s), the Serbs' right to individual national consciousness never became widely and sincerely accepted in Croatia. The Ustasha ideology, with its demand for a state with a homogeneous population, the desire to reestablish the much-exaggerated Croatian "historical" borders, and the pseudo-romantic mythologizing of the medieval state, was simply an extreme expression of traditional Croatian nationalism. But when all this was fused with religious intolerance, terrorism, and the dynamics of modern fascist and Nazi movements, the struggle for an independent Croatian state became a campaign of genocide.

Yugoslav Communists in the interwar period correctly pointed out that neither the Croatian nor the Serbian nation was one united whole with one interest and one destiny, as the majority of Croatian and Serbian nationalists wanted to see them, but that they were divided into different social classes. (There were, of course, other divisions too, such as political parties, provinces, and regions, but the Communists, to their disadvantage, did not attach great importance to them.) But Yugoslav Communists, like Communists elsewhere, exaggerated the intensity of the "class struggle" and consequently underestimated the propensity of the "oppressed classes" to identify with members of the "ruling class" and perceive them as their leaders and champions. Both Croats and Serbs had a fully formed and widely disseminated national consciousness in which historical memories (including those of men who, according to the Yugoslav Communist party, should be considered "oppressors" and "exploiters") were an essential ingredient. These historical memories could not be wiped out.

Cleavages between Serbian Orthodoxy and Roman Catholicism were not of crucial importance in the formation and preservation of national ideologies, although most advocates of Yugoslavism (and especially Yugoslav Communists) thought that they were. As a rule, for Serbs the battles they had won (and lost) and for Croats the rulers they had had (and, in some cases, imagined they had had) were a much more important part of their national identity than were Orthodox and Catholic dogma and ritual. Consequently, the decrease in the influence of the churches as a result of the Communist revolution did not, as the Communists expected, bring the Croats and Serbs much closer, nor did it cause a commensurate increase in support of the Yugoslav idea.

The CPY intended postwar federalism and Yugoslavism to be irreversible steps toward both national equality and harmonious relations among the nations of Yugoslavia. Inequalities had indeed been abolished, and the postwar organization of Yugoslavia seemed an obvious improvement over prewar Serbian predominance. Yet the new relations between the nations of Yugoslavia were not based upon durable foundations. They depended primarily on the Communist ideology and the CPY's monopoly of power. As long as the CPY was one, united, monolithic, all-Yugoslav force, with a complete monopoly of power, no disintegrative nationalist forces could come to prominence, and the federal structure remained strong. In the early 1950s the party claimed that in the near future self-managing units would govern the society and economy in its place. The idea that the party and the state would wither away through the development of self-managing socialism proved to be chimerical, and in the late 1960s the CPY began to disintegrate and to be replaced by the parties of the six republics and two provinces. This process also directly threatened the unity of Yugoslavia, since there was no other political force to keep it together. In addition, the legend of the Partisan struggle, which was a powerful force integrating the nations of Yugoslavia for many years after the war, was bound to lose its attractiveness the more it became part of the official dogma. Finally, the party had promised that the future Communist society of freedom, equality, and affluence would bring about, among other things, the final triumph of Yugoslavism and internationalism. Yet as soon as social, economic, and other realities showed that such a society was unrealizable, traditional national ideologies reappeared, sometimes allied with the party bureaucracy of the republics, sometimes with the anti-Communist intelligentsia. Based on an ideology that proved utopian and on a power structure that was both undemocratic and bound to be inefficient and deteriorate, the Communist solution of the national question in Yugoslavia was destined to be only transient.

Notes

Sources are cited by author's last name and date of publication. Full documentation is provided in the Bibliography.

Introduction

1. American media use the term *nation* to describe the people in the territory of one state, under one government. In this book the term *nation* means a community of people with territory, culture, and identity based on historical memories. This is also how Serbs, Croats, and so on see themselves—they never describe themselves as "ethnic groups."

2. The area of Yugoslavia and of its republics and autonomous provinces is from *Enciklopedija Jugoslavije.* The 1981 census figures are from *NIN,* 28 February 1982.

3. In this study the term *South Slavs* refers to all South Slav nations of today's Yugoslavia: (alphabetically) Croats, Macedonians, Montenegrins, Muslims, Slovenes, Serbs, and declared Yugoslavs; and to the ethnic groups and states from which they emerged. It does not refer to Bulgarians. There are numerous precedents in literature, historiography, and the everyday vocabulary of politics for both the exclusion and inclusion of Bulgarians.

4. Most self-declared Yugoslavs live in large industrial cities with mixed Croatian-Serbian or Croatian-Muslim-Serbian populations in Croatia, Bosnia and Herzegovina, and Serbia. Many are young and have secondary education or more.

5. Dvorniković (1939) provides a wealth of information (esp. chaps. 3–5) about ethnological and other characteristics shared by the South Slavs.

6. For Byzantine influences in Dalmatia, see Ferluga (1957); for Byzantine influences on Slavs in religion, law, social and political organization, art, and culture in general, see Obolensky (1971b). In the nineteenth century Croatian nationalists always tried to absolutize the difference between the "westernness" of Croats and the "easternness" of Serbs. For a general history of the Byzantine

empire, see Vasiliev (1953); Ostrogorsky (1956); Diehl (1957); Obolensky (1971a). Obolensky provides the most information about the South Slavs.

7. For the geographic obstacles to the creation of strong and centralized states, see Lampe and Jackson (1982). Cvijić (1966) is a seminal work crucial for understanding the geographic background to the history of the South Slavs.

8. See Obolensky (1948), a general study, but dealing mostly with Bulgaria. See also Šidak (1949); Brockett (1969).

9. See Ćirković (1964).

10. See Jiriček (1952); Grafenauer et al. (1953), 229–255, 328–514.

11. See Novaković (1960).

12. See Mirković (1965). For a general history of the Serbian Orthodox church in the Middle Ages, see Slijepčević (1962), vol. 1.

13. Both the Habsburg monarchy and the Ottoman Empire were agglomerations of many areas, kingdoms, provinces, peoples, and churches, all with differing relations to the ruler. Some of the kingdoms were protonational states. On the place of Croats and Serbs in the Habsburg monarchy and the complexity of relations among its component elements, see Evans (1979), pt. 2.

14. On Serbian migrations to Croatia, see Ivić (1926). For a detailed account of the migration of Serbs into depopulated southern Hungary (today's autonomous province Vojvodina) toward the end of the seventeenth century, see Čakić (1983). Emperor Leopold I recognized all Serbian religious rights and gave the Serbs considerable autonomy. Full text in Macartney (1970), "The 'Serb Privilege' of 1691."

15. See Donia (1981). Until the establishment of Communist Yugoslavia in 1945, the leading Muslim political organization was the Muslim People's Organization (Muslimanska narodna organizacija), in the interwar period called the Yugoslav Muslim Organization (Jugoslovenska muslimanska organizacija). Though formally created only in December 1906, its party organization was to a large extent active in 1900. Its goals were primarily protection of religious institutions and the preservation of traditions and culture. It was led by landowners who under Austria-Hungary had lost political privileges but preserved their social and economic status.

16. See Tomasevich (1955), "The Agrarian Institutions of the Croato-Slavonian Military Border."

17. According to the Habsburg census of 1786–87; Lampe and Jackson (1982), 625.

18. Croatia's struggle to regain the Military Frontier and the complicated history of its legal status in relation to Vienna and Zagreb are analyzed in Čulinović (1969).

19. Rothenburg (1960, 1966) gives an almost complete history of the Military Frontier.

20. See Jazsi (1971), "Cohesion Created by the Turkish Pressure."

21. Ibid., "Alliance between the Dynasty and the Oppressed Classes of the People" and "The Fight of the Absolutism against the Estates."

22. Mill (1864b), 53.

23. In postwar Yugoslavia, the history of the interwar Communist movement, the Second World War, and the civil war has been written under the supervision of

the Communist party. Accordingly, most works have proclaimed Communists and the Communist-led Partisan movement as heroic and patriotic, and their adversaries as villains and traitors. This Manichean division of the complex and multifaceted history of Yugoslavia has been one of the means legitimating the party's monopoly of power. Yet in spite of the party's historiographic orthodoxy, rich and varied well-researched accounts of particular events have emerged. Though rarely risking fundamentally new interpretations, and sometimes remaining silent about events that were, from the party's point of view, particularly "sensitive," many Yugoslav historians have not been ready to misrepresent historical events in order to corroborate official dogmas. In general, broader historical works have tended to be ideologically orthodox, and detailed, well-researched monographs to be more objective. Since the death of President Tito in May 1980, however, the liberalization of intellectual life has brought many serious challenges to the official "macro"-interpretations of modern Yugoslav history.

This study is not an attempt to give a comprehensive account of the party's policies toward Yugoslav unity in the 1919–1953 period. Rather, its primary aim is to reveal the sociological and historical factors determining those policies. Greater attention is therefore given to certain periods and events (as well as to certain ideas) because they show in most detail, with most "relief," the structures and patterns of these determining factors, or the "internal logic" of crucial ideas and ideologies.

One. From the Origins of Yugoslavism to Socialist Internationalism, 1740–1918

1. Most historians agree that this was the first all-Yugoslav political party in history. See, e.g., Shoup (1968), 13.

2. Croatian Yugoslavism is more important than Serbian because the effect of "progressive" ideas and Yugoslavism on Croatian-Serbian relations can be seen only through the analysis of the politics in nineteenth- and early twentieth-century Croatia, and not in Serbia, since Croatia had a mixed Croatian-Serbian population, while Serbia was to a large extent a one-nation state. Moreover, in the beginning of the nineteenth century proto-Yugoslavism was stronger in Croatia, in part because the denationalizing pressures exerted by modern Austrian (German) and Hungarian nationalisms were stronger than those the Serbs encountered in the Ottoman Empire. This primarily Croatian proto-Yugoslavism (called Illyrianism) was in the realm of language and culture already Yugoslavism. It lacked only a political dimension—the demand for the unification and independence of the South Slavs.

3. In order to understand the connection between "progressive" ideas and Yugoslavism, however, it is not necessary to present the whole history of the struggle for the unification of the South Slavs, nor to attempt to give a complete and systematic account of the development of Yugoslavism. It is sufficient to focus attention on those episodes and movements that reveal the "nature" and "internal logic" of Yugoslavism, and especially those aspects of it that are relevant to the understanding of the attitudes of the CPY toward the conflict between Croats and Serbs and to Yugoslavia in the period 1919–1953.

4. See, e.g., Cassirer (1932).

5. See ibid., chap. 4, esp. "Die Idee der Toleranz und die Grundlegung der natürlichen Religion."

6. The possible exception was Dalmatia toward the end of the First World War, when the specter of Italian occupation and the military successes of Serbia made the Yugoslav idea very popular. (Before the First World War Yugoslavism had been strengthened in Dalmatia by fear of assimilation into Italian language and culture.)

7. More attention has been devoted to the socialist movement in Croatia than to its counterpart in Serbia because the Croatian socialists were more Yugoslavist. Also, Croatia provided examples of mixed Croatian-Serbian socialist groups, and these were important for the understanding of the nationally mixed CPY.

8. For Communist elitism and its connection with the national question, see Kolakovski (1981).

9. For the religious reforms by Maria Theresa and Joseph II, see Macartney (1970), "The Habsburgs and the Churches, 1740–92." Josephinism was a much more radical implementation of Enlightenment ideas; it was a veritable "counter-counter-reformation," a term used by Evans (1979), 445.

10. For the full text of the peasant patents issued by Joseph II, see Macartney (1970), "The Habsburgs and the Peasant Question, 1740–90." Tomasevich (1955), "Intervention of the Central Government in Feudal Relationships," provides an excellent analysis of the reforms of Maria Theresa and Joseph II.

11. Jaszi (1971), "The System of the Revolutionary Absolutism," gives a vivid picture of the intensity of resistance to Josephinism by Croatian and Hungarian nobility.

12. Kombol (1945), 313.

13. For the occupation of Dubrovnik by Napoleon's troops, see Bjelovučić (1970).

14. For the relative economic decline of the Ottoman Empire, see Lampe and Jackson (1982).

15. His name was Djuro Jelačić. See Marjanović (1913), 108.

16. The term *Serbian revolution* was first used by Leopold von Ranke in his *Die Serbische Revolution* (1829). This work was later expanded into *Serbien und die Türkei im neunzehnten Jahrhundert* (1879). Both works were largely based on accounts and materials supplied to Ranke by the Serbian scholar Vuk Stefanović Karadžić.

17. For an excellent account of Illyrianism see Horvat (1936), "Polet i pad ilirstva."

18. For the "logic" of the connection between Illyrianism and the Croatian national identity, see A. Djilas (1985).

19. For the Illyrianism of Starčević's youth, see Spalatin (1975), "The Illyrian Movement, 1835–1848."

20. For a comprehensive account of Gaj's activities in the Illyrianist movement, see Despalatović (1975).

21. For a general account of Illyrianism and language, see Vince (1978). Letters and account books preserved from the first half of the nineteenth century show that many Croatian tradesmen found the *štokavski* dialect most useful for trade, since it was the most widespread.

22. For Drašković's life and activities, see Horvat (1936), "Idejna grupa iz Kapucinske ulice."

23. Even the traditional Croatian peasant costumes became fashionable among educated middle-class women. See ibid., 92.

24. This somewhat Marxist-Leninist-sounding English translation of the name Narodna stranka seems more accurate than the usual translation "National Party." German offers the exact equivalent: *Volkspartei.*

25. For a criticism of "rationalism" in politics, see Oakeshott (1962).

26. For the theory that the only legitimate way of comprehending social reality is by learning through practice ("intimations"), see ibid.

27. See Banac (1984), 78–80.

28. For pan-Slavism in general, see Kohn (1960). For the pan-Slavism of the Illyrianist movement, see ibid., "The Illyrian Movement."

29. For the romanticism of Illyrianist pan-Slavism see Horvat (1936), "Idejna grupa iz Kapucinske ulice" and "Polet i pad ilirstva." Gaj's pan-Slavism often became childlike Slavophile and Russophile euphoria. In one of his memoranda to Nikolai I, Gaj depicted the west as a "bloody demon" and the czar and Russia as the "Majestic Genius of the Eastern Sun" leading the Slav "tribes"; ibid., 113.

30. See Horvat (1936); Čubrilović (1958); Macan (1971).

31. Under Habsburg rule, from 1878 to 1918, the post-1945 republic of Bosnia and Herzegovina was called Bosnia-Herzegovina.

32. For pan-Slavism as the ideology of Russian expansionism, see Kohn (1960), pt. 2. For Serbian relations with Russia on the eve of the First World War, see Ekmečić (1973).

33. For a political biography of Garašanin, described as the "Serbian Bismarck," see Mackenzie (1985).

34. For Garašanin's political activities and their effect on later Serbian politics, see Čubrilović (1958).

35. For a general account of the establishment of Balkan states, see Jelavich and Jelavich (1977).

36. The influence of monarchy on political life was considerable in other European countries too, even those with parliamentary regimes such as Belgium and Holland. Yet in contrast to these countries, parliamentarism in Serbia was not deeply rooted, nor did it enjoy the mass support necessary to contain the ever-increasing power of the regent and the military.

37. See Pavlowitch (1971), 53: "The toll for Serbia and Montenegro amounted to about 0.75 million. (Serbia's military losses alone were relatively 2.5 [times] higher than those of France.)"

38. Many on the right did not consciously pursue hegemony but were simply unable to see Yugoslavia as anything but an extension of Serbia. Some were even ready to give up the Serbian name and part of Serbia's identity and traditions for the greater concept. Yet their failure to see the difference between Serbia and Yugoslavia and their effort to impose the Serbian concept of the state on Yugoslavia inevitably meant that non-Serbian nations, Croats in particular, perceived their Yugoslavism as Serbian hegemony in disguise.

39. See, e.g., Strugar (1956); Perović (1984), pt. 2.

40. See, e.g., Perović (1984), ibid. See also Milenković (1974), "Uvod," 1: "Kratak pregled razvitka socijalreformističkog pravca u radničkom pokretu

jugoslovenskih zemalja"; pt. 1. Milenković deals with period after the First World War, but his analysis reveals the origins of the policies of the social-democratic groups toward the national question.

41. Horvat (1936), 307–311.

42. For Khuen-Hedervary's rule, see ibid., "Khuenovština"; Šidak et al. (1968), "Khuenov režim g. 1883–1887," "Khuenov režim 1887–1895," and "Khuenov režim g. 1895–1903."

43. Starčević's opinion of Serbs (whom he called "Slavoserbi"), is quoted in Spalatin (1975), 111–112: "[Serbs are] a race of slaves, the most loathsome of beasts . . . They have no conscience, they do not know how to read properly, they cannot learn anything, they cannot be better or worse than they are. They are all completely alike, except that they differ in their craftiness and agility." For a Croatian nationalist defense of Starčević's views, see M. Starčević (1936), esp. chaps. 5, 8.

44. See Horvat (1936), "Pad grofa Khuena"; Šidak et al. (1968), "Khuenov režim g. 1895–1903," esp. "Srpsko-hrvatski odnosi." The conflict between Croats and Serbs over recognition of the Serbian name and Cyrillic script had already been intense in the 1870s; see Andrija Radenić, "Srbi u Hrvatskoj i Slavoniji 1868–1878," esp. "Borba za ravnopravnost u sporu oko jezika i imena," in *Istorija srpskog naroda*, vol. 5, bk. 2.

45. For the political activities of Stjepan Radić, see Gaži (1973–74). For the beginnings of the Croatian peasant movement of the Radić brothers, see Vuković-Todorović (1940).

46. See Marjanović (1913); Kosta Milutinović, "Nastanak politike novog kursa na Primorju," in *Istorija srpskog naroda,* vol. 6, bk. 1. For the general history of the Croatian-Serbian coalition see Gross (1960); Šidak et al. (1968), "Hrvatski narod u razdoblju od g. 1903 do 1914." For the economic preconditions of the policy of the "new course," see Gross (1960), pt. a, "Uvod"; and chap. 2.

47. See Gross (1960), pt. a, "Uvod"; chap. 1; and chap. 2, "Riječka i zadarska rezolucija."

48. Of course the Illyrianist program was a predecessor, but its goals were primarily cultural rather than political. The same is true of the neo-Illyrianism of the Catholic bishop Josip Juraj Strossmayer. This educated and liberal clergyman was the principal founder of the Yugoslav Academy in 1867, which was meant, together with various other cultural and educational institutions, publications, and activities he helped and financed, to promote the cultural unification of the South Slavs. His ecumenical efforts toward the reconciliation between Roman Catholicism and Orthodox Christianity were largely inspired by his desire to achieve the spiritual unification of Croats and Serbs. Together with his close collaborator Canon Franjo Rački, who was the first head of the academy, he envisaged the future creation of an independent South Slav state. But Strossmayer, Rački, and their followers refrained from creating a Yugoslavist political program, judging the Croatia of their time too weak and provincial for such ambitious designs. For the activities of Strossmayer and Rački, see, e.g., Horvat (1936), "Reakcija," "Na raskršću," "Voljom Bismarckovom," and "Graditelj Mažuranić."

49. For the Serbian view of the Croatian-Serbian Coalition, see Kosta Milutinović, "Hrvatsko-srpska koalicija," in *Istorija srpskog naroda*, vol. 6, bk. 2.

50. See Gross (1960), pt. d; Horvat (1936), "Hrvatsko pitanje u žarištu europske politike" and "U znaku veleizdajničkih procesa."

51. For the revolutionary ferment among South Slavs in the Habsburg monarchy, especially in Bosnia-Herzegovina, see Dedijer (1966).

52. For the ideas of Young Bosnia, see Palavestra (1965). Three reasons are usually given by historians to explain why on the eve of the First World War the Serbian youth was most active and most radical in demanding changes in the political and social structure and national relations: (1) the inspiring victories of Serbia and Montenegro in the First and Second Balkan Wars; (2) the exceptionally difficult position of Serbian peasants in Bosnia-Herzegovina (Austria-Hungary had not carried out the expected agrarian reform after its occupation in 1878, and most of the land remained in the hands of the Muslim nobility); and (3) the persecution of Serbian politicians in Austria-Hungary for their sympathies for Serbia and contacts with it. (For a general account of the position of Serbs in Bosnia-Herzegovina and their national movement at the turn of the century, see Milorad Ekmečić, "Društvo, privreda i socijalni nemiri u Bosni i Hercegovini" and "Nacionalni pokret u Bosni i Hercegovini," in *Istorija srpskog naroda*, vol. 6, bk. 1.

53. See Šidak et al. (1968), "Počeci radničkog pokreta u hrvatskim zemljama," esp. 75–76.

54. For the stagnation of the Croatian economy under Hungarian political and economic pressure, see ibid., 125.

55. Ibid., 78.

56. Ibid., 78–79, 199.

57. Ibid., 199.

58. For an analysis of the attitude of Croatian social democrats to the national question in the last decade of the nineteenth century, see Gross (1956). For a broader approach to the South Slav social democrats and the national question, see Strugar (1956); Perović (1984), pt. 2.

59. Šidak et al. (1968), 202.

60. Ibid., 204.

61. For an analysis of the political ideas among the educated youth of Croatia on the eve of the First World War, see Horvat (1936), "Rezultati politike oportunizma" and "Komesarijati i atentati"; Gross (1968).

62. See Gross (1956).

63. See Šidak et al. (1968), "Razvoj socijalističkog pokreta u Hrvatskoj od g. 1897. do 1902."

64. See Gross (1956); Strugar (1956).

65. Šidak et al. (1968), "Socijalistički pokret u Dalmaciji i Istri, g. 1895–1902."

66. Ibid., 197.

67. See ibid., "Nova obilježja socijalističkog pokreta."

68. See Gross (1956).

69. Šidak et al. (1968), "Nova obilježja socijalističkog pokreta" and "Socijalistički pokret u vrijeme 'novog kursa.'"

70. See, e.g., Perović (1984), pt. 2; Vlajčić (1984), chap. 1.

71. See Strugar (1956).

72. See Bauer (1924).

73. See Strugar (1956); Pešić (1983), "Uvod—Stav socijalističkih partija jugoslovenskih zemalja prema nacionalnom pitanju krajem prvog svetskog rata"; Morača, Bilandžić, and Stojanović (1977), "Uvod," esp. "Prve radničke organizacije, stvaranje i djelatnost socijaldemokratskih partija"; Milenković (1974), "Uvod," chap. 1; and pt. 1; Vlajčić (1984), chap. 1; Perović (1984), pt. 2.

74. For similar views of the social democrats in Bosnia-Herzegovina, see Babić (1974).

75. Strugar (1956). Perović (1984), pt. 2, chap. 2, 1, "Stanovišta radničkog pokreta u jugoslovenskim zemljama o nacionalnom pitanju do I svetskog rata" and "Srpska socijaldemokratska partija."

76. These ideas would influence the writings of Sima Marković on the organization of Yugoslavia. After the First World War he became a leading Communist theoretician on the national question.

77. Šidak et al. (1968), 314–315.

Two. The Yugoslavism and Separatism of the Communist Party of Yugoslavia, 1918–1925

1. Kolakovski (1981), 186, stresses the uniqueness of Lenin's views among the pre-1914 social democrats: "Lenin was the first to notice in the national question the great reserve of power that social democracy can and must use for its cause, instead of seeing national conflicts solely as an obstacle."

2. For a general discussion of the Bolshevik attitude to the national question, on which this chapter is partly based, see Carrère d'Encausse (1979).

3. See Heller and Nekrich (1986), "An Indissoluble Union," esp. 155–156.

4. On Stalin as the head of the Commissariat of Nationalities during the civil war, see Ulam (1987), "The Taste of Power," esp. 157–170.

5. See A. Djilas (1987b).

6. The process had already begun under Lenin. See Lazitch and Drachkovitch (1972), 322–323.

7. "The world revolution will be born from the world war," declared Grigori Zinoviev; quoted in Lazitch and Drachkovitch (1972), 234.

8. Ibid., 406.

9. Ibid., 234.

10. See Kolakovski (1981). Ulam (1966), chap. 6, esp. "On the World Stage: 1912–1917," notes that by Marxist standards the policy of alliance with nationalism, especially when it was conservative nationalism, represented an astonishing innovation.

11. Lazitch and Drachkovitch (1972), 467–468.

12. Ibid., 221–222.

13. As a "traitor" of revolution and competitor for the allegiance of the working class, social democracy was the greatest evil for the Bolsheviks. It was difficult to ascertain whether the main task of the Communists was to combat capitalism or their former socialist comrades; ibid., chap. 9, esp. "The World of the Comintern."

14. Quoted in Lazitch and Drachkovitch (1972), 358.

15. Ibid., 382–391.

16. See Heller and Nekrich (1986), "An Indissoluble Union."

17. For Stalin's views on the national question and Lenin's general approval, see, e.g., Ulam (1966), chap. 6, esp. "On the World Stage 1917"; Tucker (1973), 155–156, 168–170.

18. See McNeal (1963), "The October Upheaval and the Question of Nationalities."

19. For a similar analysis, see ibid., 69–70.

20. On Bolshevik attempts to rally the support of the 16 million Muslims of the Russian empire, see Heller and Nekrich (1986), 73–75.

21. For Serbia's foreign policy, see Ekmečić (1973).

22. For the Yugoslav program of Croatian, Slovene, and Serbian politicians, with particular reference to Serbia and Montenegro, see Andrej Mitrović, "Jugoslovenski program," in *Istorija srpskog naroda*, vol. 6, bk. 2. For Serbia and the Yugoslav question in 1914–1915, see Janković (1973). Unification of the South Slavs was one of Serbia's war aims in 1914; see Ekmečić (1973).

23. For Rakovski's career, see Souvarine (1966), 179–80; Lazitch and Drachkovitch (1972), 69–70.

24. Lazitch and Drachkovitch (1972), 198.

25. Ibid., 537.

26. See, e.g., Perović (1984), "Karakteristike u razvoju jugoslovenskih naroda do stvaranja zajedničke države."

27. Quoted in Pešić (1983), 34.

28. Yugoslavism was on the increase in the Croatian parliament after 1905 (e.g., the Croatian-Serbian Coalition). For a Croatian nationalist view of that process, see, e.g., Floegel (1985).

29. 28 June is Vidovdan, the day of St. Vitus. This feast day is prominent among the Serbs because on that day in 1389 the Ottoman Turks defeated the Serbs in the battle of Kosovo.

30. Tudjman (1969), 305.

31. Influential politicians in both the government and the opposition favored unitarism. They were especially numerous in the Democratic Party (Demokratska stranka), which played an important role in the proclamation of the centralist 1921 constitution. See Gligorijević (1970), esp. "Koncentracija Demokratske i Radikalne stranke u cilju donošenja centralističkog Ustava" and "Donošenje Vidovdanskog Ustava."

32. Pešić (1983), 33–35.

33. For Pribićević's career before King Aleksandar's dictatorship of 1929, see Matković (1972).

34. *Istina*, no. 5 (17 July 1919); quoted in Pešić (1983), 33.

35. See, e.g., Čolaković et al. (1963), "Drugi Vukovarski kongres Partije."

36. The Democratic Party was not a Serbian party *tout court* in the sense in which the Radical Party was. It began in 1919 as a coalescence of smaller parties, some of which included considerable numbers of Croats and Slovenes. In 1920 they named themselves the Democratic Party but never overcame their political and national heterogeneity. The party's support for centralism was particularly strong in the years 1919–1921. After 1925 the party modified its insistence on a

unitary organization of Yugoslavia, advocating local autonomy. But by then it had already lost much of its influence among non-Serbs. This did not change with its acceptance of federalism and its participation as a member of the United Opposition (headed by Vladko Maček, the leader of the Croatian Peasant Party) in the May 1935 elections. The participation of an important splinter group from the party in the governments after the proclamation of the royal dictatorship in 1929, the party's opposition to the Cvetković-Maček agreement of 1939 (by which Prince Pavle gave autonomy to Croatia), its support for Chetniks (Serbian anti-Communist and monarchist guerrillas) during the war, and its postwar opposition to Communist federalism as contrary to Serbian interests made the party appear to be a primarily Serbian national party, rather than Yugoslav or liberal democratic. Gligorijević (1970) gives the history of the party from 1918 to 1929.

37. The CPY received 12.36 percent of the total vote. By region, its share was 27.16 percent in Macedonia, Kosovo, and Sandžak; 14.87 in Serbia proper; 7.21 in Croatia-Slavonia; 5.46 in Bosnia-Herzegovina; 10.29 in Slovenia; 14.97 in Vojvodina; 37.99 in Montenegro; and 16.16 in Dalmatia; Banac (1983a), 202.

38. Quoted in Pešić (1983), 45.

39. For a detailed account of the revolutionary turmoil in Croatia, see Banac (1984), "The 1920 Croat Peasant Revolt against Draft-Animal Registration."

40. For a short summary of economic conditions in interwar Yugoslavia, see Bilandžić (1979), "Društveno-ekonomska kriza kapitalističke Jugoslavije."

41. Pešić (1983), 33.

42. Vlajčić (1978), 48.

43. Marković (1923a, 1923b).

44. Marković (1923a), chaps. 2 (esp. 36–37) and 8 (esp. 115).

45. For the influence of foreign capital in Croatia and the prevalence of a middle-of-the-road attitude to Croatian national demands among the "leadership of Croat capital," see Banac (1984), 407–410.

46. The Slovenian People's Party was founded in 1892 as a Catholic party and was concerned primarily with religious, educational, and social issues. *Klerikalci* (clericalists), as the members of the party were popularly known, were nevertheless regarded by the majority of Slovenes as protectors of their interests. From 1918 to 1927 the party advocated Slovenian autonomy. Nevertheless, its leader, Msgr. Antun Korošec, joined the cabinet of General Petar Živković after the establishment of King Aleksandar's dictatorship in 1929. After 1931 the party reversed its stance and in 1933, demanded autonomy for Slovenia. Until the beginning of the Second World War the Slovenian People's Party continued its policy of opposition to the dictatorship and of autonomist demands, while at the same time showing readiness to seek compromise with Serbian politicians and to join the government. It pursued similar policies even after it went into exile after the defeat of Yugoslavia in April 1941.

47. Marković (1923b), 36–37, 42. For Marković's general views on national self-determination, see Marković (1923a), chap. 4.

48. See Wilson (1984), 534–539.

49. For Marković's belief that nationally heterogeneous Yugoslavia would become a one-nation state, see Marković (1923a), chap. 8, esp. 108–112.

50. Marković (1923b), 29–35.

51. Marković (1923a), 118–122. For Marković's general views on national autonomy, see ibid., chap. 5.

52. Čolaković et al. (1963), 115.

53. Ibid., 116, 118–119.

54. Vlajčić (1978), 59–62.

55. See Pešić (1983), "Treća zemaljska konferencija KPJ"; Perović (1984), "Treća zemaljska konferencija KPJ"; Vlajčić (1984), "Treća konferencija KPJ."

56. Bilandžić (1979), 34.

57. The conference's support for the common South Slav state decisively influenced future CPY policies. See, e.g., Čolaković (1964–1968), 2: 301.

58. *Istorijski arhiv KPJ*, 2: 70–75.

59. Vlajčić (1978), 89. For a more extensive account of Radić's attitude to world Communism and the CPY, see S. Cvetković (1972); Janjatović (1983).

60. Quoted in Vlajčić (1978), 87. See also *Istorijski arhiv KPJ*, 2: 420.

61. See Stalin (1925).

62. Lenin was the first Communist to make the distinction between the right of separation and the need to separate. See Marković (1923b), 32.

63. Stalin (1925). For Marković's defense of his position, see Semić (1925).

64. Even during the Second World War Yugoslav Communists still wrote about the national oppression in "Versailles Yugoslavia"; see, e.g., Tito (1942).

65. In 1924, for example, the party had only seventy organizations and a total of 688 members (Serbia had 124 members, Macedonia 68, Montenegro 40, Dalmatia 168, Slovenia 84, Croatia 99, Bosnia 64, and Vojvodina 41); Banac (1983b), 205.

66. For some not very persuasive arguments about the presence of Serbian nationalism in the CPY in the shape of a demand for a "leading role" for the Serbian cadres, see Banac (1983a, 1984). The views of a leading Serbian Communist, Života Milojković, with their extreme mixture of Marxist orthodoxy and insensitivity to the national problems of non-Serbs could, however, be interpreted as an unconscious form of nationalism; see Pešić (1983), 96–98, 107–109, 149–153, 198–200. A similar indication of unconscious nationalism is the excessive tolerance shown to Croatian nationalism by a leading Croatian Communist, Ante Ciliga; for Ciliga's views, see Perović (1984), "Nacionalni pokreti ugnjetenih naroda u jugoslovenskoj državi"; Pešić (1983), esp. 127–131, 166–171. Yet the cases of Milojković and Ciliga seem isolated, and even their statements present little evidence of overt nationalism.

67. For Marković's personality and the development of his views in pre-1914 Serbia, see D. Jovanović (1973), 430–431.

68. "The Bolshevik program on the national question was authentically Marxist in the sense that it embraced two mutually contradictory principles: the self-determination of nations, and the centralized state. Lenin favored a centralized party and extended the centralist principle to the state. For him, the nationalities problem was above all a problem of political power"; Heller and Nekrich (1986), 76.

69. For the Yugoslavism of the small Socialist Party of Yugoslavia (Socijalistička partija Jugoslavije), see Milenković (1974), pt. 5, and pt. 6, chap. 4. The SPY was created in December 1921 from two parties recently formed from the right-wing

factions of the prewar social-democratic parties, and from the Yugoslav Social Democratic Party, the party of Slovenian social democrats. Most members of the SPY firmly believed that Yugoslavs were one nation, and in 1920 the party declared its support for a united South Slav state with one parliament but with local autonomies. A staunch proponent of unitarism and centralism, the party voted for the constitution of 1921.

The party's influence was very small. In the February 1925 elections for parliament, for example, it won only 22,204 votes (Milenković, 1974, 257–260). Although it participated in the elections without its main competitor, the banned CPY, it was still unable to counter the Communist influence among the workers. Another cause of these poor results was the party's orientation to trade unions, which, in a country with underdeveloped industry, confined its influence to skilled workers; a large majority of workers were unskilled and nonunionized. But the most important cause was its attitude toward the national question. In Croatia, Slovenia, and Bosnia-Herzegovina the party was perceived as supporting the status quo, and many workers switched their alliance from the SPY to the Croatian Republican Peasant Party, the Slovenian People's Party, or the Yugoslav Muslim Organization. See Milenković (1974), 258–259, 694–695.

The semifascist Zbor movement was another political group with a Yugoslavist orientation. Founded in 1934 by the Serbian politician Dimitrije Ljotić, Zbor was opposed to parliamentarism and any political system based on competition of political parties. Fanatically anti-Communist, yet also opposed to unrestrained free market capitalism, it sought the solution of economic and social conflicts through a corporate system based upon delegates of professions and trades. In the late 1930s it was secretly subsidized by Germany (see Pavlowitch, 1971, 93). After the defeat of Yugoslavia in April 1941 it was transformed into the "Serbian Volunteer Corps." Until the end of the war this small but disciplined and indoctrinated anti-Communist militia remained a dependable ally of the German forces. For a general history of Zbor, see M. Stefanović (1984).

Zbor had a diminutive following. In the May 1935 elections, for example, it did not gain a single seat in parliament. Its membership was predominantly Serbian. In Croatia, because of its advocacy of centralism and unitarism and its violent methods, it was mostly perceived as an aggressive great-Serbian organization. Yet it had a following among some Yugoslavist younger Croats in Dalmatia.

70. Quoted in Banac (1984), 332.

Three. *The Communist Party of Yugoslavia and the Popular Front, 1924–1941*

1. Radić had already been in prison for a year and a half in 1919–1920. See Gaži (1973–74), "Political Activities, 1919–1924" and "Compromise with Pašić"; also Banac (1984), "The Party of Radić" and "For a Croat Peasant Republic."

2. For the ideology of the Croatian peasant movement of the Radić brothers, see Vuković-Todorović (1940), esp. pt. 1, chap. 2; and pt. 2.

3. For political life in interwar Yugoslavia see, e.g., Pavlowitch (1971), chap. 2.

4. On his deathbed, according to Maček's account, Radić expressed his rejec-

tion of Yugoslavia and support for the creation of an independent Croatian state; Maček (1957), 113, 117.

5. See, e.g., Kulundžić (1967), esp. pt. 1. Also, corruption and bribery were not uncommon in interwar Yugoslavian politics. See Kulundžić (1968), esp. pt. 1.

6. For an impassioned condemnation of King Aleksandar's dictatorship by his former minister of the interior, see Pribićević (1952). For Pribićević in opposition to the dictatorship, see Boban (1974a).

7. The CPP initially welcomed the dictatorship and the repeal of the constitution, hoping that this would be the end of "Serbian centralism" and the first step toward solving the Croatian question. Some weeks before his wounding, amid skirmishes between Radicals and the CPP deputies, Radić had gone as far as to invite the king to appoint an extraparliamentary government. See, e.g., Pavlo-witch (1971), "King Alexander's Personal Rule."

8. See Stojkov (1969), chaps. 3, 4.

9. Neither the 1931 constitution nor the proclamation of 6 January 1929 formally pronounced a royal dictatorship. Nevertheless, through them the king acquired dictatorial powers.

10. The division of the country into *banovine* in October 1929, based on geography and named after rivers, emulated the French administrative model. Banovina was a historic Croatian name.

11. The constitution did not formally ban the parliament, but under it only the crown was sovereign. The constitution's antidemocratic nature was revealed primarily in its severe restrictions on the activities of political parties. A party could enjoy limited freedom only if it accepted the constitution. The Yugoslav National Party (Jugoslovenska nacionalna stranka), newly created from influential splinter groups of Serbian parties, mostly of the People's Radical Party, the Slovenian People's Party, and the Yugoslav Muslim Organization, recognized the constitution. The last two parties (both closely allied with Catholic and Muslim institutions) were the generally recognized representatives of Slovenes and Bosnian Muslims.

12. As early as 1918, his father, King Aleksandar, at that time still only a prince regent, had interfered in politics, primarily in foreign affairs and defense. He also influenced and sometimes vetoed the appointment of cabinet ministers and even prime ministers. Before January 1929, however, he was restrained by concerns that his candidates might not achieve a majority in the assembly.

13. Maček, for example, described Aleksandar's rule as "totalitarian"; Maček (1957), 127.

14. For similar examples, see Sugar and Lederer (1973); Sugar (1980).

15. For the development of Croatian nationalism in the 1930s (written from an extreme nationalist point of view, but with many important insights into the mood of Croatian nationalism in those years), see Kovačić (1970), chaps. 1, 2.

16. For the exceptionally difficult international situation in which Yugoslavia found itself in the mid-1930s, see, e.g., Hoptner (1962), chap. 2.

17. The constitution provided for a council of regency in case of the king's death. The council consisted, according to the king's will, of Prince Pavle and two respected but little-known figures. But all power was in Prince Pavle's hands.

18. See Stojkov (1985).

19. It is still a matter of debate whether the Muslims of Bosnia are a nation. But the point here is that the Yugoslav Muslim Organization politically represented an ethnic-religious group rather than an ideology or a social group or class. For the YMO's activities in the interwar period, see Purivatra (1974).

20. See A. Djilas (1987b).

21. For fascism and extreme nationalism in the states that succeeded the Habsburg monarchy, see Sugar (1971), esp. "Conclusion."

22. After Hitler came to power, one of the main goals of German foreign policy in southeastern Europe was to weaken and isolate Yugoslavia. See Avramovski (1977).

23. The essence of the Comintern's criticism of the CPY's attitude to the national question had been presented a year before, in July 1924, by Dmitri Manuilski, a member of the Executive Council, in a report to the fifth congress of the Comintern. See Vlajčić (1984), "Izveštaj druga Manuiljskog o nacionalnom i kolonijalnom pitanju." The resolution of April 1925 can be found in ibid., "Rezolucija V proširenog plenuma Izvršnog komiteta Komunističke internacionale o jugoslovenskom pitanju."

24. See Vlajčić (1984), "Intervencija Kominterne"; Pešić (1983), "Diskusija u komisiji KI za jugoslovensko pitanje 1925. godine."

25. Ristović (1984).

26. See Vlajčić (1984), "Treći kongres KPJ."

27. See Vlajčić (1984), "Rezolucija o političkoj situaciji i zadacima Partije," "Rezolucija III kongresa KPJ o nacionalnom pitanju," and "Rezolucija o agrarnom i seljačkom pitanju."

28. See, e.g., Vlajčić (1978), "Četvrti kongres KPJ"; Pešić (1983), 230–236.

29. *Istorijski arhiv KPJ*, 2: 215.

30. In the early 1930s the party sometimes interpreted Serbian history in a radical revisionist way, much as did the separatist groups in Yugoslavia, which were extremely conservative in their social and political views. Serbia was proclaimed an aggressive nationalist state even when it was fighting Austria-Hungary during the First World War. It was accused of only partly fighting a defensive war, and of primarily struggling to realize its own imperialist ambitions. The same applied to the two Balkan Wars of 1912 and 1913. These struggles against the Turks and the Bulgarians were not for liberation, but purely for conquest. The creation of Yugoslavia in 1918, therefore, was no less than a loss of freedom for all non-Serbian nations of Yugoslavia.

31. Čolaković (1964–1968), 2: 301.

32. Hungary was presumably meant to be a part of some Danubian—as opposed to Balkan—federation, although this was not specified.

33. See Pešić (1983), chap. 5, esp. "Uvodjenje šestojanuarske diktature i nacionalna politika KPJ."

34. Milan Gorkić, the political secretary of the CPY, would admit in the autumn of 1934 that the party had made a mistake and erroneously interpreted the gathering of arms and ammunition, as well as other activities, of openly fascist elements in Croatia as preparations by the Croats for the revolutionary struggle; Pešić (1983), 263.

35. Pešić (1983), 260.

36. Most of the cadres at the conference had achieved their positions through their activities in the trade unions or in the Communist youth organizations and were not appointed by the Comintern. They did not travel outside Yugoslavia, not even to Moscow. Josip Broz Tito, who had been released from prison in July 1934 and had become a member of the Central Committee and Politburo, was (with Blagoje Parović) the main organizer of the conference.

37. Pešić (1983), 264–269.

38. See Vlajčić (1984), "Slovensko i hrvatsko pitanje u susjednim zemljama i komunističke partije."

39. Aleksandar was a classic example of a soldier-king with great political ambitions in both internal and external affairs. Although his internal policies created no permanent unity and even exacerbated the Croatian-Serbian conflict, as a dictator of Yugoslavia he was partly successful in his foreign policy. See, e.g., Avramovski (1986), vol. 2. His resolute opposition to Mussolini's aspirations in the eastern Adriatic and in the Balkans, for example, had the support of most Croats. See Pavlowitch (1971), "King Alexander's Personal Rule" and "Prince Paul's Regency."

40. Exact figures are still unknown. For the estimate of more than 100, see Štajner (1988). Lazitch and Drachkovitch (1986) calculate that of 38 Yugoslavs who worked directly for the Comintern, 25 were Serbs, 8 were Croats, 4 were Slovenes, and 1 was Yugoslav of Ukrainian origin. Fifteen of these were liquidated in the purges. See also Souvarine (1966).

41. For the fascination that Communism had for large sections of the Yugoslav intelligentsia, see Stipetić (1980), "Komunistička partija Jugoslavije i intelektualci (1919–1945)" and "Uloga inteligencije u Hrvatskoj u moralno-intelektualnom i političkom pripremanju socijalističke revolucije (1935–1941)."

42. Bilandžić (1979), 88. Until the autumn of 1943, 75 percent of the Partisans were twenty-one years old or younger; ibid.

43. For a group portrait of the Communists of the new generation, see M. Djilas (1973), bk. 2.

44. See Bakunin (1974), esp. chaps. 4, 10.

45. See M. Djilas (1973), bk. 2, chap. 9.

46. For example, there was no resentment among Croatian cadres when in December 1939 Serb Rade Končar became the political secretary of the Communist Party of Croatia. See Pulić (1970), "Rade Končar."

47. Quoted in *Proleter*, 15, no. 9–11 (October–December 1940): 5; also Jelić (1981), vol. 1, "Prva konferencija Komunističke partije Hrvatske i njeno značenje." The founding congress of the Communist Party of Slovenia (Komunistična partija Slovenije) in April 1937 had expressed similar devotion to Stalin. See "Dokumenti," "Izvršnomu odboru Kom. internacionale—sodrugu Georgiju Dimitrovu," in *Zbornik ob štiridesetletnici ustanovnega kongresa KPS*. For the cult of Stalin in the CPY (and the CPY's defense of Stalin's purges in the 1930s), see M. Djilas (1973), bk. 2, esp. chap. 5.

48. So wrote in November 1943 Lord Birkenhead, British liaison officer at the Partisan headquarters in Croatia; quoted in Clissold (1978), 22.

49. For the Belgrade party organization and its Yugoslavism, see M. Djilas (1973), bk. 2, chaps. 2–8. For party organizations in Croatia, see Jelić (1981),

vol. 1, "Organizaciona struktura Komunističke partije Hrvatske" and "Komunistička partija Hrvatske i nacionalno pitanje."

50. For similar examples see, e.g., Humo (1984). Avdo Humo, a Bosnian Muslim intellectual, was the party secretary in Mostar and in Sarajevo in the late
1930s. Intensely pro-Yugoslav, he promoted close cooperation among Muslims,
Croats, and Serbs. In Sarajevo there were the Serbian cultural institutions Sloga
and Prosvjeta, the Muslim Narodna uzdanica and Gajret, the Croatian
Napredak, and the Jewish Lira and Benevolencija. The left-wing pro-Communist
organizations such as Collegium Artisticum were almost the only groups capable
of uniting young people despite religious and national differences. Resisting both
Serbian and Croatian nationalist claims to Bosnia-Herzegovina, they argued in
favor of its autonomy on the basis of historical traditions and a mutual tolerance
of three religions and nationalities.

51. For Nešković's journey to Zagreb, see "Nisam raspuštao partizane," *Intervju*, 23 November 1984. Likewise, in the winter of 1940–41 Milovan Djilas made
a round of Slovenian party organizations investigating accusations that most
Slovenian party functionaries were masked Trotskyites. (The accusations proved
to be unfounded.) See M. Djilas (1973), bk. 2, chap. 17, esp. 357–359.

52. An extensive account of the conference is given in Damjanović et al. (1980).

53. In December 1939 the government of Dragiša Cvetković and Vladko
Maček had decided to create concentration camps for Communists where they
could be sent without trial. Some evidence suggests that the plans for camps were
first prepared in October in the Ministry of the Army and Navy. See Damjanović
(1972), "Dokumenti generalštaba."

54. "Peta zamaljska konferencija KPJ—Zagreb, 19–23 oktobar 1940," *NIN*,
19 October 1980.

55. See Pešić (1983), "Prva kolebanja i radikalne promene u nacionalnoj politici."

56. *Istorijski arhiv KPJ*, 2: 369. Separatism increasingly identified itself with
fascism, and Communists could no longer support it. Destabilization of
Yugoslavia was now described as being in the interest of the fascist imperialists,
not of the Communist revolution and the Soviet Union; ibid., 399.

57. For the Split plenum, see Pešić (1983), 269–273.

58. *Istorijski arhiv KPJ*, 2: 369–370.

59. The political secretary (the leader of the party), Milan Gorkić, soon afterward perished in the purges.

60. *Istorijski arhiv KPJ*, 2: 400. There was an obvious similarity between the
Comintern's views and those of Marković in the early 1920s.

61. From that time on the party would regard the right of separation not as a
duty, but rather as a condition for cooperation among different nations. See
Kardelj (1958), 423. Also, Jelić (1981), vol. 1, "Komunistička partija Hrvatske i
nacionalno pitanje" and "Komunistička partija Hrvatske i pitanje odbrane
zemlje."

62. This vagueness was unintentional but not accidental; state borders were for
Communists only a temporary expedient, an instrument for the global unification
of the proletariat.

63. See *Zbornik ob štiridesetletnici ustanovnega kongresa KPS*, "Dokumenti,"

esp. "Fašistične nakane proti slovenskemu narodu." From that time on the Slovenian party would always insist that the future of the Slovenian people lay with the other nations of Yugoslavia. See Kardelj (1958), chap. 10. Fear of Italian Fascism and German National Socialism would make the Slovenian party claim that the "Serbian masses" and (an unthinkable phrase in the late 1920s and early 1930s) "Serbian democratic traditions" were an ally of the Slovenian people. See Kardelj (1958), 438; also Tone Zorn, "Protifašistično gibanje na avstrijskem Koroškem," in *Zbornik ob štiridesetletnici ustanovnega kongresa KPS.*

64. Milan Gorkić had been arrested in Moscow in July 1937, and by some accounts Tito immediately became the leader of the party. He was officially appointed only later. See Jelić (1977), "Dolazak Josipa Broza Tita na čelo Komunističke partije Jugoslavije." Tito was formally called the general secretary, although that title did not exist in the statute of the CPY. Gorkić had the title of political secretary while leader of the party. The Comintern gave Tito the right to veto any decision of the Central Committee. For Tito's dominant position inside the Central Committee, see M. Djilas (1973), 284; also M. Djilas (1980). For an extensive account of the foundation of the Communist Party of Croatia, see Jelić (1981), vol. 1, "Osnivanje Komunističke partije Hrvatske."

65. "Proglas osnivačkog kongresa Komunističke stranke Hrvatske," in *Istorijski arhiv KPJ*, 2: 406–410.

66. The most complete account of the Popular Front in Yugoslavia from 1935 to 1945 is Živković (1978). For a comprehensive account of the Popular Front in Croatia, see Jelić (1981), vol. 1, "Komunistička partija Hrvatske i stvaranje pokreta Narodne fronte"; pt. 3. For the Popular Front in Slovenia, see, e.g., Alenka Nedog, "Povezovanje revolucionarnih sil v okviru ljudskofrontnega gibanja na Slovenskem," in *Zbornik ob štiridesetletnici ustanovnega kongresa KPS.*

67. "Blagoje Parović o partiji," *NIN*, 23 December 1984.

68. See Petranović (1980), "Narodni front i komunisti."

69. Ibid., 125.

70. On the attitude of Yugoslav Communists toward European fascism, see, e.g., Kardelj (1958), "Pod pritiskom fašističke ekspanzije"; also M. Djilas (1973), bk. 2, esp. chap. 11. For the view that for their protection small nations have to ally themselves with the "progressive forces" in the world, see Kardelj (1958), 421.

71. Also, much of Serbian history would soon be rehabilitated. The party decided, for example, that Serbia's participation in the Balkan Wars and the First World War had an "anti-imperialist character." This closely resembled the party's views from the early 1920s and was the opposite of its views in the late 1920s and early 1930s. See Kardelj (1958), 329. (The first edition of Kardelj's book was published in November 1938.)

72. See Petranović and Simović (1979) for a detailed account of the Popular Front in this period.

73. For much useful information, interpreted from the Communist point of view, see Petranović (1979); also Petranović (1980), "KPJ u političkom sistemu i unutrašnjopolitički odnosi."

74. Yugoslav historians generally agree that 1935 was a year of crucial impor-

tance for the development of the party's new policy toward the national question. The most important event was the plenum of the Central Committee of the CPY in June 1935 in Split.

75. See Marković (1923a, 1923b).

76. Even the CPY admitted that the Slovenes were in a much better position in Yugoslavia than under the Habsburg monarchy. See Kardelj (1958), "Slovenci u Jugoslaviji."

77. Bilandžić (1979), 36. In April 1941 there were between 3,600 and 4,000 Communists in Croatia; the CPY as a whole had around 8,000 members. See Jelić (1981), 1: 401.

78. After 1937, for example, Dalmatian Communists preserved their regional committee and were in frequent contact with the Central Committees of the CPY and not exclusively with the Central Committee of the CPC. See, e.g., Jelić (1981), vol. 1, "Prva konferencija Komunističke partije Hrvatske i njeno značenje," esp. 387–390.

79. *Zbornik ob štiridesetletnici ustanovnega kongresa KPS*, 277. See also Marinko (1950).

80. *Zbornik ob štiridesetletnici ustanovnega kongresa KPS*, 276.

81. Blagoje Parović, *Proleter*, nos. 7–8 (July–August 1935).

82. "Blagoje Parović o partiji," *NIN*, 23 December 1984. After the plenum of the CPY Central Committee in June 1935 in Split, Blagoje Parović was entrusted with the task of explaining to the cadres that the party would remain essentially unchanged.

83. For a comprehensive account of the founding congress, see *Osnivački kongres Komunističke partije Srbije*.

84. Blagoje Parović, *Proleter*, nos. 7–8 (July–August 1935). See also "Predgovor," in *Osnivački kongres Komunističke partije Srbije*.

85. The Central Committee of the CPY did not at that time have a clear concept of how to organize the party in Serbia, Bosnia-Herzegovina, Montenegro, Vojvodina and Kosovo. Nor was it particularly concerned about not having a clear concept, since the party organizations in those regions were well-integrated into the CPY.

86. See "Ne okrećem glavu," *Duga*, 9–22 February 1985, an interview with Moma Marković, wartime political commissar of all Partisan units in Serbia and member of the regional committee of Serbia. The regional committee was actually the Serbian equivalent of the central committees of Slovenia and Croatia, but it was not called the Central Committee until the Communist Party of Serbia was formally constituted in May 1945. See also Marković (1985).

87. See "Govor druga Kardelja," in *Osnivački kongres Komunističke partije Srbije;* also "Iz govora Edvarda Kardelja—Osnivački kongres Komunističke partije Srbije: 8–12 maj 1945," *NIN*, 12 May 1985.

88. See A. Djilas (1984).

89. In the summer of 1936, for example, the Central Committee of the CPY criticized those party cadres in Croatia who looked to Maček as the leader of the Croatian nation and uncritically accepted his policies on the Croatian national question; Pešić (1983), 273.

90. In 1932, when the party's support of Croatian separatism was at its peak, the slogans were similar only in part to those of the Ustashas and Frankovci. (For

an account of the nationalism of the Ustashas and Frankovci, see Chapter 4.) The party's slogan was, for example, "Out with all Serbian occupiers, bureaucrats, and police." No slogans even implicitly demanded discrimination against Serbs, let alone their expulsion (Pešić, 1983, 251). During the fifth party conference, in Zagreb in October 1940, Metodije Šatorov Šarlo, the party secretary for Macedonia, came into conflict with Milovan Djilas, a member of the Politburo who had drafted the resolution on the national question in the name of the Central Committee. Šatorov demanded that all Serbs who had come as colonists to non-Serbian lands, and not only the "oppressors" (i.e., police, military personnel, and civil servants) should be expelled (M. Djilas, 1973, 354). At the time this proposal was rejected by all leading Yugoslav Communists except Miladin Popović, who described colonists as the "pillar of the hegemony" (see "Tragom jednog dokumenta," *NIN*, 28 February 1988). Delegates at the conference also criticized Šatorov for his nationalist attitude toward the Serbs who lived in Macedonia (Petranović, 1980, 133–134).

Four. National State and Genocide

1. See Spalatin (1975). For a favorable account of Starčević's intellectual development, see Ladan (1971). The fact that such an ardent Croatian nationalist as Starčević could consider the Serbian population to be Croatian is in itself stark proof of the similarity between Croats and Serbs.

2. Bracher (1970), chap. 1, traces the transformation of German nineteenth-century nationalism into Nazism. For extreme nationalism, see Deutsch (1966), chap. 8, esp. "Extreme Nationalism and Self-Destruction: The Inner Problem of the Will."

3. Starčević's writings reveal an attitude similar to that of the Frankovci and the Ustashas in the 1930s: all political, social, and economic problems were subordinate to the national one and would be easily solved once national emancipation and statehood had been achieved. See A. Starčević (1941, 1943, 1971); also M. Starčević (1936).

4. Šišić (1975), 500.

5. The full title of the 1868 Agreement was "Državo-pravna ugarsko-hrvatska nagodba." On the Nagodba, see Šidak et al. (1968) "Hrvatski narod u razdoblju od g. 1860 do 1871," "Hrvatsko-ugarska nagodba"; also Horvat (1936), "Voljom Bismarckovom."

6. See Banac (1984), "Croat Mnemonists."

7. The word *ustaša* originally meant a participant in an uprising, an insurgent. In the uprisings against the Turks in the nineteenth century, for example, the word was used by both Croats and Serbs. Only in the 1930s and especially during the Second World War did it primarily designate a member of Pavelić's organization.

8. See Krizman (1983a), chap. 2.

9. See ibid., chaps. 3, 4.

10. There were also significant numbers of Frankovci working for other institutions devoted to Croatian culture and history, e.g., the cultural literary society Matica Hrvatska.

11. The event most publicized by the Ustashas was their attack on the police

station in the village of Brušani on 6 and 7 September 1932. The organizer was Andrija Artuković, who in April 1941 became minister of interior in the first government of the NDH. See Krizman (1984–85).

12. "Ustaški pokret u hrvatskim zemljama," *Proleter,* vol. 4, no. 28 (December 1932). This proclamation is sometimes interpreted as an anti-Serbian document, in which the Communists supported the movement that later committed genocide against the Serbian people. Yet such interpretations do not take into account that the proclamation sharply attacked Pavelić and Perčec, the exiled leaders of the movement, accusing them, among other things, of being fascists. It also argued that rebellious peasants should be separated from such leaders and led by the internationalist CPY.

13. For background on Communists in the prisons of interwar Yugoslavia and their relations with the Ustashas, see Čolaković (1964–1968); Ristović and Kržavac (1968), vol. 2, esp. chap. 8; M. Djilas (1973), 131–137. See also Daviĉo (1963a, 1963b, 1964), three novels based on personal experiences. Ćosić's (1985) historical novel portrays Communists in prewar prisons with particular emphasis on ideological fanaticism and the boycott of all those whose ideas diverged from Stalinist dogma. In "Vreme robijanja" (*NIN,* 28 April 1985) Radivoj Davidović Kepa, a Communist who spent many years in the prisons of prewar Yugoslavia, takes issue with Ćosić, giving numerous examples of Communist solidarity, fraternity, and attempts at self-education (the prisons were called "Communist universities").

14. For the social composition of the Ustashas, see Krizman (1983a), 564–573, who provides a list of all Ustashas exiled in Italy in the 1930s, complete with basic biographical facts. Over 70 percent described themselves as peasants; only about 5 percent were middle class (professionals, merchants, and officers); the rest were workers and sailors. The social composition of the Ustashas inside the country was similar.

15. Nevertheless, the Ustashas remained primarily a nationalist movement. In some of their policies during the Second World War they resembled German Nazis more than Italian Fascists. The massacres of Serbs, for example, are not essentially different from the attempt by the Third Reich to exterminate Jews. In contrast, Italian and Spanish fascists did not exterminate national groups. In this sense it could be said that the Ustashas were "worse" than fascists.

16. Toward the beginning of the war, however, Pavelić was accepted as an all-powerful leader who always had to be obeyed.

17. See, e.g., M. Djilas (1973), 131.

18. In the 1930s Communist prisoners were mostly Croats and Serbs, and they worked together without any national conflicts. Some were distinguished intellectuals, who in their lectures devoted special attention to the national question.

19. The Comintern also used the term *national revolutionary* for the "anti-imperialist" national movements.

20. For the Ustashas' and Communists' ideological debates and conflicts, as well as their occasional cooperation against prison authorities, see M. Djilas (1973), 218–224.

21. For Pavelić's views on the CPY and Yugoslavism as its inherent political orientation, see Krizman (1983a), 240–244.

22. For definitions and analyses of fascism and Nazism, see Nolte (1965), pt. 1; pt. 4, esp. chap. 5; pt. 5, esp. "The Concept of Transcendence." See also Bracher (1970), chaps. 1–3 and chap. 5, "Weltanschauung and Ideological *Gleischaltung*," and "The National Socialist Elite."

23. For Ustasha anti-Communism, see Pavelić (1974), esp. pt. 1.

24. They respected the church only insofar as it represented a traditional, national, social, family, and peasant value. But they rejected the individualism of Christian teaching and the internationalism (i.e., globalism and universalism) on which the Catholic church based its doctrine; they would not accept a church that did not conform to their own view of Croatia. Their ideology sometimes sounds like social-Darwinian racism, and at other times like the early German "organic" doctrine of Johann Gottlieb Fichte and Ernst Moritz Arndt. See Smith (1982), chap. 1; Kohn (1951), chap. 5.

25. E. Weber (1966) notes "the Legion's strength in the theological seminaries and agronomical faculties where most of the peasant students went, its popularity with village priests and those village teachers who did not lean towards the Peasant Party, and the number of legionnaires who were country born." For fascism in Romania, see also Fischer-Galati (1971). Catholic clericalism and the Ustashas' attempt to solve the "Serbian question" through forced conversion (especially after the massacres proved difficult to continue) resembles the crusading ideology of the Hlinka movement in Slovakia (Hory and Broszat, 1965, 178). For the Ustashas, however, Catholicism was primarily an instrument for strengthening the state rather than a goal in itself, whereas the Hlinka movement was genuinely Catholic and was led by priests. See Jelinek (1976), esp. chaps. 4, 8.

26. Smith (1982), 56: "No longer simply a body of citizens seeking their autonomy and identity in a secure homeland, the fascist 'nation in arms' becomes an authoritarian elite of warriors engaged in a biologically determined struggle for survival and domination." Ibid., 57: "fascism . . . elevates the brutal, youthful, realistic 'whole man' above the weak, lethargic masses. It can be said that the selection of such a power elite is a principal goal of fascism but rarely appears in nationalisms." This description of fascism to a large extent does not fit the Ustashas.

27. But from 1941 on the Ustashas increasingly aped the fascist and Nazi models. It is therefore possible that if they had prevailed they would not have satisfied themselves with the creation of an ethnically "clean" national state but would have turned their aggressive militarism toward some new goal.

28. It could be argued, however, that the difference in methods eventually becomes a difference in nature. Also, many other nationalisms (e.g., Italian) blended into fascism. For the genesis of fascism, see, e.g., Mosse (1966).

29. Krizman (1983a), chap. 5.

30. Jelić-Butić (1977), 159. An extensive account of Ustasha legislation can be found in ibid., esp. "Rasna politika i sistem terora ustaškog režima"; also Hory and Broszat (1965), chap. 5.

31. No civilized country enacts criminal laws with retroactive powers, since this would contradict one of the basic principles of all legislation: "Nullum crimen sine lege, nulla poena sine lege."

32. See Jelić-Butić (1977), "Tumačenje osnivanja NDH kao konačnog nacionalnog oslobodjenja hrvatskog naroda."

33. Pavelić's views on Croatian history were almost a replica of Starčević's. He elaborated them in "Uspostava hrvatske države—trajni mir na Balkanu." See Krizman (1983a), 74–76.

34. On the role of Catholicism in Ustasha ideology and the position of the Catholic church in the NDH, see Jelić-Butić (1977), "Uloga Katoličke crkve."

35. During 1941 alone, 334 priests of the Serbian Orthodox church in the territory of the NDH were murdered or deported to concentration camps (Alexander, 1979, 25). Most of the churches were also destroyed. Paris (1961), 285–290, gives the names of 171 Serbian Orthodox clergymen and 47 rabbis killed by the Ustashas.

36. For example, a village called Srpsko polje (Serbian Field) had to change its name to Hrvatsko polje (Croatian Field), and Karadjordjevo (named after Karadjordje, the leader of the uprising in Serbia against the Turks in 1804) to Tomislavovac (after Tomislav, the first medieval Croatian king).

37. And Pavelić would then suddenly state: "There were very few real Serbs in Croatia. They were mostly Croats of Orthodox confession and 'Vlasi'" (from *Neue Ordnung,* a weekly published by the Ustashas in German; quoted in Jelić-Butić, 1977, 173). The "Vlasi" (Vlachs), who called themselves Aromuni (Aromanians), were Romance-speaking descendants of Latinized Illyrian population. In the twentieth century there were hardly any non-Slavicized Vlachs among the South Slavs. While no South Slav group was without some Vlach ingredient, there is no evidence that all or most Serbs in Croatia were of Vlach origin. The thesis that Croatian Serbs were "Vlasi" occurred regularly in Ustasha propaganda—without any serious evidence to support it. Pavelić's minister Mladen Lorković said about "Vlasi": "They are the remnants of Romanic and Gypsy halfbreeds . . . Although racially they are neither Croats nor Serbs, they represent an unstable element, open to foreign influences, which because they belong to the Serbian Orthodox church succumbed to political Serbization" (*Neue Ordnung,* 7 September 1941; quoted in Jelić-Butić, 1977, 173). The Ustashas' use of the concept "Vlasi" strongly resembles Starčević's use of "Slavoserbi."

38. Ustasha anti-Semitic legislation was a copy of the Nazi Nuremberg laws of September 1935. See Jelić-Butić (1977), "Sprovodjenje terora nad Židovima." For the Nuremberg laws see, e.g., Bracher (1970), 253–254. Ustasha crimes against Jews are documented in Loewenthal (1957), pt. 2; Hillberg (1961), chap. 8, esp. "Satellites par Excellence" and "Croatia"; Reitlinger (1961), chap. 14, esp. "Jugoslawien (Kroatien)"; Romano and Kadelburg (1977), esp. 687–688. *Encyclopedia Judaica,* 16: 884, describes Pavelić's regime as one of "savage cruelty and terror." For a relatively favorable account of the treatment of Jews by the Italian army and police, see Sabille and Poliakov (1955), "The Attitude of the Italians to the Persecuted Jews in Croatia." The little-researched destiny of the Gypsies in the NDH was also tragic: of the 40,000 who lived in the territory of the NDH in April 1941, fewer than 1,000 survived the massacres by Ustasha racists; Jelić-Butić (1977), 182. (However, Kočović, 1985, 126, estimates Gypsy losses for the whole of Yugoslavia at 27,000, or 31.4 percent of their population; and Jewish losses at 60,000, or 77.9 percent.)

39. *Novi list,* 3 June 1941; quoted in Novak (1948), 606.

40. Immediately after its establishment, Pavelić's state began to turn away from Italy. The power of the Reich and the similarity between the Ustashas' rule and the Nazi regime brought Croatia closer to Germany, although in the late 1930s Italy and Germany had agreed that Germany would have only economic interests in Croatia.

41. Most Serbs did not initially perceive the creation of the NDH as a tragedy. See, e.g., "Borbe i pobede nadomak Čapljine," in *Hercegovina u NOB-u.* The book also gives insight into the support for the NDH and Ustashas by a considerable number of Croats in Herzegovina. In the CPP, the most enthusiastic were those who were also members of the prewar paramilitary Peasants' Defense.

42. See, e.g., Krizman (1980), chap. 2, esp. "Ustaški teror u zamahu."

43. For initial Serbian disbelief about extermination as the real goal of Ustasha policies, see, e.g., Ćopić (1963). This documentary–historical novel, written by an eyewitness and a member of the Partisan movement, gives a vivid account of the Ustasha terror in the region of Bosanska Krajina and the beginning of the Partisan-led Serbian uprising. See also Ćopić (1964).

44. The first actions of mass terrorism were committed by Ustashas returning from abroad, but soon they were joined by volunteer recruits. In the summer of 1941 there were between 25,000 and 30,000 Ustashas. Toward the end of the year *domobrani,* regular conscript soldiers of the NDH, numbered around 70,000; Jelić-Butić (1977), 122.

45. For the Communist and Partisan attitude to the Ustashas' massacres see M. Djilas (1977), esp. 192–193, 211–212.

46. In general, no educated Serbs were to be accepted as converts; Jelić-Butić (1977), 219. The Ustashas believed that these Serbs had a national consciousness that was independent from their confessional affiliation, whereas illiterate peasants were expected to forget their Serbian identity once they were forced to abandon their Serbian Orthodox religion. In 1941–42 around 240,000 Orthodox Serbs converted to Roman Catholicism; ibid., 175.

47. In joint operations with the German army the Ustashas were always under German command. German military commanders frequently interfered in the internal affairs of the NDH, even appointing local civil authorities. In May 1943 Himmler visited Zagreb and organized the German police in the NDH (Hory and Broszat, 1965, 148–151). The German representative in Zagreb, Siegfried Kasche, described the Ustasha regime as capable of wishing and complaining but not of making decisions. In July 1944 there were about 100,000 Croatian workers employed in Germany. Some German commanders in the NDH even thought of giving the whole territory to Italy to occupy, but the Ustashas had support at the highest levels of the Nazi hierarchy, including Hitler himself. (Hitler was deeply distrustful of Serbs, probably as a result of anti-Serbian propaganda he encountered in pre-1914 Vienna. The Serbian-led antifascist coup of 27 March 1941 transformed this suspicion into fury and open enmity. For Hitler's anti-Serbian views see ibid., 39–43.) Soon after the establishment of the NDH Hitler became aware how badly organized and unpopular the Ustasha regime was, yet he continued to support it because he knew that it was tied to the Third Reich, primarily through its crimes. On 31 August 1943 the German minister of foreign affairs,

Joachim von Ribbentrop, urged that the link with the Ustashas be maintained at all costs, since they were ideologically firm and by their very nature bound with Germany. Hitler agreed. On the Nazi leadership's support for the Ustasha regime, see Krizman (1983b). There were also tensions and clashes between the Italian occupation forces and the Ustashas. Even outside their zone of occupation, Italian troops often took over civilian and military power from the Ustashas.

48. See Krizman (1983a), chap. 7.

49. See Jelić-Butić (1977), pt. 4.

50. For the minor role played by the Ustashas in the two largest German offensives against the Partisans in the NDH, see Krizman (1980), chap. 6. "Vrijeme pothvata 'Weiss'" (Fourth Offensive) and "Vrijeme pothvata 'Schwarz'" (Fifth Offensive).

51. See ibid., chap. 5.

52. *Vojna enciklopedija,* 10: 321.

53. Neubacher (1956), 31–32.

54. Rendulic (1952), 161–162.

55. Bušić (1969), 2–3.

56. Tudjman (1981), 163.

57. Yugoslav historians are becoming increasingly aware that genocide in the NDH has been insufficiently explored; Petranović (1983), 1: 10.

58. See Kočović (1985), "Hrvatska," "Bosna i Hercegovina." Kočović's estimates of Jewish and Gypsy victims are given in note 38, above. Total South Slav losses, according to Kočović, were 869,000, or 5.9 percent of the population. Of these, Serbs accounted for 487,000, or 6.9 percent, Croats, 207,000, or 5.4 percent; Muslims, 86,000, or 6.8 percent; Montenegrins, 50,000, or 10.4 percent; Slovenes, 32,000, or 2.5 percent; and Macedonians, 7,000, or 0.9 percent; ibid., 126.

59. It is, of course, true that Jews were persecuted in the Third Reich from its very foundation, and Hitler had announced the extermination of the Jews as the goal of the Nazi party before the outbreak of the Second World War; see, e.g., Bracher (1970), chap. 8, "The Murder of the Jews." Further, before the NDH was even created in April 1941, hundreds of thousands of Jews had already died in ghettos, been executed by *Einsatz* units, or been murdered in Nazi-organized pogroms. Nevertheless, the plan for the total extermination of Jews (men, women, and children) began to be systematically implemented in 1942 (the decision having been taken at the Wannsee conference in January 1942); ibid., 426. The Ustasha attempt to exterminate the Serbs had begun already in the summer of 1941.

Ustasha crimes against the Serbs, Jews, and Gypsies, like the Nazi crimes against the Jews and Gypsies, are a clear case of genocide and are crimes against humanity; see, e.g., *International Encyclopedia of the Social Sciences,* vol. 7, s.v. "International Crimes," esp. "The Law of Nuremberg" and "The Genocide Convention." The term *genocide* was first used during the Second World War. The United Nations General Assembly adopted the Convention on Genocide on 9 December 1949 (entered into force on 12 January 1951). Article 2 defines genocide as "any of the following acts committed with intent to destroy, in whole or in part, a national, ethnic, racial, or religious group as such: (a) Killing members of the group; (b) Causing serious bodily or mental harm to members of the group; (c) Deliberately inflicting on the group conditions of life calculated to bring about its physical destruction in whole or in part; (d) Imposing measures intended to prevent births within the group; (e) Forcibly transferring children of the group to another group"; ibid., 518.

The Ustashas committed genocide against Serbs, Jews, and Gypsies under categories a, b, and c. The Nuremberg trials defined in particular these three categories as the most dreadful and the most universally condemned. Incitement to genocide is also punishable under the Convention on Genocide. In connection with genocide committed in the NDH, this charge would apply to groups of Croatian intelligentsia that engaged before and during the war (and sometimes also in exile after the war) in Starčević-like anti-Serbian and anti-Semitic propaganda.

Count four of the indictment during the Nuremberg trials defined "crimes against humanity" as "violations of international conventions, of internal penal laws and of the general principles of criminal law as derived from the criminal law of all civilised nations"; ibid., 517. The defense argued that the sovereign state, rather than individuals, was responsible for delictual behavior and also that there was no relevant law at the time the acts had been committed, and therefore they were not crimes and there could be no trial: "Nullum crimen sine lege, nulla poena sine lege." The court, however, decided that "crimes against international law are committed by men, not by abstract entities, and only by punishing individuals who commit such crimes can the provisions of international law be enforced." It further stated that "all transgressions mentioned in all of the counts were in fact recognized as crimes under positive international law at all relevant times." Finally, it pronounced that "crimes against humanity" are based on a higher concept of law and that some things are recognized as crimes by all men and all legal systems; ibid., 517.

60. Several high-ranking German military commanders in the NDH opposed the Ustashas' policy of exterminating the Serbs; see Krizman (1980), chap. 2, esp. "Nekoliko njemačkih izvještaja o situaciji u ljetu 1941."

61. The Italians then used their Serbian Chetnik allies against the NDH in an effort to increase their influence there, especially in the regions bordering Dalmatia, which was under Italian occupation. Toward the end of 1941 Chetniks in northern Dalmatia and Lika became little more than auxiliary troops of the Italians. Anti-Communist and great-Serbian, they were used against the Partisans. The conflict between the Chetniks and Partisans further increased Chetnik dependence on the Italians and lost them much support from Serbs. They indirectly collaborated even with the Ustashas, particularly when these participated in the German-Italian operations against the Partisans, and further increased their own isolation. See Milazzo (1975), chap. 3. Most accounts estimate the number of Croatian and Muslim civilians murdered by Chetniks at around 20,000; see *Sudjenje članovima političkog i vojnog rukovodstva organizacije Draže Mihailovića*. For Chetnik attacks on Croatian and Muslim civilians, inspired primarily by the belief in collective retribution held by many Chetnik commanders, see Tomasevich (1975), chap. 7, "Chetnik Terror."

62. See, e.g., Jelić-Butić (1983).

Five. Croatian and Serbian Political Parties, 1939–1945

1. Shortly before the Second World War the CPP's "leaders appeared to believe that Croatia's interests could best be served by keeping a foot in every camp. Despite its impressive numerical strength, it was realised that the party was far from monolithic or secure in its stance"; Clissold (1978), 2–3.

2. Boban (1974a), vol. 1, gives many detailed accounts of diplomatic activities in Croatia, in particular by the British, in support of some form of Croatian-Serbian settlement; see also ibid., vol. 2, pt. 2, chap. 3, "Do travnja 1940. godine"; Avramovski (1986), esp. vol. 2.

3. After invading Czechoslovakia in March 1939, Germany established a Slovak state under its control, but with independence in international law and with foreign representations. As a result many extreme Croatian nationalists hoped to achieve independence with German help.

4. Prince Pavle was a staunch anti-Communist too, but his anti-Communist measures were generally less repressive than those of King Aleksandar.

5. For an analysis of the many reasons for Stojadinović's fall (including his ambitious foreign policy and the semifascist character of some of his political maneuvers), see Hoptner (1962), 121–129.

6. On Maček as the leader of the United Opposition, see Boban (1974a), vol. 1; for a short summary of its activities, see ibid., 2: 449.

7. Maček (1957), 162.

8. Ibid., 182; M. Djilas (1973), 306–307.

9. Maček (1957), 185. In both the 1935 and 1938 elections voters were under considerable pressure to vote for the government candidates. See, e.g., Pavlowitch (1971), 89–90, 97.

10. See Boban (1974a), vol. 2, pt. 1, chap. 2.

11. For Cvetković's account of the Sporazum, see Cvetković (1962). For a history of the Sporazum, see Boban (1965).

12. For the full text of the decree that established the Banovina of Croatia, see *Službene novine*, vol. 21, no. 194-A-68 (26 August 1939), 1198–1201.

13. The Banovina of Croatia was not explicitly constituted on the principle of nationality. But neither was it constituted from a historical territory, even though it seemed so to many contemporaries, since it united most of the three historical Croatian lands (Slavonia, Dalmatia, and inner Croatia). First, for Croatian nationalists, the historical territory of Croatia encompassed also Bosnia-Herzegovina and some other smaller territories, that is, an area much larger than the Banovina. Second, the inclusion in the Banovina of some districts of Bosnia-Herzegovina was based on the fact that most of the population there was Croatian, and not on the basis of Croatian "historical rights." Finally, the exclusion of eastern Srem, the historical part of Slavonia, and of Boka Kotorska, a historical part of Dalmatia, was based on the fact that the majority of the population there was non-Croatian. So the principle of nationality, though not openly invoked, was still more important than the historical one. Pešelj (1970–71), 25, gives similar arguments: "The 1868 Compromise [with Hungary] considered the historical borders of Croatia and her established constitutional rights. The 1939 Agreement considered the ethnic character of the population on the territory to be included in the Banovina of Croatia."

14. Inside the Banovina there was a Serbian minority, which in some regions was a majority. No autonomy, self-rule, or minority rights were provided to these Serbs.

Although the Banovina of Croatia encompassed primarily territories in which Croats were in the majority, rather than those that Croatian nationalists traditionally demanded on the basis of what they considered to be Croatian "historical rights," during negotiations for the Sporazum Maček urged the inclusion of Vrbaska *banovina,* that is, a large part of Bosnia-Herzegovina, in the Banovina of Croatia (Maček, 1957, 186). This demand was tantamount to requesting the creation of Greater Croatia and was based primarily on historical rights, as well as on the claim, typical among extreme Croatian nationalists, that Bosnian Muslims were Croats.

Maček's views about the Muslims of Bosnia-Herzegovina closely resembled those of Starčević: Bosnia was a part of the old Croatian kingdom, Muslims were Croatian blood brothers, and so on (see Maček, 1937, "Govor predsjednika Dr. Vladka Mačeka hrvatskim seljacima muslimanske vjere prilikom njihovog posjeta Zagrebu, kao glavnom gradu svih Hrvata"). Maček urged Muslims to be loyal to *hrvatstvo* (Croatdom) and asserted that they "carried in their soul Croatian national consciousness, sucked in with their mothers' milk" (ibid., 23).

15. Serbian jurists described the constitutional basis of the Banovina of Croatia as monarchical federalism, whereby the monarchy with all its constitutional privileges remained the pivot of the state. Croatian jurists, however, interpreted the Sporazum (the constitutional decree of 26 August 1939) as the constitution of Croatia, an act representing the will of the Croatian nation. See Pešelj (1971–72), 23–24.

16. *Službene novine,* vol. 21, no. 194-A-68 (26 August 1939), 1197.

17. Maček's memoirs (1957) give insight into his political mind. During the First World War he supported the preservation of Austria-Hungary under the Habsburg dynasty, won a medal for his participation in the battles against Serbia, and was proud when the monarchy finally defeated it (ibid., 62–65). He almost justifies the Ustasha massacres, saying they were caused primarily by Serbian prewar domination, and blaming the Chetniks for supposedly being the first to attack certain Croatian villages in Herzegovina in 1941 (ibid., 231). Maček seems to see no difference between the Ustashas and Chetniks (ibid., 238). Like the Frankovci and the Ustasha leaders, he also claims that the Serbs in Croatia were "Vlasi."

18. See Boban (1974a).

19. For the CPY's attitude to the Sporazum, see Kardelj (1958), 20–22. See also Boban (1974a), vol. 2, chap. 1, "Komunistička partija Jugoslavije i Sporazum Cvetković-Maček." As a part of its Popular Front policy, the CPY had supported the struggle of the United Opposition, recognizing it as "a step toward assembling all democratic and progressive forces in the struggle for the liquidation of the remnants of the military-fascist dictatorship" (Boban, 1974a, 2: 258). The CPY demanded both the abolition of the 1931 constitution and the fulfillment of Croatian demands. Yet the CPY saw the Sporazum as only a partial solution, primarily because it had not been combined with democratic reforms but also because other non-Serbs had not had their demands satisfied.

20. The Honved was the Hungarian national army before the First World

War; the Heimwehr was the local militia in the Austrian parts of the Habsburg monarchy. Yet Croatian nationalists often seemed intentionally to use the two terms interchangeably. They wanted a national Croatian army but for tactical reasons claimed to aspire only to the creation of local militia. Maček's demands for military and police autonomy were far greater than the concept of the Heimwehr would allow. Pavelić also confused the terms, probably deliberately. See, e.g., his conversation with the Italian foreign minister, Count Ciano, in January 1940 (Boban, 1974a, 2: 315–317). In somewhat crude terms, in its strength and level of organization the Citizens' and Peasants' Defense resembled the Heimwehr but aspired to be like the Honwed.

For the Citizens' Defense in Zagreb joining the Ustashas, see, e.g., Maček (1957), 231. For the actions of the Citizens' and Peasants' Defense against the Yugoslav army during the April war, its joining the NDH armed force, and its misdeeds against the Serbs, see Jelić-Butić (1983), 45–62.

21. For the reasons for Maček's failure to control the extreme right wing of his party, see, e.g., Seton-Watson (1962), 239.

22. Traditionally, the Serbian Orthodox church was anti-Catholic but not anti-Croatian, except when it perceived Croatian nationalism as an ally (or instrument) of Catholic expansion. As a centralist institution, the army had been apprehensive of Croatian separatism since the creation of Yugoslavia. Anti-Croatian sentiment, however, became prevalent only after the Sporazum.

23. See, e.g., Pešelj (1970–71), "Political Appraisal"; Boban (1974a), vol. 2, pt. 2, chap. 2.

24. See Pavlowitch (1971), 99–100; Petranović (1980), 147–149.

25. During the local elections in the Banovina of Croatia in May 1940, the CPP wanted to rid the local executives of those who had achieved their positions under pre-Sporazum centralism, and install its own people. Public (open) voting was preserved, even though the United Opposition had denounced it as a form of pressure on the voters. (The United Opposition, censuring the pseudo-representation of the 1931 constitution, had demanded a secret ballot; this continued to be the demand of the Serbian parties after the Sporazum.) The CPP claimed that since the great majority of people supported the party, the elections were nonpolitical. Yet many Serbs in the Banovina saw the elections as crucial for establishing the borders of the Banovina (i.e., deciding whether certain mostly Serbian regions would be under the rule of Zagreb or Belgrade). After the elections the CPP claimed, without strong evidence, that the elections had proved that the majority of Serbs in the Banovina supported the Sporazum. See Boban (1974a), vol. 2, pt. 2, chap. 1, "Općinski izbori u Banovini Hrvatskoj."

26. Maček showed little knowledge of or sympathy for the ideology of National Socialism. Yet he was not reluctant to praise Germany and Hitler when he judged that doing so could bring short-term tactical gains. In conversation with some diplomats in Zagreb, for example, a few days before the German attack on Yugoslavia on 6 April 1941, he stated that Hitler would achieve his greatest glory if he would free Russia from Bolshevism and save Europe from the catastrophe that threatened her from the Soviet Union. See Boban (1974a), 2: 404.

27. The Sporazum was modeled in part on the 1868 Nagodba (Agreement)

between Croatia and Hungary, which recognized the state rights and symbols of Croatia, and Croats as a political nation. (The Sporazum recognized Croatian state rights only implicitly and partially.) Yet the Nagodba subjected Croatia to a joint parliament in Budapest, where Magyars had the majority. This, of course, was not something the CPP desired to repeat with Serbs in Belgrade. On the contrary, it had great national ambitions and wanted Croatia to establish with Belgrade the kind of relationship that Hungary had had with Vienna during the last half-century of the Habsburg monarchy. So the Sporazum was even more influenced by the example of the Magyar compromise (Ausgleich) with Vienna in 1867, through which Hungary achieved special status inside the monarchy and became a Magyar nation state in the territory of "historical Hungary." The CPP wanted to attain a similar special status for Croatia inside Yugoslavia. It also hoped to annex all territories of "historical Croatia" (e.g., Bosnia-Herzegovina), but had to satisfy itself, at least for the time being, with the territories in which Croats were in the majority. (In fact, however, the Banovina also included some regions in which Croats were not a majority, such as Serbian parts of Lika, Kordun, Banija, and Dalmatinska Zagora. In addition, a few hundred thousand Croats remained outside Banovina.) For the CPP, the Sporazum was a major step, but only the first, toward these two goals.

28. For a similar comparison of the Yugoslav-Croatian problems after the Sporazum with the British-Irish ones, see S. Jovanović (1976), 57.

29. Toward the end of the seventeenth century the Polish parliament (Sejm) had been all but paralyzed by the *liberum veto*. This integral part of the Polish constitution, based on the principle of political equality among all Polish nobles, required that all measures and laws be adopted unanimously by the Sejm.

30. Germany, Italy, and Japan had signed the Tripartite Pact in September 1940 in Berlin. This document went beyond the anti-Bolshevism of the anti-Comintern pact signed by Germany and Japan in November 1936 and by Italy in November 1937. The Tripartite Pact asserted that "every nation in the world shall receive the space to which it is entitled" and that a "new order" would be established in Europe and "Greater East Asia." For the text of the pact, see Hoptner (1962), app. B.

31. For German pressure on Yugoslavia to join the Tripartite Pact, see Krizman (1977a). For the German-Italian prewar plans to divide Yugoslavia into spheres of influence, see Kljaković (1977).

32. Those chiefly involved in deciding Yugoslav foreign policy were Prince Pavle, Cvetković, Maček, Foreign Minister Aleksandar Cincar-Marković, and Ivo Andrić, the Yugoslav diplomatic representative in Berlin. For the changes in Yugoslav foreign policy that led to the pact of 25 March, see Hoptner (1962), chaps. 5–7. For the full English text of the "Protocol of Adhesion of Yugoslavia to the Tripartite Pact," see ibid., app. B.

33. The other two coregents resigned with Prince Pavle. Formally, they were equal in authority with Prince Pavle and had exercised the powers of the crown together with him as a Council of Regency.

34. See Damjanović et al. (1972), "Peta konferencija i razvoj političkih prilika u zemlji" and "U susret martovskim dogadjajima"; M. Djilas (1973), bk. 2, chap. 18; Čolaković et al. (1963), pt. 5, chap. 3.

35. For a summary of the dangers from this superficially undemanding pact for the independence of Yugoslavia, see Mitrović (1984).

36. See S. Jovanović (1976), "Konferencija od 5. aprila."

37. The view that the coup was primarily an anti-Croatian event is widespread among the Croatian nationalist intelligentsia.

38. Clissold (1978), 6: "Two days before the coup, the British Minister had telegraphed to Eden: 'Germans and Frankovci are already becoming uppish; and it is probable that the leaders of the CPP to whom the Yugoslav ideal is only important in so far as it assures them autonomy, will be pushed more and more towards separatism . . . Opposition to Germany is strongest in Serbia, and our main hopes of resistance to Germany must therefore lie there.'"

39. See S. Jovanović (1976), "Pregovori s Mačekom" and "Hrvati."

40. For British attempts to arouse Croatian interest in fighting the Germans, see Šepić (1975); Barker (1976a), 87–88.

41. For example, Maček recommended that Yugoslavia offer to allow German troops to cross its territory. See S. Jovanović (1976), 12.

42. For Hitler's decision to defeat Yugoslavia and destroy the Yugoslav state, see Čulinović (1970), 49–50.

Most Yugoslav historians claim that the coup of 27 March and the Axis invasion soon thereafter were the major causes of the six-week postponement of the German attack on the Soviet Union; without the Belgrade putsch, German troops would have reached Moscow earlier and probably captured it. However, van Creveld (1973), 182–83, states: "As for the Yugoslav campaign, it was far less 'unexpected' in a military sense than is usually believed. Although it drew forces from 'Barbarossa,' it cannot really be said to have delayed, much less disrupted, its build-up . . . The factor which really determined the starting date of 'Barbarossa' was, it seems, the general shortage of equipment in the German army." See also van Creveld (1972).

43. The number killed is estimated at between 10,000 and 20,000 out of a population of 250,000; Pavlowitch (1971), 107.

44. See Čulinović (1970), "Planovi o razdiobi Jugoslavije."

45. For an account of the short war, see *Aprilski rat 1941—Zbornik dokumenata* (1969).

46. But see Pavlowitch (1983), 450: "Hitherto the stress has been placed on the all-too-obvious weaknesses of the Yugoslav armed forces in 1941 (lack of preparedness, technological backwardness, defeatism, nationalist disloyalty, "moling" by Axis and communist propaganda, etc.). German and Italian evidence appears to suggest a performance in April 1941 that was, perhaps, less discreditable than Yugoslavs will as yet believe."

47. See Terzić (1982).

48. See Bogdanov (1961); Barker (1976a), "The Croats and the Defense of Yugoslavia."

49. For the most important documents in connection with the government in exile until January 1943, see Krizman (1981). See also Wheeler (1980). Pavlowitch (1981) gives the most succinct account.

50. For a sketch of Simović, see S. Jovanović (1976), "Simovićev pad"; for his mistrust of politicians, see ibid., 23.

51. Slobodan Jovanović argued (with full support from the representatives of political parties) that the coup had restored national representation as constitutionally equal to the crown. In spite of this, no government was constitutional without the king's approval. See Pavlowitch (1981), 90.

52. Outside the government, there were other conflicts among the Serbs: between junior and senior officers, between the king and "king's men" and others, between different branches of the army, and between those who had organized or supported the coup and those who had opposed it.

53. See S. Jovanović (1976). Pavlowitch (1971), 146, cites "the endemic deadlock of the Serbo-Croatian disagreement" in the government in exile as the main reason why "it was unable to provide united leadership for the pro-Yugoslav moderate forces in the country" and why it lost prestige in British eyes.

54. See S. Jovanović (1976), 19. The Yugoslav National Party had been formed as a government party in July 1932 but went into opposition after Stojadinović took over in 1935. In the government in exile it comprised those politicians who had not gone over to the Yugoslav Radical Union, founded by Stojadinović in August 1935. The party formed part of the United Opposition in the 1938 elections (except in Croatia, where local leaders joined the government list). It was the creation of King Aleksandar and was committed to unitarism and centralism. In the eyes of many Croats it was still the party of Aleksandar's dictatorship.

55. Slovenes were represented in the government in exile by the Slovenian People's Party.

56. See S. Jovanović (1976), "Jugoslovensko pitanje."

57. For a general account of the policies of the Yugoslav government in exile toward Croatia and the Croatian question, see Kljaković (1971–1973).

58. The chronic conflict between Croatian and Serbian ministers made the British government and the Foreign Office doubt that Yugoslavia would endure. They considered the Yugoslav government in exile incompetent and repeatedly interfered in its affairs. Later (especially after mid-1943) they influenced the choice of the prime minister, the appointment of ministers, and the content of certain important political declarations. See Clissold (1978); Krizman (1981).

59. See Maček (1957), chaps. 14, 15.

60. For Maček's proclamation, see Čulinović (1968), "Kako je došlo do Mačekovog proglasa na zagrebačkoj radio-stanici."

61. For the Ustasha version of Krnjević's anti-Serbian activities in the government in exile, see Kovačić (1970), 98–99, 205, 277.

62. There were three deputy prime ministers, one for each of the three recognized nations of Yugoslavia.

63. See Šepić (1975).

64. See S. Jovanović (1976), "Hrvati." For Krnjević's deeply entrenched dislike of the Serbs and belief that no dialogue or compromise between Croats and Serbs was possible, see, e.g., the letter of his collaborator and friend Branko M. Pešelj to *Naša reč*, vol. 41, no. 395 (May 1988), 18.

65. For example, in a memorandum to the British government in the spring of 1939 he discussed the possibility of an independent Croatia under British protection; Boban (1974a), 122–124.

66. See Krizman (1981), no. 20, "Izjava Dra Jurja Krnjevića."

67. Most ministers felt under no obligation to report to the government about their extragovernment activities, which included engaging independently in politics with foreign governments and intelligence agencies or with members of exiled communities of their nations, mostly in the United States.

For Krnjević's postwar support of an independent Croatian state, his refusal to condemn the Ustashas' crimes or to distance himself from former Ustashas, and his fear of Ustasha competition for leadership of the Croatian exiles, see "Pismo Dr. Dinka Šuljka," *Na pragu sutrašnjice*, 2, no. 2 (March 1976). See also his speech at the CPP conference in Cleveland, 5 September 1952, reported in *Danica*, 17 September 1952 (quoted in Kovačić, 1970, 279).

68. After the Ustasha massacres, some vocal Serbian politicians in exile lost all hope that Serbs and Croats could ever live together, and came to favor the creation of an independent Serbian state. The more extreme wanted to include in such a state not only Bosnia-Herzegovina but also large parts of today's Croatia. Some even imagined that these territories would have to be made ethnically "clean," that is, that Croats (and even Muslims) should be expelled from them, and that the Chetnik movement should be used for this purpose. For Fotić's anti-Croatian propaganda in Serbian communities in the United States, see Krizman (1981), no. 130, "S. Kosanović—S. Jovanoviću"; no. 186, "I. Šubašić—S. Jovanoviću i ministrima." For Krnjević's belief that there was a Serbian conspiracy behind Fotić's activities, see ibid., no. 203, "Zapisnik sjednice vlade."

69. See S. Jovanović (1976), "Hrvati."

70. For example, the British Foreign Office considered Momčilo Ninčić, the minister of foreign affairs, "to be anti-Croat to an almost fanatical degree"; Clissold (1978), 8. However, the Foreign Office's hostility to Ninčić may have been partly a result of his attempts to conduct Yugoslav foreign policy independently of any great power. See Pavlowitch (1981), 99–101; (1985), chap. 2.

71. Milan Grol, a member of the cabinet and the leader of the Democratic Party, wrote in March 1943 to Prime Minister Slobodan Jovanović: "The very idea of the [Yugoslav] state is in crisis." The main cause was the conflict between Croats and Serbs both in Yugoslavia and in the government in exile. See "Pismo Milana Grola," *Naša reč*, no. 219, 9; Krizman (1981), no. 219, "Zapisnik sjednice vlade"; no. 226, "Zapisnik sjednice vlade."

72. Pavlowitch (1981), 102, astutely remarks: "In exile and under the shock of recent events in the occupied homeland, party leaders were faced again with the prewar Serbo-Croatian issue, hideously magnified." Pavlowitch further states (ibid., 102): "The Serbo-Croatian problem, from a mere political or constitutional issue, turned into a fundamental one about the very existence of the state." Yet the Croatian issue was always about the existence of the Yugoslav state, since it was closely connected with separatism. It was never a mere political or constitutional question.

For the reports about the massacres in the NDH and their effect on the London government, see Krizman (1981), no. 81, "Lj. Hadži-Djordjević—Dušanu Simoviću"; no. 89, "I. Šumenković—Ministarstvu vanjskih poslova"; no. 98, "I. Šumenković—M. Ninčiću"; no. 122, "Episkop Dionizije—Ivanu Šubašiću"; no. 177, "I. Šumenković—S. Jovanoviću."

73. R. W. Seton-Watson, a British historian of Austria-Hungary and the Balkans who was generally sympathetic to Croatian demands, believed that Croats were the most quarrelsome of all Slavs. Although this is of course both an exaggeration and a simplification, it is true that Croats, lacking an independent state in which their political elites could learn the responsibilities of government, and without sufficient strength to challenge Vienna or Budapest through revolution, often put up opposition by issuing declarations and resolutions. Over time it left a mark on the Croatian political mentality.

Krišković (1925), 24, notes that "desperate struggle against more powerful opponents over centuries had pushed Croats toward this sterile field of negations, principled reservations and protests." And again (ibid., 24–25): "Abhorring any revolution . . . weak in conceiving new political ways and means, too feeble to arouse the interest of European public opinion in its honest struggle, [Croatia's] politics were mostly ideological, philosophical, dogmatic, and sectarian."

74. See S. Jovanović (1976), 62. Interestingly, Jovanović, who correctly perceives that it was wrong to consider the Ustasha massacres as almost the same thing as the mass dismissal of Croatian schoolteachers, describes these dismissals as a case of "ordinary party persecution." In fact they were much worse; they were a case of national persecution.

75. George Rendel, the British minister to the Yugoslav government in exile, writes about Croatian unwillingness "to issue some clear and unequivocal statement condemning and repudiating the atrocities perpetrated by the Ustase. But, with what seemed typically short-sighted obstinacy, they refused to be either wise or generous and continued to flog the dead horse of Croat grievances in and out of season. By this time both parties [Croats and Serbs] had lost sight of the fact that the world war was at its crisis"; Rendel (1957), 216.

Rudolf Bićanić, the CPP member of the London government, wrote a memorandum in which he tried primarily to blame the Muslims for the massacres of Serbs and at the same time accused the Germans of organizing them. Although he considered the Ustashas and Frankovci to be culpable, he described them as the tools of German policy. None of these claims, however, was true. Germans in general opposed the massacres, and the Ustasha units were mostly Catholic Croatian, although many Muslims participated. Among the Ustasha leadership and officers, there were only a few Muslims. Also, Bićanić believed that in general the Serbs in the NDH were as much to blame for the massacres as the Croats. In a memorandum he described the "real state of affairs" as follows: "(1) Croats are killing Serbs; (2) Croats are slaughtered by Croats; (3) Serbs are slaughtering Croats; (4) Serbs are slaughtering Serbs" (quoted in Krizman, 1981, no. 118, "Memorandum Dra Rudolfa Bićanića").

Given that there were far more Serbian victims than Croatian, it was inevitable that views such as Bićanić's would appear to Serbs both in the London government and in the exiled Serbian community in the United States as an insufficient condemnation of the Ustashas.

76. In his letter to Prime Minister Slobodan Jovanović, Milan Grol blamed the government crisis on, among other things, the failure of Croatian members of the government to condemn the Ustasha massacres. See "Pismo Milana Grola," *Naša reč*, no. 221, 2. While Croats were reluctant to attack Ustasha policies and to

participate wholeheartedly in the government, and Serbs were unprepared to abandon completely Serbian centralism and unitarism and halt the Chetniks' persecution of Croats and Muslims, the CPY was energetically pro-Yugoslav. Opposing both the Chetniks and the Ustashas, it tried to prevent all nationalist conflicts. It rejected "Serbian hegemony" and favored a federal system. Led by a united "war cabinet," i.e., the Politburo and the Supreme Staff, it succeeded in uniting people of different nationalities both in the leadership and among cadres and ordinary soldiers.

77. See S. Jovanović (1976), "Simovićev pad."

78. For Simović's Yugoslavism, see ibid., 18.

79. Throughout the interwar period Serbs constituted the absolute majority of the officers corps. Of the approximately 230 Yugoslav generals in 1941, 21 were Croats and 10 were Slovenes. All the rest were Serbs. In the late 1930s, however, there had been a slow but continuous increase in the number of non-Serbian generals and other officers. See Pavlowitch (1983).

80. The fact that Simović had already accepted Maček's demands was insufficient reassurance to the Croats.

81. For Croatian perceptions of the Serbian parties as a bloc, see S. Jovanović (1976), "Simovićev pad," esp. 19–22. In reality, the Serbian parties, with or without Simović, were less of a bloc than Croats believed. The Serbs were also less united than the Croats, although they had important points of agreement. See ibid., "Srbi," esp. 73.

Jovanović (1976), 22, comments that Simović's fall was caused "by a major crisis in Serbian-Croatian relations. Of course, he could excuse himself by saying that this crisis, precisely because of its magnitude, would have caused the fall of most others in his place."

82. A portrait of Slobodan Jovanović as a scholar can be found in Vlajić (1959). For Jovanović as both historian and politician, see D. Djordjević (1974).

83. Contact between the Yugoslav government in exile and the country was primarily through the British. Contact with Mihailović was via the British military command in the Middle East. See S. Jovanović (1976), "Pitanje generala Mihailovića," esp. 33.

84. For the similarity between Jovanović's and Mihailović's views and aims, see Pavlowitch (1981), 96.

85. For the history of the Mihailović movement, see, e.g., Roberts (1973) and Tomasevich (1975).

86. Mihailović was generally considered by the British to be anti-Croatian. In order to stop the Ustasha massacres, for example, Mihailović urged the Allies in 1942 to threaten to bomb "the Ustasha centers of Zagreb, Karlovac, and Varaždin" in order to stop the extermination of the Serbs. See Krizman (1981), no. 240, "M. Ninčić—K. Fotić."

87. For a general account of British wartime policy in southeastern Europe (including the switch of support from the Chetniks to the Partisans), see Barker (1976a). A lucid and well-argued (though not completely persuasive) defense of British policy is in ibid., "Postscript." For the critical period 1942–43, see Barker (1979).

88. For an analysis of Mihailović's attitude toward the occupying powers, see, e.g., Milazzo (1975), chap. 5 and "Conclusion."

89. See S. Jovanović (1976), "Jugoslovensko pitanje."

90. Jovanović also wanted to use it to counter claims by Croatian politicians and the CPY that Serbs were interested in reestablishing their prewar "hegemony"; ibid., 54–55.

91. Ibid., 55.

92. Krnjević had supported Trifunović's nomination for prime minister in place of Jovanović, even though Jovanović was a more moderate critic of the Sporazum, and although Krnjević had accepted Jovanović's draft of the declaration. (For Trifunović's criticism of the Sporazum and his belief that the CPP ministers were continuing the nationalism of Ante Starčević, see Krizman, 1981, no. 224, "Zapisnik sjednice vlade".) Obviously, Krnjević was obstructing any form of common policy or declaration by the Yugoslav government, probably because he saw the paralysis of the government as a chance for Croatian independence.

93. Since April 1942 the king had wanted to marry Princess Alexandra of Greece, niece of King George II of the Hellenes. Most Serbian ministers opposed the idea, fearing (as it turned out, correctly) that in its propaganda the CPY would exploit a display of conjugal festivity as proof of the king's lack of sympathy for Serbian wartime suffering. The Croatian ministers and the British used this situation to manipulate the king and to get rid of those Serbian politicians of whom they disapproved, beginning with Jovanović. (King Petar II and Princess Alexandra were married in London in March 1944.) See Pavlović (1975); S. Jovanović (1976), "Kraljeva ženidba."

94. In the beginning of 1942 the government in exile had appointed Mihailović minister of defense (minister of the army, navy, and air force, which encompassed the "Yugoslav Army in the Fatherland," as well as the units in the Middle East). He was given the highest military rank, that of army general, although he was only a colonel when the war started. Mihailović was also the chief of staff of the Supreme Command (Načelnik štaba Vrhovne Komande). The king was formally the supreme commander of the armed forces; but in wartime, according to the regulations of the kingdom of Yugoslavia, the General Staff became the Staff of the Supreme Command, and the effective commander of the armed forces was its chief of staff.

95. S. Jovanović (1976), "Hrvati." On the wartime conflict between Croatian and Serbian communities in the United States, see Krizman (1981), no. 116, "M. Trifunović—Dušanu Simoviću"; no. 164, "K. Fotić—M. Ninčiću."

96. For the fear of Mihailović among Croats living in the United States and their consequent support of the Partisans, see, e.g., Petranović (1983), 2:379. For some activities of Croatian organizations in the United States, see "Pismo Dr. Dinka Šuljka," *Na pragu sutrašnjice*, vol. 2, no. 2 (March 1976). A congress of the People's Council of American Croats (Narodno Vijeće Američkih Hrvata) in February 1943 in Chicago was attended by more than 900 delegates from various Croatian organizations. The Executive Committee of the People's Council consisted of leading Communist supporters and representatives of the CPP. Among

other things, the congress criticized King Petar II for giving indirect support to certain Yugoslav diplomats who were Serbian nationalists; ibid., 136–137.

97. See Radica (1974). The author's animosity toward Serbs prevents him from fairly presenting Croatian-Serbian relations in the last year of war and civil war in Yugoslavia. Yet he gives many memorable and picturesque details of the prevailing atmosphere and of the depth and severity of the conflict between Croatian and Serbian non-Communist political groups. There is also a somewhat caricatured but still perceptive account of the intrigue and strife in the government in exile.

98. For accounts of Mihailović's help to Allied airmen and a portrayal of him as a resistance leader rather than as a collaborator, see, e.g., Martin (1946, 1978); Yourichitch (1950); Avakumović (1969).

99. Many Serbian nationalists combined their rigid anti-Communism with halfhearted support of parliamentarism and liberal-democratic institutions. They accepted the latter only insofar as they did not allow Croats or Communists to endanger Serbian interests and undermine the unity of the state. This type of nationalism was particularly strong in the People's Radical Party.

100. Activities of many members of the London government demonstrated the high correlation that existed between moderation on the national question, dedication to liberal-democratic (pluralist parliamentary) political institutions, and readiness to seek compromise with the CPY. One Serb in the government who showed great openmindedness to Croatian demands was Srdjan Budisavljević, president of the Independent Democratic Party, which was influential among Serbs in Croatia and an ally of the CPP. This party was pro-Yugoslav, favoring federalism and seeking compromise with Croats. (See S. Jovanović, 1976, "Simovićev pad" and "Srbi".) Many Independent Democrats in the country had joined the Partisans. Other Serbs in the government in exile accused the Independent Democrats of being much more arduous in the suppression of Serbian than of Croatian extremism (ibid., 69). Budisavljević also favored compromise with the Partisans. The exiled politician who cooperated most with the Communists was Sava Kosanović, another leader of the Independent Democrats and minister of information in the Communist-dominated provisional government of March 1945. For his account of the London government and the political situation among exiles in general, see Kosanović (1984).

Ivan Šubašić's Croatian nationalism definitely played a role in the abandonment of Mihailović. Yet he was, in comparison with Krnjević, a moderate Croatian nationalist, and this, among a number of personal and political reasons, made it possible for him to cooperate with the Partisan leadership, even though it was leading a Yugoslav, and not Croatian, movement. Juraj Šutej, another moderate among the CPP ministers, likewise reached accommodation with the Communists. Krnjević, unswerving in his nationalist convictions, stayed in exile.

The Democratic Party has a special place in connection with the relation between nationalism, liberalism, and anti-Communism. It had opposed the 1929 dictatorship and the 1931 constitution. Because of its insistence on full and strict application of all democratic procedures, its opponents sometimes accused it of "democratic and parliamentary purism." (A number of distinguished Democrats, however, participated in the pseudo-representative post-January 1929 governments, and the party's opposition to the dictatorship was not energetic.) Moreover, the party favored some compromise with Croats, and its more liberal members supported federalism as early as 1933. In the government in exile Milan Grol, the leader of the party, was still primarily concerned with Serbian interests. (For example, in March 1943 he had written to Prime Minister Slobodan Jovanović: "The value of the common Serbian-Croatian-Slovene state I measure according to the value it represents for insuring Serbdom"; see "Pismo Milana Grola," *Naša reč,* no. 221, 2.) Together with Radicals and Agrarians he supported the Chetnik movement and made minimal efforts to change the Chetnik policies toward Croats, Muslims, and the Partisan movement. In spite of all this, he was not an intransigent Serbian nationalist. He was in conflict with the Croats far less often than the Radicals and Agrarians, and he often tried to mediate between Croatian and Serbian ministers. Grol's devotion to parliamentary pluralism somewhat moderated both his nationalism and his anti-Communism. (For his perceptive analysis of how persecution of the CPY in interwar Yugoslavia increased the sympathies for Communists, see Krizman, 1981, no. 219, "Zapisnik sjednice vlade," 419.) After the war, he returned to Yugoslavia and tried unsuccessfully to establish the opposition to the Communist regime.

Six. Federalism and Yugoslavism, 1943–1953

1. Seton-Watson (1956); Russinow (1977), 13.

2. Schöpflin (1983) maintains that the Communists' rise to power in eastern Europe was made possible by Germany and its wartime ideological allies, such as the Arrow Cross in Hungary, the Iron Guard in Romania, and the predominantly Serbian Ljotić movement in Yugoslavia. However, in Yugoslavia it was primarily the Ustasha movement, installed and supported by Italians and Germans, that committed the worst atrocities against civilians and pushed them into joining the Partisans. (For Ljotić's semifascist Zbor movement, see Chapter 2, note 69.)

3. Roberts (1973), 321, states: "Although the Partisans received outside military help after the middle of 1943, that material aid did not determine their victory: Tito and his followers won the civil war because they were from the first militarily more active and later politically more astute than the Chetniks. Only an Allied landing in Yugoslavia—which Churchill would have welcomed but Roosevelt and Stalin opposed for military reasons—might have altered the outcome of the internal Yugoslav struggle."

4. Without Soviet help, however, the Partisans would not have captured Belgrade as early as October 1944. The control of the capital was an important political victory for the CPY. Also, help from the Anglo-American Allies in the form of weapons, equipment, and propaganda had increased the strength, confidence, and influence of the Partisans.

5. This generalization is valid on the whole, although the CPP and the Slovenian People's Party still had considerable support among peasants. In Serbia, no individual party enjoyed similar influence, but the pre-1929 (and even pre-1914) traditions of parliamentarism had not been forgotten.

6. See Kulundžić (1968), which, though not a scholarly study, contains much interesting information.

7. See N. Jovanović (1974), esp. chap. 4.

8. See Bodrožić (1973). On Partisan efforts to win over the CPP for the war effort, see M. Djilas (1977), 317–318: "At that time [August 1943] we received a radiogram from Slavonia containing the offer by several leaders of the CPP to collaborate with the Partisans, on condition (1) that a "Radić Brothers Brigade" be organized; (2) that the Brigade have not just Communist political commissars, but also commissars from the CPP; and (3) that the Brigade be used not to fight the Home Guards [Domobrani] but only the Ustashi and the invaders . . . The proposals were considered acceptable, on condition that the "Radić Brothers Brigade" be subject to the orders of our own high command and that it not be exempted from fighting against the Home Guards."

Yet at the last moment the Slavonian CPP leaders changed their minds. When Djilas went to Slavonia early in September 1943 they did not even show up at the meeting. "What else could we do but seek to divide the CPP as persistently and cleverly as possible, and win over those who were for the armed struggle?"; ibid., 325.

9. Memorandum from the Middle East Intelligence Centre in Cairo to the Foreign Office; Clissold (1978), 20.

10. During the First World War Stjepan Radić frequently referred to the Habsburgs as "the August Dynasty" and reaffirmed what he considered to be the traditional Croatian loyalty to it. See Gaži (1973–74), 41–44.

11. See Koštunica and Čavoški (1983), chap. 3. For *Slobodni dom* and the press on Partisan-controlled territories, see *ZAVNOH, zbornik dokumenata 1943* and *ZAVNOH, zbornik dokumenata 1944*.

12. See, e.g., *ZAVNOH, zbornik dokumenata 1943*, nos. 115, 127.

13. Toward the end of the summer of 1943 the Partisans had survived the so-called fourth and fifth German offensives: of the Neretva River (four German and three Italian divisions) and of the Sutjeska River (five German and three Italian divisions, which together with other troops numbered more than 120,000). These were to be the last large-scale operations against the Partisans. The Communists' confidence was further increased by the capitulation of Italy in September 1943; at that point they could begin to plan for the postwar regime. Postwar Yugoslav historians describe the Jajce meeting as an event crucial for the creation of a new Yugoslavia, and the date on which it began is a national holiday.

14. J. Stefanović (1960) shows that the party considered the proclaimed federalism to be irreversible but for tactical reasons did not propagandize it as such. Stefanović's evidence also indicates that during the war the Communists considered the whole postwar constitutional organization of Yugoslavia (elections for the Constitutional Assembly, the drafting and proclamation of the constitution, etc.) to be merely the formal legalization of an already-established political system. See also J. Stefanović (1962), 32–33.

15. The Treaty of Rapallo proclaimed Rijeka (Fiume) a free city. Local fascists organized a *putsch* in March 1922, and in September 1923 Italian troops marched in. The Rome agreement of January 1924 between Yugoslavia and Italy gave Rijeka to Italy.

16. There is general acknowledgment that most people in Yugoslavia, including Croats, would probably have voted for the CPY anyway. Milan Grol, the leader of the Democratic Party, which constituted the main opposition to the CPY in the immediate postwar period, expressed this opinion privately on numerous occasions (conversation between the author and Milan Grol's son, Dr. Vojislav Grol). The Politburo of the CPY's Central Committee estimated that the CPY would have won about 60 to 65 percent of the vote. See "Milovan Djilas: 'Ja sam vjernik komunizma,'" *Omladinska iskra,* no. 60 (24 June 1988), 1; M. Djilas (1983), 26.

17. Also, 5 percent of the electorate was deprived of the right to vote; Pavlowitch (1971), 177.

18. Kardelj (1949) points out the continuity between the Partisan movement's policies on the national question and the organization of the postwar Yugoslav federation.

19. See *Ustav FNRJ.*

20. See Šnuderl (1956).

21. In the minds of most people this "nation blindness" did not apply to non-Yugoslav nations. See "Revolution and the New Nationalism" later in this chapter.

22. The idea that a nation and nation only should be the subject of international law was first promoted in the nineteenth century. It was an essential element of the ideology of national revolutionary movements, which directly challenged the legitimacy of the multinational nondemocratic monarchies of that time. An important implication of these new democratic and national criteria of legitimacy was the idea that only wars of national liberation were just, while any other kind of war was one of conquest and subjugation. If the nations and republics of Yugoslavia were fully sovereign, then only they, and not their citizens, would be the subject of Yugoslav law. In such a case, Yugoslav law or the Yugoslav constitution could not regulate the rights and duties of the citizens or workers of the republic of Croatia or the republic's social and political order. They could only define inter-republic relations and agreements that had been freely accepted by the republics. For a similar analysis, see, e.g., Lapenna (1982).

23. If Croatia was sovereign, and Serbs in Croatia were a part of the Serbian nation, then the following question, posed by Shoup (1968), 117, inevitably arises: "was Croatia 'multinational,' in fact a multinational state within a multinational state?"

24. The question of Serbian sovereignty in a sovereign Croatia was discussed in the late 1960s and the early 1970s by the Croatian nationalist intelligentsia, who wanted for Croatia not only what political theorists traditionally considered sovereignty—that is, complete independence from any "outside" influences (including those of the central federal bodies in Belgrade)—but also Croatian sovereignty in the sense of the Croatian nation being the only political subject inside Croatia. This developed into a demand that political rights be granted only to members of the Croatian nation. The most extreme version stated that Serbs could not have any political rights—that is, could not have their own political organizations, meetings, or press—since this would be an infringement on Croatian sovereignty. (See Perić, 1976). Another way of interpreting the sovereignty of

the republics (sometimes utilized by leading Yugoslav Communists) was to state that they were sovereign in relation to other republics (that is, no republic—and no nation—dominated the others), but not in relation to the Communist party, which was a supranational force of historical progress. This kind of interpretation was essentially faulty; the party was supranational in relation to the individual republics and nations of Yugoslavia, but "national" in relation to other states and Communist countries. It was, after all, a Yugoslav party and did not have some transcendent, global role. This interpretation also made Yugoslavia vulnerable to the hegemonist aspirations of the Soviet Communists, who also saw themselves as a supranational force of historical progress. For, if the nations of Yugoslavia had accepted the leadership of one supranational force, then why not of another one, i.e., of the Soviet party? It was, however, very difficult for the Yugoslav Communist Party to define itself as a "national" party. Yugoslav Communists, for example, never used the term *national communism,* since in this way they would have negated the universal validity of their Communist ideology, and by implication would also have placed limitations on their own rule within the country.

25. Strictly speaking, a Macedonian in Croatia, for example, could vote about matters important for Croatian sovereignty. This was implied in article 48 of the Yugoslav constitution: "Unified citizenship is established for all citizens of the Federal People's Republic of Yugoslavia. Every citizen of one of the people's republics is at the same time a citizen of the Federal People's Republic of Yugoslavia. Every citizen of one republic enjoys in every republic the same rights as its citizens." Political rights are obviously included.

26. The inconsistency of the official attitude to the South Slav Muslims is demonstrated in the 1953 census, which defined them as Yugoslavs.

27. It seems that there were fewer Croats from inner Croatia and from Slavonia in the Partisan army in the summer of 1941 than there had been members of the party a few years earlier. (The Italian-occupied Dalmatia and northern Adriatic region were much more active in the Partisan movement.) This is one more proof that the criteria for party membership were more relaxed in Croatia, where the party still had some characteristics of a trade union party, rather than of a party of revolutionary cadres.

28. For Tito's praise of the Serbs in December 1942, see Tito (1959–1967), 1: 132–133. Three events in the summer of 1941 induced Serbs to join the Partisan army in 1941–42 in larger numbers than any other nation: the mass uprising of Serbs in the NDH, primarily in response to the Ustasha massacres; the mass uprising in Montenegro against the Italian occupation; and the Partisans' successes in western Serbia, where they temporarily controlled a considerable territory.

29. The final stage in the development of postrevolutionary Communist society would, of course, be the creation of a global society without individual national consciousness, though not necessarily without individual national languages and cultures.

30. *Global* seems to be a more appropriate word than *international* which necessarily presumes the existence of a national consciousness.

31. For Tito's views on the CPY as the guardian of Yugoslav independence through economic development and "the building of socialism," see, e.g., M.

Djilas (1980), 52–61. This biographical essay also contains numerous insights into Tito's attitude toward Yugoslavia and Yugoslavism.

32. See Tito (1959–1967), 1: 292–293.

33. Shoup (1968), 113, states that the "primary purpose" of the "introduction of the federal system . . . was to serve as a lightning rod for national emotions, without limiting the power of the Party and the jurisdiction of the centralized administration built up during the war."

34. "Govor Generalnog sekretara KPJ Josipa Broza Tita," in *Osnivački kongres KP Srbije (8–12 maja 1945)*.

35. Federalism had enormously contributed to solving the national question and in this way strengthened the "brotherhood and unity" of the Yugoslav people; ibid. See also Tito (1946).

36. For Stalin's constitution, see Ulam (1987), esp. 403–404. "Neither J. S. Mill nor Thomas Jefferson could have objected to a single provision"; ibid., 403.

37. Kardelj (1946), 199, stated that the Soviet constitution of 1936 was the most successful solution (of all times and of all countries) for the relations among different nations.

38. The right to national self-determination is included in the United Nations Charter as well as in other documents of international law. It is implied by basic human rights. See Ivanović and Djilas (1983); Reibstein (1949); Heidelmeyer (1977), 270–272 and chap. 8.

39. This right was a part of the program of the Social Democratic party of the pre-1914 kingdom of Serbia.

40. Until the mid-1980s, most Yugoslav constitutional experts agreed that none of the post-1945 constitutions gave the republics the legal right to secession.

41. See Lapenna (1982), 17.

42. The endorsement by antifascist councils of Croatia, Slovenia, and elsewhere of the decisions of the second meeting of AVNOJ cannot be considered such an act, since neither the councils nor AVNOJ itself was democratically elected. And the Communists did not insist that this was the moment when "new" Yugoslavia was created by its peoples, because they did not want to imply that these councils, which would soon become assemblies of republics, were the creators of Yugoslavia.

43. See Lapenna (1982), 17.

44. The CPY was convinced that the Communist society of abundance was imminent. Party leaders, for example, were confident that within a decade Yugoslavia would overtake Great Britain in per capita industrial production. See M. Djilas (1983), 20.

45. The most thoroughly researched study of the expulsion of the Germans from Yugoslavia is Schieder (1953–1961), vol. 5. See also "Wurden Deutsche aus Jugoslawien 'vertrieben'?" *Bundesinstitut für ostwissenschaftliche Studien,* no. 7 (22 July 1987); "Sudbina Folksdojčera u Jugoslaviji," *NIN,* 19 July–2 August 1987. For the wartime struggle of these *Volksdeutschers* against the Partisans, see Miletić (1977).

46. After the Second World War, which was called the "Great Patriotic War," Soviet party and state documents referred to the Russians as the "great Russian people"; no other nation in the Soviet Union was so extolled.

47. Although the National Socialist ideology defined all Slavs as an inferior race, the Third Reich formally recognized the Bulgarian, Slovak, and Croatian states and maintained diplomatic relations with them during the war.

48. For criticism of the CPY's criteria for the postwar creation of borders between the republics, see Čavoški (1987).

49. See Dedijer (1981–1984), 3: 172, 340–348. According to M. Djilas (1983), 84, Hebrang felt that Bosnia and Herzegovina should also be part of Croatia but refrained from openly demanding its incorporation, since Bosnia and Herzegovina had already become a republic.

50. See M. Djilas (1983), 84–85. Djilas was the chairman of the parliamentary committee for establishing borders between Croatia and Serbia. See also Dedijer (1981–1984), 3: 172.

51. There are different estimates of how far to the south and north of the western Adriatic Dalmatia actually extends. But the point here is that Croatian nationalists believe that Boka Kotorska should be a part of Dalmatia on the basis of historical rights, rather than according to the nationality (and the wishes) of the population.

52. See Shoup (1968), 118; Dedijer (1981–1984), 3: 172.

53. For the requests by leading Dalmatian Communists for Dalmatian autonomy, and the opposition of the Central Committee of the CPC, see Dedijer (1981–1984), 3: 171. Dalmatia had been a separate province in the Austrian part of the Habsburg monarchy, and before that it had been one of the dominions of the Venetian republic. It had its own cultural and political identity.

54. About one-quarter of the CPC's members after the war were of Serbian nationality. Since according to the 1948 census (Shoup, 1968, 266) there were 2,975,399 Croats and 543,795 Serbs in Croatia, it was obvious that Serbs were overrepresented. Yet neither their numerical strength nor the positions they held were sufficient to make their influence decisive in Croatian politics.

55. For Serbs' postwar predominance in the party of Bosnia and Herzegovina and for the underrepresentation of Croats, see ibid., 121.

56. Bilandžić (1979), 106–111, explains the connection between centralism and the ruling economic ideas in the CPY.

57. Whereas the January 1929 dictatorship introduced unitarism with the aim of creating one Yugoslav nation by, among other things, eradicating Croatian, Slovene, and Serbian national consciousnesses, the Communists after the war wanted to create a Yugoslav national consciousness in the sense of a mixing and merging of cultures and of one political and ideological loyalty, but without erasing the individuality of any nation.

58. In general, Tito was more directly involved in Croatia's affairs than in those of any other republic. For example, he appointed his personal friend Ivan-Stevo Krajačić as Croatia's minister of the interior. Krajačić was personally responsible only to Tito, maintained regular contact with him, and was not supervised or controlled by the federal ministry of the interior. This was contrary to the 1946 constitution, since the ministries of the interior had a "mixed" federal-republican character.

59. Anić (1984), 71, states: "More substantive aid began to come from the

Allies only in the final stages of the war . . . In the period between 1943 and May 15 1945, the Allies (the Soviet Union and the Anglo-Americans) sent a total of 1,283 guns, 6,024 minethrowers, 172 tanks, 482 aircraft, 81,447 machineguns and 233,000 rifles."

60. For example, Ljudevit Gaj, Petar II Petrović Njegoš, Josip Juraj Strossmayer, Svetozar Marković, Dositej Obradović, Svetozar Miletić, and Frano Supilo. See Čulinović (1952), "Federalizam u jugoslavenskim zemljama do Prvog svjetskog rata."

61. One example was the Yugoslavism of Miroslav Krleža, the most influential Croatian intellectual figure in this century (see Lasić, 1982, 349–352). Krleža was the main organizer of the exhibition of medieval art of the nations of Yugoslavia, held in Paris in March 1950.

62. Russinow (1977), chap. 2, gives a balanced account of the complexity of the attempt to democratize Yugoslavia, with the crucial role played by a political elite that itself held the monopoly of power.

63. See *VI kongres Komunističke partije Jugoslavije (Saveza komunista Jugoslavije), 2–7 novembra 1952, Stenografske beleške.*

64. For an analysis of the constitutional law of 1953, pointing out its originality in relation to the 1946 constitution, see J. Djordjević (1964), 33.

65. The Soviet Union had been praised as a model of a justly solved national question until the Soviet-Yugoslav conflict in 1948. In his speech at the sixth congress of the CPY in November 1952, Tito sharply attacked Soviet policies toward their non-Russian nationalities (comparing them even with the Nazi extermination of "inferior" races) and severely censured the Stalinist theory of the Russians as the "leading nation." See *VI kongres Komunističke partije Jugoslavije.*

66. See *Ustav SFRJ sa ustavima socijalističkih republika i statutima autonomnih pokrajina.*

67. The constitutional changes of 1953 promoted Yugoslavism to such an extent that it almost contradicted the idea of federalism. See, for example, J. Djordjević (1964), esp. chap. 4. Djordjević states that the economic and political role of the republics was neglected by the 1953 constitutional law. He further argues (ibid., 267): "In the period in which the constitutional law of 1953 was valid, that is, for about ten years (from 1953 to 1963), the process of social-economic development . . . strengthened . . . the federation as a social community."

68. The examples are legion. According to Čolaković (1950), 53, the national question in Yugoslavia was basically solved during the war.

69. See M. Djilas (1953).

70. Until the 1960s, "local patriotism"—the inclination of some party officials to gain advantages (primarily economic) for their regions—was a greater problem for the party than nationalism.

71. Kardelj (1953a) described the Yugoslav federation as a "united socialist community of Yugoslav workers" both fundamentally different from and superior to any "old" form of either centralism or federalism.

72. See Kardelj (1953b).

Conclusion

1. Seton-Watson (1977).

2. Smith (1983), 122, based on Sugar and Lederer (1973) and Sugar (1980).

3. Therefore, Yugoslavia is not a "polyethnic state," as Smith (1983), 123, calls it.

4. *Plamen,* 1 (January–March 1919), 24–32; quoted in Pešić (1983), 34.

5. Banac (1984), 407.

6. See, e.g., ibid., "Conclusion."

7. *Encyclopaedia Britannica,* 15th ed; "Parliamentary Politics, 1922–28," s.v. "Yugoslavia," 29:1052.

Bibliography

Books and Articles

Acton, Lord. 1919. "Nationality." In Figgis and Laurence (1919).

Alexander, S. 1979. *Church and State in Yugoslavia since 1945*. New York.

Anić, N. 1984. "The Armed Forces of the National-Liberation Movement of Yugoslavia (1941–1945)." *Socialist Thought and Practice*, 24, no. 10: 55–72.

Anić, Ž., et al., eds. 1977. *The Third Reich and Yugoslavia 1933–1945*. Belgrade.

Antonijević, T. S. 1939. *Hrvatski ustavni program u državi Srba, Hrvata i Slovenaca*. Belgrade.

Auty, P., and R. Clogg, eds. 1975. *British Policy towards Wartime Resistance in Yugoslavia and Greece*. London.

Avakumović, I. 1964. *History of the Communist Party of Yugoslavia*. Aberdeen.

—— 1969. *Mihailović prema nemačkim dokumentima*. London.

—— 1971. "Cooperation and Conflict between Germany and the Yugoslav Right, 1933–1945." Paper presented at the Annual Meeting of the Pacific Branch of the American Historical Association, Los Angeles.

Avineri, S. 1969. *Karl Marx on Colonialism and Modernization*. New York.

Avramovski, Ž. 1968. *Balkanske zemlje i velike sile, 1935–1937*. Belgrade.

—— 1977. "The International Isolation of Yugoslavia: An Objective of German Foreign Policy in the Period from 1933–1939." In Ž. Anić et al. (1977).

—— 1986. *Britanci o Kraljevini Jugoslaviji 1921–1938*. 2 vols. Zagreb.

Babić, N. 1974. *Rat, revolucija i jugoslovensko pitanje u politici Socijaldemokratske stranke Bosne i Hercegovine*. Sarajevo.

Baerlein, H. 1922. *The Birth of Yugoslavia*. 2 vols. London.

Bakarić, V. 1979. *Društvene klase, nacija i socijalizam*. Zagreb.

Bakunin, M. 1974. *Selected Writings*, ed. A. Lehning, trans. S. Cox and O. Stevens. New York.

Banac, I. 1983a. "The Communist Party of Yugoslavia during the Period of Legality, 1919–1921." In Banac (1983b).

Banac, I., ed. 1983b. *War and Society in East Central Europe*. N. p.

Banac, I. 1984. *The National Question in Yugoslavia: Origins, History, Politics.* Ithaca, N.Y.

Barker, E. 1976a. *British Policy in South-East Europe in the Second World War.* London.

—— 1976b. "Fresh Sidelights on British Policy in Yugoslavia, 1942–3." *Slavonic and East European Review,* 54 (October): 572–585.

—— 1979. "British Wartime Policy towards Yugoslavia." *South Slav Journal,* 2 (April): 3–9.

Basta, M. 1971. *Agonija i slom NDH.* Belgrade.

Bauer, O. 1924. *Die Nationalitätenfrage und die Sozialdemokratie.* 2d ed. Vienna.

Behschnitt, W. D. 1980. *Nationalismus bei Serben und Kroaten, 1830–1914. Analyse und Typologie der nationalen Ideologie.* Munich.

Belz, H. G. 1962. *Die Idee des Föderalismus in der Verfassung der UDSSR von 1936.* Göttingen.

Bićanić, R. 1938. *Ekonomska podloga hrvatskog pitanja.* 2d ed. Zagreb.

Bilandžić, D. 1979. *Historija Socijalističke Federativne Republike Jugoslavije— glavni procesi.* Zagreb.

Bilandžić, D., et al., eds. 1969. *Komunistički pokret i socijalistička revolucija u Hrvatskoj.* Zagreb.

Bjelovučić, H. T. 1970. *The Ragusan Republic: Victim of Napoleon and Its Own Conservatism.* Leiden.

Blažević, J. 1986. *Brazdama partije.* Zagreb.

Boban, L. 1965. *Sporazum Cvetković-Maček.* Belgrade.

—— 1974a. *Maček i politika Hrvatske seljačke stranke 1928–1941.* 2 vols. Zagreb.

—— 1974b. *Svetozar Pribićević u opoziciji 1929–1936.* Zagreb.

Bodrožić, M. 1973. "O nekim pitanjima politike Hrvatske seljačke stranke prema NOP-u u Hrvatskoj 1943. godine." *Časopis za suvremenu povijest,* 5, no. 1: 33–63.

Bogdanov, V. 1934. "Marks i Hrvati." *Danas,* 1, no. 4: 116–123.

—— 1957. "Historijski uzroci sukoba izmedju Hrvata i Srba." *Rad JAZU,* no. 311: 353–477.

—— 1961. *Porijeklo i ciljevi šovinističkih teza o državanju Hrvata 1941.* Zagreb.

Boshkovich, B. [Filip Filipović]. 1929. *Krestianskoe dvizhenie i natsionalni vopros v Jugoslavii.* Moscow.

Božić, I., S. Ćirković, M. Ekmečić, and V. Dedijer. 1973. *Istorija Jugoslavije.* 2d ed. Belgrade.

Bracher, K. 1970. *The German Dictatorship.* New York.

Britovšek, M. 1972. "Stavovi Marksa i Engelsa prema slovenskim narodima— istorijski prikaz." *Medjunarodni radnički pokret,* no. 1: 73–95.

Brockett, L. P. 1969. *The Bogumils of Bulgaria and Bosnia.* Philadelphia.

Bukvić, D. 1986. "Gavranica hrišćanska grobnica." In *Hercegovina u NOB-u.* Sarajevo.

Bulut, V. 1986. "Borbe i pobede nadomak Čapljine." In *Hercegovina u NOB-u.*

Burks, R. V. 1961. *The Dynamics of Communism in Eastern Europe.* Princeton.

Bušić, B. 1969. "Žrtve rata." *Hrvatski književni list,* 2, no. 15: 2–3.

Čakić, S. 1983. *Velika seoba Srba 1689/90 i patrijarh Arsenije III Čarnojević.* Novi Sad.

Čalić, D., and L. Boban. 1976. *Narodnooslobodilačka borba i socijalistička revolucija u Hrvatskoj 1944 godine.* Zagreb.

Carrère d'Encausse, H. 1979. *Bolchévisme et nation.* Paris.

Carter, F. W. 1972. *Dubrovnik (Ragusa): A Classic City State.* London and New York.

Cassirer, E. 1932. *Die Philosophie der Aufklärung.* Tübingen.

Čavoški, K. 1987. *Iz istorije stvaranja nove Jugoslavije.* London.

Cerić, S. 1968. *Muslimani srpskohrvatskog jezika.* Sarajevo.

Cesarec, A. 1923a. "Nacionalno pitanje i naši zadaci; II. Razvoj i pouke naše nacionalne revolucije." *Borba,* 23 August.

———— 1923b. "Nacionalno pitanje i naši zadaci; IV. Federacija kao etapa od nacionalne revolucije k proleterskoj." *Borba,* 6 September.

———— 1962. *Izbor članaka.* Belgrade.

Ciano, G. 1947. *Ciano's Diary 1930–1943.* London.

Ciliga, A. 1951. "Nacionalizam i komunizam u hrvatskosrpskom sporu." *Hrvatska revija,* 4 (December): 365–396.

———— 1972. "Uloga i sudbina hrvatskih komunista u KPJ." *Bilten Hrvatske demokratske i socijalne akcije,* 9–10, no. 67: 1–68.

Ćirković, S. 1964. *Istorija srednjevekovne bosanske države.* Belgrade.

Clissold, S. 1949. *Whirlwind: An Account of Marshal Tito's Rise to Power, 1939–1945.* London.

Clissold, S., ed. 1966. *A Short History of Yugoslavia.* Cambridge.

———— 1975. *Yugoslavia and the Soviet Union 1939–1973: A Documentary Survey.* London.

Clissold, S. 1978. "Britain, Croatia and the Croatian Peasant Party, 1939–1945." Manuscript. London.

Čolaković, R. 1950. "Rješenje nacionalnog pitanja u Jugoslaviji." *Komunist,* nos. 4–5.

———— 1959. *Borba KPJ za rješenje nacionalnog pitanja.* Belgrade.

———— 1964–1968. *Kazivanje o jednom pokoljenju.* 2 vols. Zagreb.

Čolaković, R., et al., eds. 1963. *Pregled istorije Saveza komunista Jugoslavije.* Belgrade.

Ćopić, B. 1963. *Prolom.* Rijeka.

———— 1964. *Gluvi barut.* Belgrade.

Ćorović, V. 1933. *Istorija Jugoslavije.* Belgrade.

Ćosić, D. 1985. *Grešnik.* Belgrade.

Čubrilović, V. 1958. *Istorija političke misli u Srbiji XIX veka.* Belgrade.

Čubrilović, V., ed. 1967. *Jugoslovenski narodi pred Prvi svetski rat.* Belgrade.

———— 1973. *Ustanak u Jugoslaviji 1941 godine i Evropa.* Belgrade.

Čulinović, F. 1951. *Seljačke bune u Hrvatskoj.* Zagreb.

———— 1952. *Razvitak jugoslavenskog federalizma.* Zagreb.

———— 1954. *Državnopravna historija jugoslavenskih zemalja XIX i XX vijeka.* Zagreb.

———— 1955. *Nacionalno pitanje u jugoslavenskim zemljama.* Zagreb.

———— 1958. *Slom stare Jugoslavije.* Zagreb.

—— 1959. *Stvaranje nove jugoslavenske države.* Zagreb.

—— 1961. *Jugoslavija izmedju dva rata.* Zagreb.

—— 1963. *Državno-pravni razvitak Jugoslavije.* Zagreb.

—— 1965. *Dvadeset sedmi mart.* Zagreb.

—— 1968. *Dokumenti o Jugoslaviji—historijat od osnutka zajedničke države do danas.* Zagreb.

—— 1969. *Državno-pravni razvitak Vojne krajine.* Zagreb.

—— 1970. *Okupatorska podjela Jugoslavije.* Belgrade.

Cummins, I. 1980. *Marx, Engels and National Movements.* London.

Cvetković, D. 1962. "Smisao, značaj i posledice srpsko-hrvatskog sporazuma." *Glasnik SIKD Njegoš* (December): 8–27.

Cvetković, S. 1972. "Stjepan Radić i komunistički pokret 1923–1925 godine: Prilog pitanju odnosa HRSS i KPJ." *Istorija XX veka, zbornik radova,* 12: 375–402.

Cvijić, J. 1966. *Balkansko poluostrvo i južnoslovenske zemlje: osnovi antropogeografije.* 2d ed. Belgrade.

Damjanović, P. 1972. *Tito tred temama istorije.* Belgrade.

Damjanović, P., et al., eds. 1980. *Peta zemaljska konferencija KPJ (19–23. oktobar 1940).* Belgrade.

Davičo, O. 1963a. *Ćutnje.* Belgrade.

—— 1963b. *Gladi.* Belgrade.

—— 1964. *Tajne.* Belgrade.

Davidović, R. 1985. "Vreme robijanja." *NIN,* 28 April.

Dedijer, V. 1953. *Tito Speaks.* London.

—— 1966. *Sarajevo 1914.* Belgrade.

—— 1970. *Dnevnik.* 3 vols. 3d ed. Belgrade and Sarajevo.

—— 1981–1984. *Novi prilozi za biografiju Josipa Broza Tita.* 3 vols. Rijeka.

Despalatović, E. M. 1975. *Ljudevit Gaj and the Illyrian Movement.* Boulder, Colo.

Deutsch, K. 1966. *Nationalism and Social Communication.* 2d rev. ed. Cambridge, Mass.

Diehl, C. 1957. *Byzantium: Greatness and Decline.* New Brunswick, N.J.

Djilas, A. 1980a. "Koliko je 'ruski' Sovjetski Savez." *Naša reč,* 33, no. 315 (May).

—— 1980b. "Sovjetska imperijalistička tradicija." *Naša reč,* 33, no. 319 (November).

—— 1981a. "Pravo na nacionalizam." *Naša reč,* 34, no. 325 (May).

—— 1981b. "The Cross of Yugoslavia." *New Society,* 56, no. 969 (11 June).

—— 1984. "Communists and Yugoslavia." *Survey,* 28, no. 3 (Autumn).

—— 1985. "The Foundations of Croatian Identity." *South Slav Journal,* 8, nos. 1–2 (27–28), 3–4 (29–30).

—— 1986. "Creeping Confederalisation of Yugoslavia." *Soviet Analyst,* 15, no. 3 (5 February).

—— 1987a. "The Illyrianist Movement and the Logic of the Yugoslav Idea." *South Slav Journal,* 10, no. 1 (Spring).

—— 1987b. "Kominterna i stvaranje Jugoslavije." *Naša reč,* 40, no. 385 (May).

—— 1987c. "Nationalismus und Kommunismus in Jugoslawien." *Kontinent,* 13, no. 43 (October–December): 54–65.

Djilas, M. 1947a. *Članci, 1941–1945*. Belgrade.

—— 1947b. "O rješenju nacionalnog pitanja." In M. Djilas (1947a).

—— 1949. "O nacionalnoj istoriji kao vaspitnom predmetu." *Komunist*, no. 1 (January): 57–82.

—— 1953. "Jugoslavija." *Borba*, 18 October.

—— 1973. *Memoir of a Revolutionary*. New York.

—— 1977. *Wartime*. New York.

—— 1980. *Druženje s Titom*. London.

—— 1983. *Vlast*. London.

Djordjević, D. 1974. "Historians in Politics: Slobodan Jovanović." In Laqueur and Mosse (1974).

Djordjević, D., ed. 1980. *The Creation of Yugoslavia*. Santa Barbara.

Djordjević, J. 1953. *Ustavno pravo*. Belgrade.

—— 1954. *Političko i državno uredjenje Federativne Narodne Republike Jugoslavije*. Belgrade.

—— 1964. *Novi ustavni sistem*. Belgrade.

Djurdjev, B., et al., eds. 1959. *Historija naroda Jugoslavije*. 2 vols. Zagreb.

Dolenc, M. 1936. "Die strafrechtliche Bekämpfung des Kommunismus im Königreiche Jugoslawien." *Zeitschrift der Akademie für Deutsches Recht*, 3, no. 11–12: 562–566.

Donia, R. J. 1981. *Islam under the Double Eagle: The Muslims of Bosnia and Hercegovina, 1878–1914*. New York.

Drachkovitch, M., and B. Lazitch, eds. 1966a. *The Comintern: Historical Highlights, Essays, Recollections, Documents*. New York.

—— 1966b. *The Revolutionary Internationals, 1864–1943*. Stanford.

Drachkovitch, M., and B. Lazitch. 1966c. "The Third International." In Drachkovitch and Lazitch (1966b).

Dugandžija, N. 1983. *Religija i nacija*. Zagreb.

Durman, M. 1936. *Hrvatska seljačka buna 1573*. Zagreb.

Dvornik, F. 1949. *The Making of Central and Eastern Europe*. London.

Dvorniković, V. 1939. *Karakterologija Jugoslovena*. Belgrade.

Ekmečić, M. 1973. *Ratni ciljevi Srbije*. Belgrade.

Evans, R. J. W. 1979. *The Making of the Habsburg Monarchy, 1550–1700*. Oxford.

Ferluga, F. 1957. *Vizantijska uprava u Dalmaciji*. Belgrade.

Figgis, J. N., and R. V. Laurence, eds. 1919. *The History of Freedom and Other Essays*. London.

Fischer-Galati, S. 1971. "Fascism in Romania." In Sugar (1971).

Floegel, R. 1985. "Prodor jugoslovenstva u Hrvatski Sabor poslije 1905. godine." *Republika Hrvatska*, 35, no. 148 (10 April): 6–28.

Foot, M. R. D. 1976. *Resistance: European Resistance to Nazism 1940–1945*. London.

Fricke, G. 1972. *Kroatien 1941–1944: Der "Unabhängige Staat" in der Sicht des deutschen Bevollmächtigten Generals in Agram, Glaise von Horstenau*. Freiburg im Breisgau.

Gaži, S. 1973. *A History of Croatia*. New York.

—— 1973–74. "Stjepan Radić: His Life and Political Activities (1871–1928)." *Journal of Croatian Studies*, 14–15: 13–73.

Gellner, E. 1964. *Thought and Change*. London.

———— 1983. *Nations and Nationalism*. Ithaca, N.Y.

Gellner, E., and G. Ionescu, eds. 1970. *Populism, Its Meaning and National Characteristics*. London.

Gizdić, D. 1958. *Dalmacija 1941*. Zagreb.

Gligorijević, B. 1970. *Demokratska stranka i politički odnosi u Kraljevini Srba, Hrvata i Slovenaca*. Belgrade.

Goodwin, A., ed. 1953. *The European Nobility in the Eighteenth Century*. London.

Grafenauer, B., et al., eds. 1953. *Istorija naroda Jugoslavije*. 2 vols. Belgrade.

Gross, M. 1956. "Socijalna demokracija prema nacionalnom pitanju u Hrvatskoj, 1890–1902." *Historijski zbornik*, 9, nos. 1–4: 1–27.

———— 1960. *Vladavina Hrvatsko-srpske koalicije 1906–1907*. Belgrade.

———— 1968. "Die 'Welle.' Die Ideen der nationalistischen Jugend in Kroatien vor dem 1. Weltkrieg." *Österreichische Osthefte*, 10, no. 2: 65–86.

———— 1973. *Povijest pravaške ideologije*. Zagreb.

———— 1981. *Društveni razvoj u Hrvatskoj od 16. stoljeća do početka 20. stoljeća*. Zagreb.

Hadžijahić, M. 1974. *Od tradicije do identiteta: Geneza nacionalnog pitanja bosanskih Muslimana*. Sarajevo.

Halperin, E. 1957. *Der siegreiche Kätzer*. Cologne.

Hasanagić, E., ed. 1959. *Komunistička partija Jugoslavije, 1919–1941: Izabrani dokumenti*. Zagreb.

Heidelmeyer, W., ed. 1977. *Die Menschenrechte*. Paderborn.

Heller, M., and A. M. Nekrich. 1986. *Utopia in Power: The History of the Soviet Union from 1917 to the Present*. New York.

Hilberg, R. 1961. *The Destruction of the European Jews*. Chicago.

Hoffman, G. W., ed. 1971. *Eastern Europe: Essays in Geographic Problems*. London.

Hoffman, G. W., and F. W. Neal. 1962. *Yugoslavia and the New Communism*. New York.

Hoptner, J. B. 1962. *Yugoslavia in Crisis, 1934–1941*. New York.

Horvat, J. 1936. *Politička povijest Hrvatske*. Zagreb.

———— 1938. *Politička povijest Hrvatske 1918–1929*. Zagreb.

Hory, L., and M. Broszat. 1965. *Der kroatische Ustascha-Staat 1941–1945*. 2d ed. Stuttgart.

Humo, A. 1984. *Moja generacija*. Sarajevo.

Huntington, S., and C. Moore, eds. 1970. *Authoritarian Politics in Modern Society: The Dynamic of Established One-Party States*. New York.

Ivanović, I., and A. Djilas, eds. 1982. *Demokratske reforme*. London.

———— 1983. *Zbornik o ljudskim pravima*. London.

Iveković, M. 1970. *Hrvatska lijeva inteligencija 1918–1945*. 2 vols. Zagreb.

Ivić, A. 1926. *Migracije Srba u Hrvatsku tokom XVI, XVII i XVIII stoleća*. Subotica.

Jackson, G. D. 1966. *Comintern and Peasant in East Europe, 1919–1930*. New York.

Janjatović, B. 1983. *Politika HSS prema radničkoj klasi*. Zagreb.

Janković, D. 1973. *Srbija i jugoslovensko pitanje 1914–1915. godine.* Belgrade.
Janković, D., and B. Krizman, eds. 1964. *Gradja o stvaranju jugoslovenske države.* 2 vols. Belgrade.
Jaszi, O. 1971. *The Dissolution of the Habsburg Monarchy.* Chicago.
Jelavich, C. 1962. "Serbian Nationalism and the Question of Union with Croatia in the Nineteenth Century." *Balkan Studies,* 3, no. 1: 29–42.
Jelavich, C., and B. Jelavich. 1977. *The Establishment of the Balkan National States.* Seattle.
Jelić, I. 1977. *Komunisti i revolucija.* Zagreb.
———— 1978. *Hrvatska u ratu i revoluciji, 1941–1945.* Zagreb.
———— 1981. *Komunistička partija Hrvatske, 1937–1945.* 2 vols. Zagreb.
———— 1987. *Tragedija Kerestinca.* Zagreb.
Jelić-Butić, F. 1977. *Ustaše i Nezavisna država Hrvatska 1941–1945.* Zagreb.
———— 1983. *Hrvatska seljačka stranka, 1941–1945.* Zagreb.
———— 1986. *Četnici u Hrvatskoj.* Zagreb.
Jelinek, Y. 1976. *The Parish Republic: Hlinka's Slovak People's Party.* New York.
Jiriček, K. 1952. *Istorija Srba.* 2 vols. Belgrade.
Jovanović, D. 1973. *Ljudi, ljudi . . . Medaljoni 56 umrlih savremenika.* Belgrade.
Jovanović, N. 1974. *Politički sukobi u Jugoslaviji, 1925–1928.* Belgrade.
Jovanović, S. 1976. *Zapisi o problemima i ljudima, 1941–1944.* London.
Kardelj, E. 1946. *Put nove Jugoslavije, Članci i govori iz narodnooslobodilačke borbe 1941–1945.* Belgrade.
———— 1949. "O narodnoj demokratiji u Jugoslaviji." *Komunist* (July).
———— 1951. *Deset godina narodne revolucije; referat na III kongresu Osvobodilne fronte 27. aprila 1951.* Belgrade.
———— 1953a. "Les bases sociales et politiques de la R.F.P.Y." *Questions actuelles du socialisme,* no. 16 (January–February): 1–9.
———— 1953b. "Govor na šestoj redovnoj sednici Narodne Skupštine FNRJ." *Borba,* 13 January.
———— 1953c. *O osnovama društvenog i političkog uredjenja FNRJ.* Belgrade.
———— [pseud. Sperans]. 1958. *Razvoj slovenačkog nacionalnog pitanja.* 3d ed. Ljubljana.
———— 1975. *Nacija i medjunacionalni odnosi.* Belgrade.
Kedourie, E. 1960. *Nationalism.* London.
Keršovani, O. 1971. *Povijest Hrvata.* Rijeka.
Kiszling, R. 1956. *Die Kroaten. Der Schiksalsweg eines Südslawenvolkes.* Graz and Cologne.
Klaić, N. 1976. *Povijest Hrvata u razvijenom srednjem vijeku.* Zagreb.
Klaić, V. 1972. *Povijest Hrvata od najstarijih vremena do svršetka XIX stoljeća.* 5 vols. Zagreb.
Kljaković, V. 1971–1973. "Jugoslavenska vlada u emigraciji i Saveznici prema pitanju Hrvatske 1941–1944." *Časopis za suvremenu povijest,* nos. 2–3; 97–138; no. 1: 5–31.
———— 1977. "The German-Italian Agreement on Spheres of Influence in the Balkans with Particular Reference to Yugoslavia." In Ž. Anić et al. (1977).
Kočović, B. 1985. *Žrtve Drugog svetskog rata u Jugoslaviji.* London.

Kohn, H. 1951. *The Idea of Nationalism: A Study of Its Origins and Background.* New York.

———— 1955. *Nationalism, Its Meaning and History.* Princeton.

———— 1960. *Pan-Slavism: Its History and Ideology.* 2d ed. New York.

Kolakovski, L. 1981. "Postanak lenjinizma." *Dijalog,* no. 4: 183–211.

Kombol, M. 1945. *Povijest hrvatske književnosti do preporoda.* Zagreb.

Korać, V. 1929–1933. *Povijest radničkog pokreta u Hrvatskoj i Slavoniji od prvih početaka do ukidanja ovih pokrajina 1922 godine.* 3 vols. Zagreb.

Kosanović, S. 1984. "Jugoslavija: bila je osudjena na smrt." *NIN,* May–June.

Koštunica, V., and K. Čavoški. 1983. *Stranački pluralizam ili monizam.* Belgrade.

Kovačić, M. 1970. *Od Radića do Pavelića.* Munich.

Krišković, V. 1925. *Dokle smo došli?* Zagreb.

Krizman, B. 1977a. *Raspad Austro-Ugarske i stvaranje jugoslavenske države.* Zagreb.

———— 1977b. "Yugoslavia's Accession to the Tripartite Pact." In Ž. Anić et al. (1977).

———— 1980. *Pavelić izmedju Hitlera i Musolinija.* Zagreb.

———— 1981. *Jugoslavenske vlade u izbjeglištvu, 1941–1943; dokumenti.* Zagreb.

———— 1983a. *Ante Pavelić i Ustaše.* Zagreb.

———— 1983b. *Ustaše i treći Reich.* 2 vols. Zagreb.

———— 1984–85. "Andrija Artuković—jugoslavenski Himmler." *Danas,* 27 November–5 February.

———— 1986. *Pavelić u bjekstvu.* Zagreb.

Kulundžić, Z. 1967. *Atentat na Stjepana Radića.* Zagreb.

———— 1968. *Politika i korupcija u kraljevskoj Jugoslaviji.* Zagreb.

Ladan, T. 1971. "Ante Starčević." In Starčević (1971).

Lampe, J. R. 1980. "Unifying the Yugoslav Economy, 1918–1921: Misery and Early Misunderstandings." In D. Djordjević (1980).

Lampe, J. R., and M. R. Jackson. 1982. *Balkan Economic History, 1550–1950: From Imperial Borderlands to Developing Nations.* Bloomington, Ind.

Lanović, M. 1928. *Zapadno-evropski feudalizam i ugarsko-hrvatski donacionalni sustav.* Zagreb.

Lapenna, I. 1964. *State and Law: Soviet and Yugoslav Theory.* New Haven.

———— 1982. "Suverenitet i federalizam u Ustavu Jugoslavije." In Ivanović and Djilas (1982).

Lasić, S. 1982. *Krleža—Kronologija života i rada.* Zagreb.

Laqueur, W., and G. Mosse, eds. 1974. *Historians in Politics.* London.

Lazitch, B. 1966. "Stalin's Massacre of the Foreign Communist Leaders." In Drachkovitch and Lazitch (1966a).

Lazitch, B., and M. Drachkovitch. 1972. *Lenin and the Comintern.* Stanford.

———— 1986. *Biographical Dictionary of the Comintern.* Stanford.

Lenin, V. I. 1958. *O nacionalnom i kolonijalnom pitanju (zbornik).* Zagreb.

Loewenthal, Z., ed. 1957. *The Crimes of the Fascist Occupants and Their Collaborators against the Jews in Yugoslavia.* Belgrade.

Lukač, D. 1972a. *Radnički pokret u Jugoslaviji i nacionalno pitanje 1918–1941.* Belgrade.

—— 1972b. "Učesnici iz Hrvatske u diskusiji o nacionalnom pitanju u NRPJ 1923. godine." *Časopis za suvremenu povijest,* 4, no. 3: 31–42.

Lybeyer, H. 1913. *The Government of the Ottoman Empire in the Time of Suleiman the Magnificent.* Cambridge.

Macan, T. 1971. *Povijest hrvatskog naroda.* Zagreb.

Macartney, C. A. 1970. *The Habsburg and Hohenzollern Dynasties in the Seventeenth and Eighteenth Century: Selected Documents.* London and Melbourne.

Maček, V. 1937. *Bit hrvatskoga seljačkoga pokreta.* Zagreb.

—— 1957. *In the Struggle for Freedom.* New York.

Mackenzie, D. 1985. *Ilija Garašanin, Balkan Bismarck.* N.p.

Marjanović, M. 1913. *Savremena Hrvatska.* Belgrade.

Marinko, M. 1950. *Politički izveštaj CKKPS na II kongresu Komunističke partije Slovenije.* Zagreb.

Marković, M. 1985. *Sazrevanje revolucije.* Belgrade.

Marković, S. 1923a. *Nacionalno pitanje u svetlosti marksizma.* Belgrade.

—— 1923b. *Ustavno pitanje i radnička klasa Jugoslavije.* Belgrade.

Martin, D. 1946. *Ally Betrayed.* New York.

—— 1978. *Patriot or Traitor: The Case of General Mihailovich.* Stanford.

Marx, K., F. Engels, and V. I. Lenin. 1973. *Nacionalno pitanje.* Sarajevo.

Matković, H. 1972. *Svetozar Pribićević i Samostalna demokratska stranka do šestojanuarske diktature.* Zagreb.

McNeal, R. H., ed. 1963. *Lenin, Stalin, Khrushchev: Voices of Bolshevism.* Englewood Cliffs, N.J.

Milatović, M. 1952. *Slučaj Andrije Hebranga.* Belgrade.

Milazzo, M. J. 1975. *The Chetnik Movement and the Yugoslav Resistance.* Baltimore.

Milenković, T. 1974. *Socijalistička partija Jugoslavije, 1921–1929.* Belgrade.

Miletić, A. 1977. "The Volksdeutschers of Bosnia, Slavonia, and Srem Regions in the Struggle against the People's Liberation Movement (1941–1944)." In Anić et al. (1977).

Mill, J. S. 1864a. *Dissertations and Discussions: Political, Philosophical, and Historical.* 3 vols. Boston.

—— 1864b. "Vindication of the French Revolution of February, 1848." In Mill (1864a), vol. 3.

Mirković, M. 1965. *Pravni položaj i karakter srpske crkve pod turskom vlašću.* Belgrade.

—— 1968. *Ekonomska historija Jugoslavije.* Zagreb.

Mitrany, D. 1951. *Marx versus the Peasant: A Study in Social Dogmatism.* Chapel Hill, N.C.

Mitrović, A. 1984. "Pakt i rat." *Politika,* 27 March.

Morača, P., D. Bilandžić, and S. Stojanović. 1977. *Istorija saveza komunista Jugoslavije.* 2d ed. Belgrade.

Mosse, G. L. 1966. "Introduction: The Genesis of Fascism." *Journal of Contemporary History,* 1, no. 1: 14–26.

Nešović, S., ed. 1951. *Zakonodavni rad Predsedništva AVNOJ-a i Predsedništva Privremene Skupštine Demokratske Federativne Jugoslavije.* Belgrade.

Nešović, S., and B. Petranović. 1983. *AVNOJ i revolucija.* Belgrade.

Neubacher, H. 1956. *Sonderauftrag Südost, 1940–1945. Bericht eines fliegenden Diplomaten.* Göttingen.

Nolte, E. 1965. *Three Faces of Fascism: Action française, Italian Fascism, National Socialism.* London.

Novak, V. 1948. *Magnum Crimen.* Zagreb.

Novaković, S. 1960. *Srbi i Turci u XIV i XV veku.* Belgrade.

Oakeshott, M. 1962. *Rationalism in Politics and Other Essays.* New York.

Obolensky, D. 1948. *The Bogumils: A Study in Balkan Neo-Manicheism.* Cambridge.

———— 1971a. *The Byzantine Commonwealth: Eastern Europe, 500–1453.* New York.

———— 1971b. *Byzantium and the Slavs: Collected Studies.* London.

Ostrogorsky, G. 1956. *History of the Byzantine State.* Oxford.

Palavestra, P. 1965. *Književnost Mlade Bosne.* 2 vols. Sarajevo.

Paris, E. 1961. *Genocide in Satellite Croatia, 1941–1945: A Record of Racial and Religious Persecutions and Massacres.* Chicago.

Pašić, N. 1973. *Nacionalno pitanje u savremenoj epohi.* Belgrade.

Pavelić, A. 1941. *Die Kroatische Frage.* Berlin.

———— 1954. *Lijepa plavka; roman iz borbe hrvatskog naroda za slobodu i nezavisnost.* 2d ed. Buenos Aires.

———— 1974. *Strahote zabluda: komunizam i boljševizam u Rusiji i u svietu.* 4th ed. Madrid.

———— 1977. *Putem hrvatskog državnog prava.* Madrid.

———— 1986. *Doživljaji.* Madrid.

Pavlović, K. S. 1958. "Pad Simovićeve vlade." *Glasnik SIKD 'Njegoš,'* no. 2 (December): 67–81.

———— 1959. "Pad Jovanovićeve vlade." *Glasnik SIKD 'Njegoš,'* no. 4 (December): 1–16.

———— 1975. *Ženidba Kralja Petra II prema britanskim dokumentima.* London.

Pavlowitch, S. K. 1971. *Yugoslavia.* London.

———— 1981. "Out of Context—The Yugoslav Government in London 1941–1945." *Journal of Contemporary History,* 16, no. 1: 89–118.

———— 1983. "How Many Non-Serbian Generals in 1941?" *East European Quarterly,* 16, no. 4 (January): 447–452.

———— 1985. *Unconventional Perceptions of Yugoslavia, 1940–1945.* New York.

Perić, I. 1976. *Suvremeni hrvatski nacionalizam.* Zagreb.

Perović, L. 1984. *Od centralizma do federalizma.* Zagreb.

Pešelj, B. M. 1970–71. "Serbo-Croatian Agreement of 1939 and American Foreign Policy." *Journal of Croatian Studies,* 11–12: 3–82.

Pešić, D. 1983. *Jugoslovenski komunisti i nacionalno pitanje, 1919–1935.* Belgrade.

Petranović, B. 1964. *Političke i pravne prilike za vreme privremene vlade Demokratske Federativne Jugoslavije.* Belgrade.

———— 1969. "Gradjanske stranke u Jugoslaviji 1944–1948. i njihov karakter." *Istorijski glasnik,* no. 1: 71–85.

———— 1976. *AVNOJ—revolucionarna smena vlasti, 1942–1945.* Belgrade.

———— 1979. "Narodni front u političkom sistemu Jugoslavije (1945–1949)." *Istraživanja,* 8: 309–397.

——— 1980. *Istorija Jugoslavije 1918–1978.* Belgrade.

——— 1983. *Revolucija i kontrarevolucija u Jugoslaviji, 1941–1945.* 2 vols. Belgrade.

Petranović, B., and V. Simović. 1979. *Istorija narodne vlasti u Jugoslaviji, 1941–1945.* Belgrade.

Petrovich, M. B. 1976. *A History of Modern Serbia.* 2 vols. New York.

Pijade, M. 1950a. *About the Legend That the Yugoslav Uprising Owed Its Existence to Soviet Assistance.* London.

——— 1950b. *Balanced Representation in a Multi-National State.* London.

Pleterski, J. 1973. "Perspektiva federativnog ujedinjenja u novoj Jugoslaviji kao faktor narodnooslobodilačke borbe." *Časopis za suvremenu povijest,* 5, no. 3: 9–24.

——— 1976. *Prvo opredeljenje Slovenaca za Jugoslaviju.* Belgrade.

Pribićević, S. 1952. *Diktatura Kralja Aleksandra.* Belgrade.

Pulić, N., ed. 1970. *Revolucija i revolucionari.* Zagreb.

Purivatra, A. 1974. *Jugoslavenska muslimanska organizacija u političkom životu Kraljevine Srba, Hrvata i Slovenaca.* Sarajevo.

Radić, S. 1971. *Politički spisi.* Zagreb.

Radica, B. 1974. *Hrvatska 1945.* Munich and Barcelona.

Ranke, L. von 1879. *Serbien und Türkei im neunzehnten Jahrhundert.* Leipzig.

Redlich, O. 1961. *Weltmacht des Barock, Österreich in der Zeit Kaiser Leopolds I.* Vienna.

——— 1962. *Das Werden einer Grossmacht.* Vienna.

Reibstein, E. 1949. *Die Anfänge des neueren Natur- und Völkerrechts.* Bern.

Reitlinger, G. 1961. *Die Endlösung. Hitlers Versuch der Ausrottung der Juden Europas, 1939–1945.* Berlin.

Rendel, G. 1957. *The Sword and the Olive: Recollections of Diplomacy and the Foreign Service, 1913–1954.* London.

Rendulic, L. 1952. *Gekämpft, Gesiegt, Geschlagen.* Wels and Heidelberg.

Ristović, Lj. 1984. "KPJ i srpsko nacionalno pitanje—lutanja je ipak bilo." *Duga,* 14–16 July.

Ristović, Lj., and S. Kržavac. 1968. *Robija—Kovačnica Komunista.* 2 vols. Zagreb.

Roberts, W. R. 1973. *Tito, Mihailović, and the Allies, 1941–1945.* New Brunswick, N.J.

Romano, J., and L. Kadelburg. 1977. "The Third Reich: Organiser and Executant of Anti-Jewish Measures and Genocide in Yugoslavia." In Ž. Anić et al. (1977).

Roth, G., and G. Wittich, eds. 1968. *Economy and Society.* New York.

Rothenburg, G. E. 1960. *The Austrian Military Border in Croatia, 1522–1747.* Urbana, Ill.

——— 1966. *The Military Border in Croatia, 1740–1881: A Study of an Imperial Institution.* Chicago.

Rothschild, J. 1974. *East Central Europe between the Two World Wars.* Seattle.

Russinow, D. 1977. *The Yugoslav Experiment 1948–1974.* London.

Sabille, J., and L. Poliakov, eds. 1955. *Jews under the Italian Occupation.* Paris.

Sadkovich, J. J. 1987. *Italian Support for Croatian Separatism, 1927–1937.* New York.

Scalapino, R., ed. 1969. *The Communist Revolution in Asia.* Englewood Cliffs, N.J.

Schieder, T., ed. 1953–1961. *Das Schicksal der Deutschen in Jugoslawien.* Vol. 5 of *Dokumentation der Vertreibung der Deutschen aus Ost-Mitteleuropa.* 5 vols. Bonn.

Schöpflin, G. 1983. "Communist Takeovers in Eastern Europe: Three Stages or Four? An Essay in Historical Reinterpretation." Paper presented at the conference "History and Historians in Central and South-Eastern Europe," 11–14 July at the London School of Slavonic and East European Studies. Abridged version published as "The Pattern of Political Takeovers: How Eastern Europe Fell," *Encounter,* 64, no. 2 (February 1985), 65–69.

Semić, M. [Sima Marković]. 1925. "K natsionalnomu voprosu v Jugoslavii." *Bolshevik,* nos. 11–12 (30 June): 20–23.

Šepić, D. 1975. "Velika Britanija i pitanje revizije jugoslavensko-talijanske granice 1941." *Časopis za suvremenu povijest,* no. 1: 121–140.

Seton-Watson, H. 1956. *The East European Revolution.* London.

———— 1960. *The Pattern of Communist Revolution: A History of World Communism.* London.

———— 1967. *Eastern Europe between the Wars, 1918–1941.* 3d ed. New York.

———— 1977. *Nations and States.* London.

Seton-Watson, R. W. 1937. "Yugoslavia and the Croat Problem." *Slavonic Review,* 16, no. 2: 102–112.

Shoup, P. 1968. *Communism and the Yugoslav National Question.* New York.

Šidak, J. 1949. *Crkva bosanska i problem Bogumilstva u Bosni.* Zagreb.

Šidak, J., et al., eds. 1968. *Povijest hrvatskog naroda, 1860–1914.* Zagreb.

Šišić, F. 1975. *Pregled povijesti hrvatskoga naroda.* Zagreb.

Slijepčević, D. 1962. *Istorija srpske pravoslavne crkve.* 3 vols. Munich.

Smith, A. D. 1981. *The Ethnic Revival.* Cambridge.

———— 1982. *Theories of Nationalism.* 2d ed. London.

———— 1983. *State and Nation in the Third World.* Brighton.

Šnuderl, M. 1953. "O državnosti Narodne Republike Jugoslavije." *Anali Pravnog fakulteta u Beogradu,* 1, nos. 3–4: 277–286.

———— 1956. *Ustavno pravo Federativne Ljudske Republike Jugoslavije.* Vol. 1. Ljubljana.

———— 1965. *Politički sistem Jugoslavije.* Vol. 1. Ljubljana.

Souvarine, B. 1966. "Comments on the Massacre." In Drachkovitch and Lazitch (1966a).

Spalatin, M. S. 1975. "The Croatian Nationalism of Ante Starčević, 1845–1871." *Journal of Croatian Studies,* 16: 19–146.

Štajner, K. 1988. *Seven Thousand Days in Siberia.* New York.

Stalin, J. 1925. "K natsionalnomu voprosu v Jugoslavii." *Bolshevik,* no. 7 (15 April): 20–23.

———— 1935. *Marxism and the National and Colonial Question.* Moscow.

———— 1946. *Pitanja lenjinizma.* Belgrade.

Stalin, J., and S. Marković. 1976. "Polemika o nacionalnom pitanju u Jugoslaviji." *Na pragu sutrašnjice,* 2, no. 2 (March).

Starčević, A. 1941. *Misli i pogledi.* Zagreb.

———— 1943. *Izabrani spisi,* ed. B. Juršić. Zagreb.

———— 1971. *Politički spisi.* Zagreb.

Starčević, M. 1936. *Ante Starčević i Srbi.* Zagreb.

Stefanović, J. 1953. "Primjena federativnog načela u saveznom ustavnom zakonu." *Anali Pravnog fakulteta u Beogradu,* 1, nos. 3–4: 257–270.

———— 1956. *Ustavno pravo FNRJ.* 2 vols. Zagreb.

———— 1960. *Ustavno pravo.* Zagreb.

———— 1962. *Federalizam i njegov razvitak u svijetu.* Zagreb.

Stefanović, M. 1984. *Zbor Dimitrija Ljotića.* Belgrade.

Stipetić, Z. 1980. *Komunistički pokret i inteligencija.* Zagreb.

———— 1982. *Argumenti za revoluciju—August Cesarec.* Zagreb.

Stojisavljević, B. 1952. *Seljaštvo Jugoslavije, 1918–1941.* Zagreb.

Stojkov, T. 1969. *Opozicija u vreme šestojanuarske diktature, 1929–1935.* Belgrade.

———— 1985. *Vlada Milana Stojadinovića, 1935–1937.* Belgrade.

Strugar, V. 1956. *Socijalna demokratija o nacionalnom pitanju u jugoslovenskim zemljama.* Belgrade.

Sugar, P. F., ed. 1971. *Native Fascism in the Successor States, 1918–1945.* Santa Barbara.

———— 1980. *Ethnic Diversity and Conflict in Eastern Europe.* Santa Barbara.

Sugar, P. F., and I. J. Lederer, eds. 1973. *Nationalism in Eastern Europe.* Seattle.

Suljević, K. 1981. *Nacionalnost Muslimana.* Rijeka.

Šuvar, S. 1970. *Nacija i medjunacionalni odnosi.* Zagreb.

———— 1974. *Nacionalno i nacionalističko.* Split.

Terzić, V. 1963. *Jugoslavija u aprilskom ratu 1941.* Titograd.

———— 1982. *Slom Kraljevine Jugoslavije: uzroci i posledice poraza.* Belgrade.

Tito, J. B. 1940/1946. "The Previous Works and the Tasks of the Party." Speech delivered at the fifth conference of the Communist Party of Yugoslavia, Zagreb, October 1940. Published in *Communist,* no. 1 (October 1946): 49–89.

———— 1946. "Temelji demokratije novoga tipa." *Komunist,* no. 2.

———— 1947. *Borba za oslobodjenje Jugoslavije 1941–1945.* Belgrade.

———— 1949. "Politički izvještaj CK KPJ." In *Peti kongres Komunističke partije Jugoslavije, stenografske beleške.* Belgrade.

———— 1959–1967. *Govori i članci.* 19 vols. Zagreb.

———— 1977. *Nacionalno pitanje i revolucija, Izabrana djela.* Vol. 3. Sarajevo.

Tomasevich, J. 1955. *Peasants, Politics, and Economic Change in Yugoslavia.* Stanford.

———— 1975. *The Chetniks.* Stanford.

Tomasic, D. 1948. *Personality and Culture in Eastern European Politics.* New York.

Topalović, Z. 1964. *Kako su komunisti dograbili vlast u Jugoslaviji.* London.

Tošić, D. 1952. *Srpski nacionalni problemi.* Paris.

Tucker, R. 1973. *Stalin as Revolutionary, 1879–1929: A Study in History and Personality.* New York.

Tudjman, F. 1969. *Velike ideje i mali narodi.* Zagreb.

———— 1981. *Nationalism in Contemporary Europe.* New York.

Ulam, A. B. 1952. *Titoism and the Cominform.* Cambridge, Mass.

———— 1966. *Lenin and the Bolsheviks*. London.

———— 1987. *Stalin: The Man and His Era*. Boston.

Ungar, A. 1981. *Constitutional Development of the USSR: A Guide to the Soviet Constitutions*. London.

van Creveld, M. 1972. "The German Attack on the USSR: The Destruction of a Legend." *European Studies Review*, 2, no. 1 (January): 69–86.

———— 1973. *Hitler's Strategy 1940–1941: The Balkan Clue*. London.

Vasiliev, A. A. 1953. *History of the Byzantine Empire, 324–1453*. Madison, Wis.

Vince, Z. 1978. *Putovima hrvatskoga književnoga jezika*. Zagreb.

Vlajčić, G. 1974. *KPJ i nacionalno pitanje u Jugoslaviji 1919–1929*. Zagreb.

———— 1976. *Osma konferencija zagrebačkih komunista*. Zagreb.

———— 1978. *Revolucija i nacije: Evolucija stavova vodjstva KPJ i Kominterne 1919–1929 godine*. Zagreb.

———— 1979. *KPJ i problem revolucije*. Zagreb.

———— 1984. *Jugoslavenska revolucija i nacionalno pitanje 1919–1927*. Zagreb.

Vlajić, B. 1959. "Slobodan Jovanović kao pravnik." *Poruka*, nos. 53–54 (January–March).

Vuković-Todorović, Lj. 1939? *Sveslovenstvo Stjepana Radića*. Belgrade.

———— 1940. *Hrvatski seljački pokret braće Radića*. Vol. 1. Belgrade.

Weber, E. 1966. "The Men of the Archangel." *Journal of Contemporary History*, 1, no. 1: 101–126.

Weber, M. 1965. *The Theory of Social and Economic Organisation*. London.

———— 1968. "Ethnic Groups." In Roth and Wittich (1968).

Wheeler, M. C. 1980. *Britain and the War for Yugoslavia, 1940–1943*. New York.

Wilson, W. 1984. *The Papers of Woodrow Wilson*, ed. Arthur S. Link. Vol. 45. Princeton.

Yourichitch, E. 1950. *Le procès Tito-Mihailovitch*. Paris.

Zečević, M. 1973. *Slovenska ljudska stranka i jugoslovensko ujedinjenje*. Belgrade.

Živković, D. 1978. *Narodni front Jugoslavije, 1935–1945*. Belgrade.

Reference Works and Published Documents

Aprilski rat 1941—Zbornik dokumenata. 1969. Belgrade.

Bolshaya Sovetskaya Entsiklopediya. 1949–1958. 51 vols. 2d ed. Moscow.

———— 1970–1978. 30 vols. 3d ed. Moscow.

Drugi kongres Komunističke partije Hrvatske, 21–25. novembar 1948. 1949. Zagreb.

Drugi kongres Narodnog fronta Jugoslavije. 1947. Belgrade.

Enciklopedija Jugoslavije. 1955–1971. 8 vols. Zagreb.

Encyclopaedia Britannica. 1988. 29 vols. 15th ed. Chicago.

Encyclopaedia Judaica. 1971. 16 vols. Jerusalem.

V Congress of the Communist International: Abridged Report of Meetings Held in Moscow, June 17th to July 18th 1935. N.d. London.

V kongres Komunističke partije Jugoslavije, 18–21 jula 1949, Stenografske beleške. 1949. Belgrade.

Hercegovina u NOB-u. 1986. 2 vols. Sarajevo.
Hrvatska enciklopedija. 1941–1945. 5 vols. Zagreb.
International Encyclopedia of the Social Sciences. 1968–1979. 18 vols. New York.
Istorija srpskog naroda. 1981–1983. 6 vols. Belgrade.
Istorijski arhiv Komunističke partije Jugoslavije—kongresi i zemaljske konferencije KPJ, 1919–1937. 1949. Vol. 2. Belgrade.
"Materijali Pete konferencije KPJ održane novembra 1940 u Zagrebu." 1946. *Komunist,* no. 1 (October): 59–122.
Narodna enciklopedija Srba, Hrvata i Slovenaca. 1929. 4 vols. Zagreb.
"Nationality and the 'National Question.'" 1975. In *Review of the Study Centre for Yugoslav Affairs.*
New Catholic Encyclopedia. 1967. 14 vols. New York.
Osnivački kongres Komunističke partije Hrvatske. 1958. Zagreb.
Osnivački kongres Komunističke partije Srbije (8–12 maja 1945). 1972. Belgrade.
Peti kongres Komunističke partije Jugoslavije, stenografske beleške. 1949. Belgrade.
Pravopis hrvatsko-srpskog književnog jezika s pravopisnim rječnikom. 1960. Zagreb and Novi Sad.
Pregled istorije Saveza komunista Jugoslavije. 1963. Belgrade.
Programme of the League of Yugoslav Communists. 1959. London.
Prvi kongres Narodnog fronta Jugoslavije. 1945. Split.
VI kongres Komunističke partije Jugoslavije (Saveza komunista Jugoslavije), 2–7 novembra 1952, Stenografske beleške. N.d. Belgrade.
Srpska pravoslavna crkva. 1969. Belgrade.
Sudjenje članovima političkog i vojnog rukovodstva organizacije Draže Mihailovića. 1945. Belgrade.
Treće zasedanje Antifašističkog veća narodnog oslobodjenja Jugoslavije, Zasedanje Privremene narodne skupštine, 7–26 avgust 1945. N.d. Belgrade.
Treći kongres Narodnog fronta Jugoslavije. 1949. Belgrade.
Ustav FNRJ. 1946. Belgrade.
Ustav SFRJ sa ustavima socijalističkih republika i statutima autonomnih pokrajina. 1963. Belgrade.
Vjesnik jedinstvene narodno-oslobodilačke fronte Hrvatske, 1941–1945. 1970. Zagreb.
Vojna enciklopedija. 1958–1969. 11 vols. Belgrade.
Zasedanje Ustavotvorne skupštine, 29. novembar 1945–1 februar 1946 (stenografske beleške). 1946. Belgrade.
ZAVNOH, zbornik dokumenata 1943. 1964. Zagreb.
ZAVNOH, zbornik dokumenata 1944. 1970. Zagreb.
Zbornik dokumenata i podataka o Narodno-oslobodilačkom ratu naroda Jugoslavije. 1949–. 13 vols. to date. Belgrade.
Zbornik ob štiridesetletnici ustanovnega kongresa KPS. 1977. Ljubljana.
Zemaljsko Anti-fašističko vijeće narodnog oslobodjenja Hrvatske. 1970. Zagreb.

Newspapers and Periodicals

Borba. Leading daily.
Danas (Zagreb). Leading weekly.
Demokratija (Belgrade). Organ of the Democratic Party.
Duga (Belgrade). Popular biweekly.
Glas slobode (Sarajevo). Organ of the Socialist Workers Party of Yugoslavia (Communists).
Intervju (Belgrade). Popular weekly.
Komunist. Journal of the CPY/LCY.
Mladina (Ljubljana). Influential youth weekly.
Naša reč (London). Yugoslav monthly.
Neue Ordnung (Zagreb). Ustasha weekly, 1941–1945.
NIN (Belgrade). Leading weekly.
Nova Hrvatska (London). Croatian biweekly.
Nova Jugoslavija. Partisan journal, 1944.
Obzor (Zagreb). Leading newspaper in the interwar period.
Organizovani radnik (Belgrade). Organ of the Independent Trade Unions, 1903–1941.
Politika (Belgrade). Leading daily in the interwar and postwar periods.
Proleter. Organ of the CC CPY, 1929–1942. Reprinted by Institut za izučavanje radičkog pokreta, Belgrade, 1968.
Radničke novine (Belgrade). Journal of the Workers Union, 1903–1941.
Službene novine Kraljevine Jugoslavije (Belgrade). Official newspaper.
Vijesnik (Zagreb). Leading postwar daily.
Vijesnik. Organ of the Front of People's Liberation of Croatia, 1941–1945.

Index

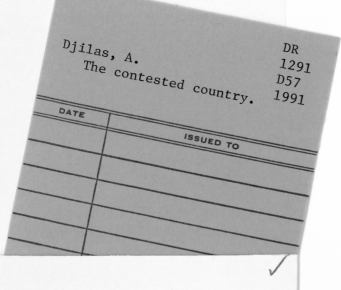